S0-AYX-683

Accessible Housing

Accessible Housing

Leon A. Frechette

McGraw-Hill

New York San Francisco Washington, D.C. Auckland Bogotá
Caracas Lisbon London Madrid Mexico City Milan
Montreal New Delhi San Juan Singapore
Sydney Tokyo Toronto

McGraw-Hill

A Division of The **McGraw·Hill** *Companies*

©1996 by **Leon A. Frechette**
Published by The McGraw-Hill Companies, Inc.

Printed in the United States of America. All rights reserved. The publisher takes no responsibility for the use of any materials or methods described in this book, nor for the products thereof.

hc   1 2 3 4 5 6 7 8 9 DOC/DOC 9 0 0 9 8 7 6

Product or brand names used in this book may be trade names or trademarks. Where we believe that there may be proprietary claims to such trade names or trademarks, the name has been used with an initial capital or it has been capitalized in the style used by the name claimant. Regardless of the capitalization used, all such names have been used in an editorial manner without any intent to convey endorsement of or other affiliation with the name claimant. Neither the author nor the publisher intends to express any judgment as to the validity or legal status of any such proprietary claims.

Library of Congress Cataloging-in-Publication Data
Frechette, Leon A., 1954–
   Accessible housing / by Leon A. Frechette.
     p.   cm.
   Includes index.
   ISBN 0-07-015748-0 (h)
    1. Dwellings—Access for the physically handicapped—United States. 2. Dwellings—Remodeling. I. Title.
TH4816.15.F74 1996
728.042—dc20
                                 96-11106
                                 CIP

McGraw-Hill books are available at special quantity discounts to use as premiums and sales promotions, or for use in corporate training programs. For more information, please write to the Director of Special Sales, McGraw-Hill, 11 West 19th Street, New York, NY 10011. Or contact your local bookstore.

Acquisitions editor: April D. Nolan
Editorial team: Lori Flaherty, Executive Editor
              Andrew Yoder, Supervising Editor
              Susan Bonthron, Book Editor
Production team: Katherine G. Brown, Director
                Toya B. Warner, Computer Artist
                Rose McFarland, Desktop Operator
                Jodi L. Tyler, Indexer
Design team: Jaclyn J. Boone, Designer   0157480
            Katherine Lukaszewicz, Associate Designer   GEN1

Contents

Appendices

A Contributing agencies, associations, organizations, and vendors   *331*

B Special offer   *341*

C Measurements   *343*

Index   *381*

About the author   *387*

To all those individuals who need a helping hand,
but especially to my grandmother, Olga Smith,
and Ing Montgomery.

Acknowledgments

I thank the many people who took time out of their busy schedules to help me turn this book into a reality. Their hard work and dedication helped to create a worthwhile tool to benefit construction professionals.

The efforts of the following are surely appreciated. These individuals supplied information and photos, answered questions, reviewed chapters so they stayed on track, and proofed materials:

- Joann M. Weeden, American Standard, Inc.
- Nancy B. Deptolla, Kohler Co.
- Kris Donnelly, HomeStyles Publishing and Marketing Inc.
- Brad Johnson, CPBD, LifeStyle HomeDesign Services
- Brian Sherry, GE Appliances
- Emily Moser, HUD USER
- Will Biddle, NAHB Research Center
- Carolyn M. Verweyst, Whirlpool Corporation
- Marie I. Overfors, Honeywell Inc.
- A. Robert Gould, *Workbench* magazine
- Lisa M. Robey, CKD, Harvey's Kitchens and Baths
- Julia Thomas, Kraftmaid Cabinetry, Inc.
- Shannon W. Flora, Northwest Hospital
- Bruce Wilson, Habitat
- Allan J. Browne, Extended Home Living Services, Inc.
- Carolyn Fitch, National Conference of States on Building Codes & Standards
- Alison DeMartino, Wilsonart International Inc.
- Dick Duncan, The Center for Universal Design–North Carolina State University
- George Cochran, Eastern Paralyzed Veterans Association
- Sharon McNaughton, Western Red Cedar Lumber Association
- Mary Jo Peterson, CKD, CBD, Design Consultant
- Corey Friedlander, Mechanical Plastics Corporation
- Gary E. White, CID, CKD, CBD, Kitchen & Bath Design

I would like to offer special thanks to Linda Nitteberg, CKD, owner of Concepts Kitchens & Baths; Diane Miller, founder of Welcome, H.O.M.E. (House of Modification Examples), Inc.; Gene Rothert, Manager, Urban Horticulture with Chicago Botanic Garden and author of *The Enabling Garden*; Barbara L. Allan, Community Access Director with the Eastern Seal Society of Washington; and Joyann Ward, Ing Montgomery's wife. These five individuals shared their personal experiences and helped to set the tone for *Accessible Housing*. Their hard work and valuable information are all through this book.

I would also like to thank Kenneth W. Smith, CKD, CBD, Director of Training with the National Kitchen & Bath Association for his insights on Effective Communication found in chapter 1; to Bob Brown, Program Director, and Richard Kuchnicki, Chief Executive Officer, of the Council of American Building Officials, for the use of diagrams in chapters 5 and 6; to Carolyn D. Geise, FAIA, of Geise Architects for input and valuable photos of Barbara Allan's home in chapter 7; to Dianne Walsh Astry and Liz Wortman of the American Lung Association, Minneapolis Affiliate, for the information that helped put chapter 8 together on the environmentally safe home; and to Patricia A. Moore, president of GUYNES DESIGN, Inc., for her wonderful foreword to *Accessible Housing* and for her assistance, input, and proofreading of the entire manuscript; to Tom Craig, Certified Plan Examiner, City of Spokane, Washington, for the hours he spent reading the text and reviewing diagrams to make sure they agreed with the codes required for multifamily and codes that should be considered for the residential market; and to Karen Craig for her hard and dedicated work in organizing, editing, and proofreading our fourth book together. The computers we both purchased sure help to move our projects along—maybe with time we just might understand the machines!

Thanks also to April Nolan, McGraw-Hill, for publishing my second book. We have only begun to scratch the surface of getting useful and needed information to the readers.

I would also like to thank my wife, Kimberly, for her support throughout all my projects, including this one. Now that she has moved me to the basement, it seems she is always sending me there. Perhaps she enjoys getting her living room back after all these years!

If I missed anyone, it certainly wasn't intentional. There just isn't enough paper—and you know who you are! This indeed was a community effort and I thank you all for your help and support on this very worthwhile project.

Again, many thanks to all.

Foreword

With each passing day, we age. And we've grown, impacted by our experiences and the events of every waking moment. The passage of time also presents us with the challenge of change: new jobs, marriage, the birth of a child, relocation, kids leaving home, retirement, catastrophic illness, loss of a spouse—all these events shape our lives.

We do not awaken each day thinking that we will end that day in a desperate fight for life in an emergency room. No, we begin with a familiar routine: shower, dress, breakfast, dash to work. Each action is taken for granted until the accident, the coronary, or the accumulated effects of aging redefine our lives. The medical community can only maintain our bodies; how well we manage depends on the quality of many other variables. Our financial capacity, the composition of our families, and our ability to work all play a major role in determining our autonomy and the quality of our life.

Perhaps the most important feature in everyone's world is the environment: those places in which we live, work, and play. Our homes, our workplaces, and our communities are the deciding factors in how we manage and how well we thrive. Without the accommodation of appropriate settings, we find our ability to perform daily tasks and ultimately, our independence, in jeopardy.

Leon A. Frechette, in a timely and highly impactful offering, provides those of us in the world of design and build with endless opportunities to make a difference in the lives of the individuals and families we serve. You will find these pages complete with the necessary resources and references to provide a knowledge base for the creation of accommodating, accessible housing beyond any text previously conceived. Regardless of your focus—appliance manufacturer, materials distributor, architect, contractor, interior designer—you will discover invaluable information for providing exemplary homes.

With the aging of America and the accommodation of people of all types of ability, the need for nests which we can happily view as responsive to any consumer's requirements has never been so keen.

We owe Leon our thanks for paving the way to homes which make a difference—for a lifetime!

Patricia A. Moore, President

GUYNES DESIGN, Inc., Phoenix, AZ

Introduction
Americans with disabilities: The statistics

Because of a variety of physical, mental, and emotional conditions, an estimated 49 million noninstitutionalized Americans (about one in five) have a disability. Of these persons, 24 million (almost one-half!) have a "severe" disability.

Difficulty with a functional activity is the most common type of disability for adults

Functional activities include lifting and carrying a weight as heavy as 10 pounds, walking 3 city blocks, seeing the words and letters in ordinary newsprint, hearing what is said in normal conversation with another person, having one's speech understood, and climbing a flight of stairs—all activities that we do every day and take for granted.

Thirty-four million adults aged 15 and older had difficulties performing at least one of these tasks; for 15 million of them, the disability was severe—they were simply unable to perform one or more of these activities. The latter figure includes 1.6 million who would be unable to see the words on this page and 900,000 who were completely unable to hear what was said in normal conversation.

Fewer adults have trouble with ADLs and IADLs than with functional activities

Activities of daily living (ADLs) consist of getting in or out of a bed or a chair, bathing, getting around inside the home, dressing, using the toilet—what amounts to your morning routine. About 8 million adults had difficulty with at least one of these tasks; 3.9 million required the assistance of another person, making the disability severe.

Instrumental activities of daily living (IADLs) include going outside the home to shop or visit a doctor's office, doing light housework (such as washing dishes), preparing meals, keeping track of money and bills, and using the telephone. Twelve million adults had trouble with one or more of these activities; nine million needed assistance.

Not only were adults with functional, ADL, and IADL limitations considered to have a disability, but so too were those who

- Used a wheelchair (1.5 million did so)
- Used a cane, crutches, or a walker for 6 months or longer (4 million)
- Had a mental or an emotional disability, such as Alzheimer's disease or mental retardation (6.9 million)
- Had a condition that limited the kind or amount of work they could do at a job (19.5 million aged 16 to 67)
- Had a condition that made it difficult to do housework (18.1 million aged 16 and over)

The elderly comprise a disproportionate share of persons with disabilities

The chances of having a disability increased with age; most persons aged 75 or older had a disability. In fact, those aged 65 or more comprised a far larger share of those with disabilities (34 percent) than of the total population (12 percent); they constituted an even greater percentage (43 percent) of persons with severe disabilities.

What is a severe disability?

Adults aged 15 and over were classified as having a severe disability if they used a wheelchair or had used another special aid for 6 months or longer, were unable to perform one or more functional activities or needed assistance with an ADL or IADL, were prevented from working at a job or doing housework, or had a selected condition that included autism, cerebral palsy, Alzheimer's disease, senility or dementia, or mental retardation.

These interesting statistics from the U.S. Department of Commerce (Economics and Statistics Administration, Bureau of the Census, "Americans With Disabilities," Statistical Brief, SB/94-1, Issued January 1994) define the scope of the problem. So what should these numbers mean to you? It's simple—there are close to 50 million disabled people in this country who deserve the same respect as nondisabled individuals. You can help. There's a large market out there, one you can serve. This market has specific needs, but don't let this deter you. You can learn.

Accessible Housing is one way to get you started. It is a nuts-and-bolts approach to incorporating universal, barrier-free, and adaptable/adjustable design into a home, possibly into an environmentally safe home. Accessible housing enables people to live independently in their homes as long as they choose, regardless of their age or physical capacities.

As a professional builder or remodeler, you'll have to venture into unfamiliar areas, which might make you uncomfortable—and that's okay. *Accessible Housing* will help you all the way. Just keep one thing in mind: You can make a difference in the lives of a persons with disabilities. You can help individuals maintain their self-worth and live comfortable, rewarding lives in their own homes. You can indeed make a difference.

Accessible Housing provides insights into accessibility, safety, security, comfort, space efficiency, and communications. The designs and information given in firsthand accounts will help you to better understand customers' wants, needs, and desires to manage life in their homes more freely, regardless of age or physical conditions. It will also identify special benefits to people who function with various chronic conditions linked to the normal aging process.

With the help of this book you can also improve the safety and well-being of frequent visitors into customers' homes, or you might be called upon to help the "sandwich generation" adapt portions of their homes for use by elderly parents or grandparents. The advice given throughout this book not only makes the home more functional but also makes it easier to sell—because a barrier-free home will appeal to a larger number of prospective buyers.

Recognizing the opportunities

You never know when the phone will ring and a customer will request your services on a project that involves universal, barrier-free, or adaptable/adjustable design. Customers might want you to make permanent modifications or even build an environmentally safe home (discussed in chapter 8).

There is a large market out there, and it is your responsibility to learn such designs as well as to learn and practice good construction techniques. You could be called upon to create, rebuild, design, build new, change, or adapt an environment (the home) to eliminate any or all obstacles that would restrict all freedom of movement in any way throughout a home.

The projects you could be involved in can enhance the home's accessibility, safety, security, comfort, space efficiency, and communications for a wide variety of people. The designs and adaptations you use will enable individuals of any age or physical condition to manage in their homes more easily, including those who function with various chronic conditions associated with the normal aging process.

You might have started out in this business by remodeling a kitchen or building a deck. Now you will be involved in the personal lives of your customers more than you ever imagined. Are you up to helping your customers live more comfortably within their own environments?

Personal rewards

The opportunity to help people presented by this specialized field is a great reward in this business. I know this from personal experience. For me, it started with my grandmother (now age 80) who has lived on her own since my grandfather passed away in 1980. It is hard for an individual to lose a loved one and even harder suddenly to have to live alone and meet all your own needs. As the years passed, Grandma's house slowly closed in around her. She was not able to function as freely as she was accustomed to, but she recognized what was happening; a few years back she purchased a deluxe safety tub bar. Unfortunately, she was not able to install it. I guess that's what grandsons are for—to love their grandmothers and take care of some of these little things.

Soon after that, my uncle added a handrail to the basement along with a phone extension at the bottom of the stairs on the floor along with a flashlight. Friends and relatives were worried about her going to the basement to do her laundry or get something from the freezer because her hip was rapidly deteriorating and it was hard for her to climb up and down the stairs. It wasn't long after that when my plumber and I converted the back room (on the first floor) to a laundry room. The old washer still sits in the basement (no dryer—Grandma never believed in using one). The remodeling project gave her an opportunity to purchase a new washer and dryer for her new laundry room. This arrangement is very convenient for her, and she sure likes that dryer, even though she still prefers to hang her clothes outside.

Within a year, Grandma had a hip replaced and while she was in the hospital, my stepsons and I installed a temporary ramp over the back steps. Using a cane made by my grandfather, she would work her way down the ramp to her garden. She never did get used to that ramp, nor did she like it. To her, that ramp stripped away her freedom to use the steps. She didn't like the fact that she had lost her independence, even for a short period of time. It was amazing to see how quickly she healed, and it wasn't long before I got a call to come and remove the ramp.

Since I started this book, the ramp has been removed from storage and reinstalled. She has had cataract surgery on one eye and an aortic valve replaced. Her refrigerator was replaced with a combination side-by-side freezer/refrigerator unit, and an accordion door has replaced the bathroom door.

For my grandmother, the little that was done has helped her feel more comfortable at home. These changes include:

- The installation of a clip-on deluxe safety tub bar
- The addition of a handrail to the basement stairway
- A phone on the floor in the basement
- Laundry facilities moved to the main floor
- A temporary ramp
- Replacement of the refrigerator with a side-by-side combination unit
- Replacement of the bi-fold bathroom door with an accordion door

Of all the things done to help make life a little easier at home, it was the presence of the ramp that disturbed Grandma the most. I'm sure it won't be long before I get another call to remove it, and that will be the day when she regains her full independence. That ramp reminds my grandmother that she has a physical disability that she will have to cope with, accept, and overcome all on her own, even though it is temporary. She has lived through the Great Depression; learned to get by, make things work, and go without; and generally lived an independent life. Individuals from that era are proud people and their dignity is important to them. No matter how small the job, your willingness to do these types of special projects can help to restore a feeling of self-worth to these people. Remember, the day might come when you and I need the same kind of help—and we never know when that day might come.

Just this summer I received the news that one of my business associates, Ing, was injured in a motorcycle accident. His fourth and fifth thoracic vertebrae (between the shoulder blades) were crushed, leaving him paralyzed from the chest down. He spent most of the summer and early fall in the hospital and in a rehab center. As difficult as all this has been for Ing, it has also been hard on his family. His wife Joyann writes,

As you might well imagine, this is very difficult and we have a lot of adjustment ahead of us. Ing is in fairly good spirits considering the extent of his back injury. Our families have been incredibly supportive . . . I simply could not have gotten through this without their support and help . . . Ing's greatest concern about the future is that he will burden me and cause me not to complete graduate school. Those of you who know us as a couple will know that he is not a burden to me; he is a delight! We all feel so fortunate that he is alive. All of us, including Ing, believe he will lead a full, active, and independent life. We are not being unrealistic; we know it will take a long time and a lot of hard work, especially for Ing . . . I have promised Ing that I will try to continue with my schooling, partly because it is what I had wanted and worked at for such a long time and partly because it will keep me from doing everything for Ing (which would be really easy to do) and thereby take away his independence and confidence . . . When something like this happens and our lives are changed forever in a fraction of a second, our priorities become crystal clear. Our relationships with those we love are foremost and all else pales by comparison.

Some people, like my grandmother, age into disabilities. Others, as Joyann writes, have their lives ". . . changed forever in a fraction of a second."

The aging population

By the middle of the next century, there could be more persons who are elderly (65 or over) than young (14 or younger). Don't think of America as a nation of young people—the numbers just don't support it.

The statistics listed below are from Sixty-Five Plus in the United States, a Statistical Brief (SB/95-8) issued in May 1995 (U.S. Department of Commerce, Economics and Statistics Administration, Bureau of the Census). The overall view they present of the potential in this market only scratches the surface.

- The older population—persons 65 years or older—numbered 33.2 million in 1994. They represent 1 in 8 Americans, while in 1900, they were 1 in 25 at 3.1 million.
- The older population is itself getting older. The "oldest old," those aged 85 and over, are the most rapidly growing elderly age group. Their numbers rose 274 percent between 1960 and 1994.
- In general, the elderly population rose 100 percent and the entire U.S. population grew only 45 percent between 1960 and 1994. The "oldest old" numbered 3 million in 1994, making them 10 percent of the elderly and just over 1 percent of the total population.

- It is expected that the "oldest old" will number 19 million in 2050. That would make them 24 percent of elderly Americans and 5 percent of all Americans.
- We are living longer. When the United States was founded, life expectancy at birth was about 35 years. In 1900 it was 47 years; in 1950 it was 68 years; and in 1991 it was 76 years (79 years for women and 72 years for men).
- Once we reach age 65, we can expect to live 17 more years.
- Men generally have higher death rates than women at every age. Elderly women outnumbered elderly men in 1994 by a ratio of 3 to 2: 20 million to 14 million. This difference grew with advancing age: women aged 65 to 69 outnumbered men only 6 to 5, but at age 85 and over, the ratio was 5 to 2.

Many elderly live alone, and the likelihood of living alone increases with age. For women in the above-quoted statistics, the figure rose from 32 percent for 65- to 74-year-olds to 57 percent for those aged 85 years or more. For men, the corresponding proportions were 13 percent and 29 percent.

It is also interesting to note that the elderly of the future will be better educated. Research has shown that the better educated tend to be healthier longer and better off economically.

Some assume that health among the elderly has improved because, as a group, they are living longer. Others hold a contradictory image of the elderly as dependent and frail. The truth actually lies somewhere in between. Poor health is not as prevalent as many assume. In 1992, about 3 in every 4 noninstitutionalized persons aged 65 to 74 considered their health to be good. Of those aged 75 or older, 2 of 3 felt similarly.

On the other hand, as more people live to the oldest ages, there might also be more who face chronic, limiting illnesses or conditions, such as arthritis, diabetes, osteoporosis, and senile dementia. These conditions result in people becoming dependent on others for help in performing the activities of daily living. With age comes increasing chances of being dependent. For instance, while 1 percent of those aged 65 to 74 years lived in a nursing home in 1990, nearly 1 in 4 aged 85 or older did. And among those who were not institutionalized in 1990–1991, only 9 percent aged 65 to 69 years needed assistance performing everyday activities such as bathing, getting around inside the home, and preparing meals, while 50 percent aged 85 or older needed such help.

As more and more people live long enough to experience multiple chronic illnesses, disability, and dependency, there will be more and more relatives in their fifties and sixties who will be facing the concern and expense of caring for them.

An upcoming report, "Sixty-Five Plus in the United States," will expand upon the information contained in the Statistical Brief cited here. As of this writing, the report had not yet been issued; call Customer Services (301-457-4100) to check on the availability of this report or to order (free) "Housing of the Elderly," Statistical Brief 94-33, which contains information on topics such as the chances of elderly householders owning their home, the type of structures they live in, and the odds of their lacking amenities such as plumbing and telephones in their homes. At the Bureau of the Census, contacts for information on the elderly population are Frank Hobbs or Bonnie Damon (301-457-2378). For information on Statistical Briefs, contact Robert Bernstein (301-457-3030).

According to the Eastern Paralyzed Veterans Association (EPVA), there are about 50 million people with disabilities. Every year 10,000 people are added to that population with spinal cord injuries received through auto accidents, sports activities (5,000 through diving accidents alone), and diseases that damage the spinal cord.

Are you aware that there are more than 23 million people who are deaf or have hearing losses? How about individuals with allergies, arthritis, heart disease, hypertension, and partial paralysis? What about children? It is easy to overlook the special needs and daily activities of such people. We take the situation for granted because we don't have the experience, can't relate to them personally or understand their feelings, simply because we are not disabled. Sometimes it is hard to understand someone if we have never "worn the same shoes." Remember, people with disabilities have the same "wants" and "needs" that we do; maybe it's time to change our perspective and make a dramatic impact on their lives by being aware of the market, understanding that market, and getting involved.

I encourage you to visit your local library to research other statistics that could affect your decision-making process as you search out a niche in this market. While the market seems to be wide open, working from "gut instincts" or "by the seat of your pants" won't guarantee success in this business. You might find yourself on the outside not able to penetrate this market. Has anyone ever told you to "measure twice, cut once" to eliminate costly mistakes? Apply the same method here and study the market; do your homework and get the facts. Use this information to your advantage to meet your goals.

Accessible Housing assures homeowners—both seniors and their adult children—that "aging in place" can be made more satisfying as well as safer. You can make this happen but you need to have both eyes open when crossing the threshold into this unfamiliar territory. This book has the tools to equip you to effectively work in this very timely market. Your knowledge can give customers more control over their own destinies and help them to live longer, more productive lives.

Yes, you can make a difference—you really can!

1

Understanding customers' needs

Nothing in life truly prepares us to play the hand we're dealt. Life constantly changes around us—we give birth, get hurt, grow old, and deal with the deaths of our loved ones. Construction also constantly changes. As professionals, we will all reach a point when we will have to venture outside our construction "comfort zone." When this happens, we will have to learn new techniques, adjust to and understand new and revised building codes and regulations, install and use unfamiliar products, and address new issues and concerns brought to us by our customers.

The natural cycle of life as well as unfortunate accidents or illness require potential customers to make changes in their homes. These changes affect the comfort and productivity of those individuals within their home environments. These are the changes (now issues!) that will soon become our responsibility. Remember, you chose to be in this field. It is your responsibility to keep up with the constant changes brought to you by customers and the construction trends required to satisfy their needs.

Don't wait for this to hit home before you understand that the homes we live in can restrict those everyday activities that we take for granted—in other words, our freedom! When "freedom" is no longer a luxury because of age, a disability, and/or the use of a wheelchair, we need to consider options to make everyday living more comfortable. The time will come when we must face the challenges of living with aging or a disability. That time is here now for many people; as contractors we can help them face it with dignity.

To understand customer needs under such conditions requires both careful listening to your customers and experience. Your customers might not be abreast of construction techniques and products that could make their lives a little simpler at home. However, don't underestimate your customers—they most likely have done their homework or have been advised by their therapists. It is important for you to read *Accessible Housing* in its entirety, read other related material, and view some (or all) of the videotapes on the subject that will be recommended throughout this book. Staying informed helps you serve your customers better. Keep in mind that this is not like selling a product with a "one-size-fits-all" approach; your potential customer has unique needs that require your full attention. Just like your nondisabled customers, though, this customer still deserves the following basics:

- A professional job at a reasonable price
- Minimal interruption of family life, i.e., the job done promptly
- Clean premises—no dirt tracked into the home
- A warranty backed by your assurance that any problems will be handled promptly, courteously, and correctly
- A contractor with a professional attitude and approach

While these guidelines seem very generic and basic, we as professionals do not always follow them as much as we should, and now is definitely not the time to forget them. If you want to specialize in this business, it is up to you to understand and work according to these basics. You will be amazed at how fast your name and reputation spread—and there is nothing like a word-of-mouth referral! Keep in mind that for a short time you will be invading your customer's privacy. Without even trying you will be emotionally involved, and your customer will come to trust you both as an individual and as a professional. That's a big responsibility. If you feel you cannot handle such responsibility and its potential emotional impact, this might not be an area of the construction trade that suits you, and it would probably be best to target some other area in the business.

Understanding and being sympathetic to your customers' needs definitely help to close a sale. Focus on why you are in business and assure customers that their needs are important to you.

Understanding the customer

The simplest things in life, like tying our shoelaces, we do without a second thought. But for those who have chronic conditions, tying shoelaces can be an everyday struggle, a challenge that they can't accomplish on their own. Chronic conditions can indeed affect independence and interfere with the activities of daily living that we take for granted. Under these conditions, the possible limitations to be faced are in the following areas:

- To see and hear
- To bend, reach, and carry
- To walk and climb

This can affect daily activities such as:

- Getting in and out of bed
- Getting on and off a toilet
- Getting in and out of a bathtub
- Brushing teeth (personal hygiene)
- Dressing
- Tying shoes
- Walking safely
- Knowing that something is protruding in the walkway
- Climbing stairs
- Knowing and responding to a ringing phone or doorbell
- Turning on a faucet
- Eating
- Taking out garbage
- Working in the garden
- Opening an envelope
- Preparing lunch
- Taking clothes out of the dryer
- Driving

This list could be endless, which should give you something to think about the next time you look at an elder or a person using a wheelchair; someone who has arthritis, a spinal cord injury, or hearing or visual impairment; a person born with a physical disability; or someone who has survived an accident. By providing solutions that best fit the needs of an individual, you can restore life in that person and help build the confidence needed to face everyday challenges as well as the opportunity to participate in the daily activities of life. People deserve the freedom to be independent within and around their own homes. We can give them that freedom.

Other considerations

The National Easter Seal Society has included some helpful tips in their brochures *Awareness is the First Step Towards Change: Tips for Portraying People with Disabilities in the Media* and *Tips for Disability Awareness*, that I think would be very helpful when meeting a potential customer who has a disability both on your initial appointment and when working and dealing with the customer during the project. For the purposes of this book, I only highlight those tips that are applicable to your services, but it would be a good idea to pick up these brochures for your library.

- Use the word "disability" when referring to persons or people with disabilities. Don't use the word "handicapped." A disabling condition might or might not be handicapping. For example, someone who uses a wheelchair has a "physical disability." This person is "handicapped" when faced with a set of stairs that has no ramp alongside.
- Emphasize the person, not the disability. Use "people with disabilities" as a first description in a piece; then, if you need to, "disabled persons" in later references.
- Because people are not conditions, don't label individuals as "the disabled," "epileptics," "post-polios," or by using other names of conditions. Refer, instead, to "people with cerebral palsy" or "someone who has epilepsy."

Never use these terms:

- "Victim." Instead, say "person who has . . ." or "person who experienced . . ." or "person with . . . ."
- "Cripple," "crippled," or "the crippled." Rather, say "person with a disability" or "individual with a disability caused by or as result of . . . ."

Avoid using the terms:

- "Wheelchair bound" or "confined to a wheelchair." Say instead, "uses a wheelchair." People can't generally sleep in them.

Some general considerations for disability etiquette:

- People with disabilities are entitled to the same courtesies that you extend to anyone. This includes their personal privacy. You wouldn't generally ask people about their sex lives or their complexions or their incomes; don't ask people with disabilities about their situation or condition.
- If you make a habit of leaning or hanging onto people you're with, then don't lean or hang onto someone's wheelchair. Wheelchairs are an extension of personal space for people who use them.
- When you offer to assist someone with a vision impairment, allow the person to take your arm. This will help you to guide, rather than to propel or lead, this person.
- Treat adults as adults. Call a person by his or her first name only when you're extending this familiarity to everyone present. Don't patronize people who use wheelchairs by patting them on the head. Reserve this sign of affection for children, even if a wheelchair user's head is at about the same height as a child's.

The following are some tips to follow in conversations:

- When talking with someone who has a disability, speak directly to that person rather than through any companions who might be along.
- Relax. Don't be embarrassed if you happen to use accepted, common expressions, such as "See you later" or "Got to be running along" that seem to relate to the person's disability.
- To get the attention of a person who has a hearing disability, tap the person on the shoulder or wave your hand. Look directly at the person and speak clearly, slowly, and expressively to establish if the person can read your lips. Not all persons with hearing impairments can lip-read. Those who do will rely on facial expressions and other body language to help in understanding. Show consideration by placing yourself facing the light source and keeping your hands and food away from your mouth when speaking. Keep your mustache well-trimmed. Shouting won't help—written notes will.
- When talking with a person in a wheelchair for more than a few minutes, place yourself at the wheelchair user's eye level to spare both of you a stiff neck.
- When greeting a person with a severe loss of vision, always identify yourself and others who might be with you. Say, for example, "On my right is Penelope Potts." When conversing in a group, remember to say the name of the person to whom you are speaking to give a vocal cue. Speak in a normal tone of voice, indicate when you move from one place to another, and let it be known when the conversation is at an end.
- Give your whole unhurried attention when talking to a person who has difficulty speaking. Keep your manner encouraging rather than correcting, be patient rather than speak for the person. When necessary, ask short questions that require short answers or a nod or shake of the head. Never pretend to understand if you are having difficulty doing so. Repeat what you do understand. The person's reaction will clue you in and guide you to understanding.

Some common courtesies:

- Offer assistance to a person with a disability if you feel like it, but wait until your offer is accepted before you help, and listen to any instructions the person might want to give.
- When giving directions to a person in a wheelchair, consider distance, weather conditions, and physical obstacles such as stairs, curbs, and steep hills.

- Use specifics such as "left a hundred feet" or "right two yards" when directing a person with a visual impairment.
- Be considerate of the extra time it might take for a person with a disability to get things done or said. Let the person set the pace in walking and talking.

It is also important to have the utmost respect and courtesy for any animal(s) that might live with a customer or potential customer; e.g., a dog or a monkey. These animals probably play a very important role in the customer's life, depending on that person's situation. In addition, they are a good source of therapy for the following reasons:

- They provide company.
- They help the customer remain independent.
- They aid the visually impaired.
- They fill a void in the person's life.

Whatever the role of the animal, remember that it is part of the family and an extension of the person who is disabled. It is your responsibility to be courteous and well-mannered in front of them as well as in front of anyone else living in the household. You never know who might be just around the corner, and the "human broadcasting system" works swiftly, so protect your reputation!

Hear it firsthand

The following individuals have been—and still are—experiencing the challenges of life with disabilities. They have seen changes over the years when it comes to products, dealing with other professionals, and dealing with the public directly. Their outlook on life, the changes they had to accept, and the barriers they had to overcome could dramatically influence how we look, act, and treat our customers with special needs. The following individuals all have something important to offer—read between the lines and choose those attributes that will help you in your next interview with a customer—whether the customer has a disability or not.

Diane Miller

In 1988 Diane started Welcome, H.O.M.E. (House of Modification Examples), Inc., a nonprofit organization that provides information on products and services to those individuals with disabilities who live independently at home. Their main thrust is to build an accessible design demonstration three-bedroom home where two of the bedrooms will be used as part of a bed-and-breakfast retreat by the fall of 1996. The model home with its hands-on environment will allow people with disabilities to sample design elements that could make their lives easier when it comes time to design or alter their existing homes.

Diane's personal battle with post-polio syndrome spurred her interest in making the world more accessible to all people. She was diagnosed with polio at the age of 3 and, until nine years ago, walked solely with the help of leg braces and crutches. Now she uses a wheelchair more and more and finds that it has put her in the forefront of helping people maintain their independence. Diane has a master's degree in rehabilitation counseling. Here is her story:

I liked what I did and was good at it, but after just three years, I was feeling tired and my body hurt (not just my legs any more). I was more fatigued than my peers—which was unusual. It seems I am not only the age of the Yuppie, I am also the age of the first generation of polio survivors who were told 30 years ago by the medical world that "no pain, no gain" was to be our life-long motto.

Those of us who were able to participate in upright mobility with assistive devices (and did so to the fullest) were suddenly being told to SIT!! Not only when it was convenient, but to trade in our walking apparatus for a wheelchair.

I complied. I got fitted for and bought my lightweight wheelchair. I traded in my station wagon for a minivan. Then I sat and stared at the six steps at both the front and back doors of my (I own it) 60-year-old duplex (which I finally sold in '94). My "normal" life was being disrupted. I didn't like it. My body allowed me to ignore the wheelchair that rode around in my van for two years; a reprieve I took advantage of.

It took awhile, but I have created a positive outlet (utilizing what for a time was the unproductive energy of anger and frustration) and directed my energy toward the Welcome, H.O.M.E. project, which is now becoming a reality. A 2,000-foot wheelchair-accessible trail along with specially designed picnic tables has been built on the 18-acre site. This gives individuals with disabilities the opportunity to meet Mother Nature up close and to enjoy the outdoors at a comfortable pace (Fig. 1-1).

Diane has a few pet peeves she would like to share that could be beneficial to those who are already in this market or for those who are considering it, hopefully to clear the air for a better understanding. They are as follows:

- It is extremely important to know that barrier-free design does not come in a "One Size Fits All" category.
- I hate to read literature that refers to people as being confined, restricted, or wheelchair bound. What's

wrong with giving this characteristic a less negative visual image? I really appreciate a critique that offers a solution. My best offer is simply "wheelchair user"—I'm sure there are better options.

- I do not enjoy having the word "disabled" used as a noun. My phrase of choice is "person living with a disability"—putting the person actively participating in life first in the visual image.
- It is not safe to assume that the ADA (Americans with Disabilities Act), FHAA (Fair Housing Amendments Act) or other specs used in constructing a home for a specific individual might meet his/her needs.
- It is not fair to expect ready answers about heights, depths, and widths. Most likely, the consumer has never been asked or given options before, so simply will have no answer.

Designing homes to accommodate persons with special needs is not difficult, nor is it expensive and it certainly does not need to be anything but pleasing to the eye. Barrier-free living not only makes sense, it also makes "cents." For example, a large percentage of all nursing home bills are paid by taxpayer dollars. Yet, if homes were built more sensibly (to create more accessible living), probably a much smaller percentage of the nursing home population would need to be there. Imagine the savings this would mean to all taxpayers across the country!!!

1-1 *Enjoying the outdoors shouldn't be a challenge for anyone with a disability.* Welcome, House of Modification Examples, Inc. (Welcome, H.O.M.E.)

Patricia A. Moore

Pat is the president of GUYNES DESIGN Inc., a design firm specializing in health care environments, rehabilitation settings, and graphic, interior, and product design. Her interest in designing for special needs emerged during her undergraduate studies at the Rochester Institute of Technology. Joining a New York design firm following graduation, Pat was frustrated by the inaccessibility of the appliances and equipment her department produced. When she challenged the system, it was explained to her, "We don't design for those people." Outraged, Pat began a journey which defined her life's work.

Utilizing the talents of a New York makeup designer, Pat set out to completely change her body's abilities and appearance so she could travel throughout the United States and Canada as a woman more than 80 years old. For more than three years, Pat experienced the indignities faced by elders when younger and weller people are rude, uncaring, violent, abusive or simply lack courtesy and civility. She almost died as a result of a vicious gang attack that was partly for theft and partly for the "fun" of beating up an older, defenseless woman.

Pat's book, *Disguised: A True Story*, tells of her experiences. Walking in someone else's shoes provided an extraordinary amount of information:

> Without this empathic experience, my colleagues would never have embraced what I felt was necessary as a focus for architecture and design. Homes which aren't manageable, appliances which are difficult to use, stores which fail to address the physical requirements of customers, and the hostility of environments which don't accommodate individual needs put every person at risk of losing their autonomy and independence!

Pat points out that with the aging of the Baby Boomers, the longevity of their parents, and the high costs of residential and nursing care, meeting the consumer needs of all people equally is the challenge of design. She is a frequent lecturer, media guest, and author of numerous articles. Pat is a renowned gerontologist and is a leading authority on the requirements and behaviors of elders and all people as they progress throughout the lifespan.

Linda Nitteberg, CKD

Linda, the owner of CK&B (Concepts Kitchens and Baths), is a nationally recognized expert in the field of universal design. She comments that "most people don't want to deal with people who have anything wrong with them, because they don't want to have to face their own mortality. . . ." She goes on to say, "There are lots and lots of people who have major limitations in their ability to function, and we as a society are not dealing with them."

When I was a child, I learned that things like disease, death, and disability could happen to anyone. Many of us live a great part of our lives thinking these things only happen to other people. It is comforting to believe intelligent, careful individuals in my social economic class are spared such misfortune.

When I was four years old, my father drowned in a fishing accident and when I was eight my mother gave birth to a microcephalic baby, as the result of rubella. My sister, Terry, didn't survive birth. Her head was smaller than a baseball and she practically had no brain. Because of this she didn't survive the birth process.

In the sixth grade I met a girl who became a lifelong friend. My friend had cerebral palsy. She was awkward when she walked, and listening to her talk took extra effort until you got used to her. Becoming closest of friends was well worth overcoming any barriers we faced. She taught me as much as possible what it was like to have cerebral palsy. And she shared her experiences with Easter Seals and let me know of special education programs. . . .

For the first time in my life I became aware of barriers faced by individuals with disabilities. The obvious types of barriers are those that are architectural in nature. People with disabilities or limited abilities might find stairs difficult to manage. They might find communication difficult. They might find it impossible to enter environments such as theaters, arenas, churches, and shopping centers. In addition to architectural barriers, I learned about social barriers. I remembered my friend saying everyone was really nice to her but most people didn't to be close friends. One year our physical education teacher gave her an "A." She knew she was not able to do the sports well enough to get an "A." The others in the class knew the only way she had earned an "A" was by being very nice. This grade caused problems for her in the class. There were educational barriers. Lots of people, including some teachers, treated her as if she were retarded.

My friend had been in special education and was kept back a year. At the time I met her she was being mainstreamed.

Over the years I was aware of people making accommodations. For example, she was allowed to use an electric typewriter.

In my college years my interests included medical research, special education, physical education classes, and psychology classes. One of my undergraduate field study assignments was to work with trainable retarded children. I tried to teach them basic physical skills such as rolling over, pushing, pulling, and going up and down stairs. I enjoyed learning how to make accommodations to adapt sports and recreational activities.

I learned that it could be possible for a blind person to play softball and a person using a wheelchair to bowl. During my junior year in college my health was getting worse. It was getting harder for me to do many of the activities that were once taken for granted. Swimming and running were becoming quite difficult.

By the time I got my bachelor's degree, I had taken several graduate-level education, psychology, and counseling classes. I was thrilled to be accepted into the rehabilitation counseling masters program.

Graduate school gave me the opportunity to learn about the physical as well as the psychological aspects of many disabling conditions. I learned a great deal about physical and mental illness. During the two-year program, I read and abstracted dozen of articles about disabilities. I spent several months working at an office of the Nebraska State Rehabilitation Department.

It was there I became interested in designing housing that would be suitable for individuals with disabilities. I had always been interested in architecture and construction. My parents had built a custom house when I was seven. I knew my short mother insisted on lower than standard kitchen counters. I remember the discussion between my 4'11" mom and my 6'3" tall dad about how high to place the mirrored medicine chest. The solution for the bath was masterful. The vanity was about 36" in height. They built an upside-down type drawer into the toe kick space of the cabinet. It had a cabinet handle installed which made it easy for me to pull. I then could reach the sink and faucet. The mirror was positioned so Mom could see herself at the bottom without too much stretching and Dad could see himself at the top without too much bending. As I recall, it was a few years before I was able to use the mirror easily.

During graduate school I actually learned how to not only read, but to draw blueprints. My first clients were two ladies, one was a post-polio survivor and the other had multiple sclerosis. They wanted to build a house and live together. The first lady could walk but had to be in a corset to hold her upright. She often was in a wheelchair and used metal devices to support and steady her arms. The second lady was just starting to experience the fatigue and lack of coordination typical of MS.

In the mid 1970s, I became actively involved in the rights of those with disabilities. In 1975 I served as a facilitator for the White House Conference for individuals with disabilities. . . . I've continued to be an advocate since that time.

Linda has lupus, an inflammatory disease that affects her heart and lungs. So what makes her an expert in this market? Besides what was previously mentioned, part of her expertise is the personal experience she has gained through use of her own wheelchair. Unable to stand for long periods of time she has learned a lot about the turning radii of wheelchairs and the heights at which counters become barriers. At 4'10" standing up, she can put a variety of twists on the word "normal." She estimates that 15 percent of her business involves adaptive uses. She advises that when your customer has a disability, you will need to ask different, and sometimes very sensitive, questions in order to come up with the special design solutions required. Her philosophy is that adaptive design should be an expression of the customer's taste and lifestyle, rather than an extension of the local hospital.

To those designers and contractors who initially might feel uncomfortable working with a customer with a disability, Linda has three simple words that really could work for you in communicating with the customer. If you understand these words and practice them, then you will have gone a long way toward adaptable design. The first word is "relax." The second one is "individualize," and the third one is "dignify." Linda continues,

I'm often asked how I start my initial contact with a person with a disability. My advice to you is first of all, relax. Realize the person you are dealing with is a person, first and foremost. He or she just happens to be unable to perform some of the specific tasks that the general population can perform. It might help you in relaxing to take a few deep breaths. Sometimes it is helpful to admit your anxiety or your discomfort in the situation. It is very important to try to get at the same eye level as the person you're talking with. Adjust your speech so that it is appropriate for your customer. That might entail changing your vocabulary. It might involve altering your pitch. It might involve varying your speed. It's sometimes helpful to ask your customers if they're comfortable. I want the person I deal with, whether able-bodied or having a disability, to be comfortable. That means physically comfortable—a pleasant temperature, comfortable sitting position—and emotionally comfortable so that they don't feel inhibited or threatened.

Oftentimes professionals tell me that they're uncomfortable about the whole issue of assistance: "Oh, but this person can't do this so I want to do it for them," or "How do I know when to push a person in a wheelchair?" Establish early on in your relationship with your customer when you may give assistance and when you may not. Avoid putting customers in situations where they have to twist or turn or look up. I cannot begin to tell you how my neck hurts from always looking up when I'm spending three or four days in a wheelchair.

Linda recommends that you never, ever talk behind a person in a wheelchair. The person in the wheelchair also wants to be part of the conversation. Basically, what all this amounts to is a little sensitivity and a little bit of good manners.

In an interview, start the process by putting yourself in a state of mind that you will be entering a long and close relationship with the customer. Linda continues, "I just finished a bathroom for a gentleman who has multiple sclerosis. I've been working with him for a year and a half. We have gotten very close. At this point, I think I probably know him better than his family members. It's an important aspect of this niche for you to be aware that that can happen, often happens, and I believe should happen."

Respect your customers both physically and emotionally. Respect their privacy. Linda says, "I tell my customer that I need to know certain things about them in order to better serve them, but I assure them that it's their choice what they choose to share with me and that anything we talk about is kept between the two of us. I value their confidentiality." Respect your customer's equipment. Consider it part

of him or herself. Avoid separating any individual who uses any kind
of adaptive equipment from that equipment. That includes people using wheelchairs, canes, hearing aids, even glasses. Don't rock, bang,
or fidget a person in a wheelchair. Offer assistance but only in such a
way that the person knows you're available if they need you. Don't
offer it in such a way as to say, "You're helpless and I'm going to rescue you." You might try saying things like, "May I turn you around?"
"Would it be easier if I pushed?" "Let me know if you need some assistance." Try to convey the attitude "I'm here for you."

There are a lot of difficulties in designing for people with disabilities, especially people in wheelchairs. When it comes to what specifically to ask the customer, try doing this in a very systematic,
grouping method. First try to identify what the customer can easily
do, what he or she can do with difficulty, what can only be done with
assistance, and what he or she is unable to do. Linda learned from a
friend that the word *ask*, "A-S-K," means: "Acquire Specific Knowledge." That's a gold mine, not just in this field of adaptive design but
in all design and all relationships. Ask the customer the following
questions:

- How much can you lift?
- How much can you carry?
- How long can you stand?
- What causes you to fatigue?
- How's your grip?
- Is one side stronger than the other?
- Can you open cabinet doors?
- What are you unable to do?
- What can you do easily?
- What can you do with difficulty?
- What can you do with assistance?
- Are you taking medications that increase your sensitivity to
  light?
- How is your vision? Can you read small print?
- Can you use both hands, one hand, palm only, some fingers,
  or all fingers?
- Does mobility vary by time of day? Are you weaker in the
  morning or at night?
- Can you feel the difference between hot and cold?
- Are there any hearing changes, hypersensitivity to sound, or
  certain sounds that can't be heard?
- What adaptive equipment do you use? A wheelchair, walker,
  or a scooter? Does there need to be room in the kitchen or
  bath for both? (The customer might have two wheelchairs: a

motorized one for outside, a manual one for inside. There is also the possibility the customer might need to transfer from a wheelchair to a walker.)

- Is there a helper who is around? All the time? (If so, you might have to design the kitchen or bath for two.)

You might want to have these questions (and any others of your own) printed up in worksheet form to help organize your thoughts and information as you communicate with the customer. This way you won't forget to discuss anything that might be important.

One thing that is important when designing for special needs is to always consider safety. Protect your customers at all times from the dangers of burns, falls, and injuries that can be caused by items falling or from cooktops. Be alert, increase safety, and prevent accidents. Consider the following:

- Good lighting
- Extra receptacles (to avoid any dangerous situations with electrical cords)
- Vision height (avoid shelves installed above the comfort zone—the area where the customer can totally see the item being reached for)
- Contrasting colors (e.g., the edge of the countertop a different color than the top)
- Highly visible controls, knobs (e.g., different in color from the background), etc.

Linda continues, "The hardest questions to ask a person with a disability have to do with prognosis. A person will probably improve after a stroke. A person with MS probably will have lots of ups and lots of downs. A person with Parkinson's most likely will get progressively worse. I find it hard to ask about prognosis. I ask because it's important information. My customers are glad that I care enough to ask." You might try saying things like:

- How's it going with you?
- Are you having an up?
- Are you having a down?
- Are you expecting to get better?
- One of Linda's favorites is, "You're looking good; I hope you're doing well."

When you find yourself in an unusual situation where you need to get personal information from the customer, try starting a conversation by referring to another customer in a similar situation and how you were able to help. If you begin slowly, the customer will gain your trust and feel comfortable enough to talk about things that are personal. If you are patient, the customer will respond willingly.

Before you can design a project for a customer, it is important to ask the questions previously listed in order to gather information you will need to conform and complete the project to your customer's needs. Acquiring this information benefits both you and the customer. Learning your customer's comfort zones makes designing for special and specific needs much easier.

Gene Rothert

Gene is a Registered Horticultural Therapist and is the Manager of Urban Horticulture at the Chicago Botanic Garden, where he also oversees their Enabling Garden for People with Disabilities (which will be discussed later in this book) and other horticultural outreach programs. He's the author of *The Enabling Garden—Creating Barrier-Free Gardens* (ISBN #0-87833-847-0, Taylor Publishing Company). Eighteen years ago, Gene went to work for Chicago Botanic Garden, fresh out of college and fresh out of rehabilitation after a spinal cord injury that requires him to use a wheelchair. Those who have done their homework on the subject of disabilities know that this was a time when placement of an individual with disabilities in the workplace was very rare.

Gene knows from experiencing a permanent disability that life becomes an exercise in adaptation. "We make the best use of our abilities along with the assistive equipment we need and we get to be very good at it out of necessity and the everyday challenges of overcoming barriers—sometimes it is just simply finding an easier way." Gene has personal remodeling experience dealing with insensitive contractors and their lack of observations on barriers in and around the home.

He comments, "In a nutshell, builders and remodelers need to focus on individual capabilities, now and in the future (as a person ages, etc.). Knowing what's out there in the way of material and special equipment that creates barrier-free living is vital but even more important is the ability to guide a person unfamiliar with all the design and component selection possibilities—to hand-hold, if necessary, so the end product works!"

Before we look at Gene's story, there are some technical medical terms with regard to the location and extent of his injuries which need explaining. Spinal cord injuries are defined by a combination of letters and numbers; in Gene's case, the injury was at the T-12/L-1 level. The letters indicate where the injury is located (i.e., in what section of the spinal or vertebral column). The numbers indicate the specific vertebra (or vertebrae) within that section. The column is made up of 33 vertebrae and it is divided into five sections of vertebrae: 7 cervical (neck), 12 thoracic (chest region), 5 lumbar (lower back), 5 fused sacral (hip region), and 4 fused coccygeal (tailbone region or coccyx). Gene's injuries were located on the last vertebra of the thoracic and the first vertebra of the lumbar section of the spinal column, which means he is paralyzed from the waist down.

This is Gene's story on the nightmares he experienced during his remodeling project.

I became a wheelchair user in 1977 as the result of a rock climbing accident which left me with a spinal cord injury at the T-12/L-1 level. Functionally, I use a manual wheelchair and have better than average upper body strength. Active as I am, the very athletic "super grip" image does not fit.

I do have a career that keeps me quite busy and in 1979, I married. My wife and I then settled into normal expectations of the American dream—save for the down payment on a house, think about having kids, get a better car. . . .

Several months before the wedding, we began looking for an accessible apartment. In those days, I think accessible housing was built by accident rather than on purpose. My needs were not unreasonable: A first-floor apartment was my preference over one requiring use of an elevator, rooms large enough to allow relative freedom of movement around furniture, doorways wide enough to allow passage of my wheelchair, and a bathroom for the basic functions of life. Sounds simple but it took three months to find such a "haven." Then, it was made accessible (widening of the bathroom door) only at my expense and through the landlord's "generosity." Once completed, we moved in for what we thought would be the usual two to three years necessary to save for a down payment. Well, that time stretched to nine years and it wasn't because we were poor! Finding an accessible house, from the outset, turned into the impossible dream. We couldn't afford to gut and remodel to my specifications while also considering the usual factors of location, price, municipal services, taxes, etc. . . .

Nine years later (the search was not continuous; we gave up altogether for varying periods of time), my wife came home almost in tears. "I've found it! You have got to see this house!!" At that time, the real estate market was very hot;

houses in the neighborhood were listed on the average only one week. The house was on the market just one day and there were three parties interested. If you snooze, you lose, so we decided quickly, made an offer and won the prize.

The house is a simple, three-bedroom/two-bath, brick and frame ranch built in the mid-1950s. It was custom designed for someone with polio, which meant doorways were wider than customary and a concrete ramp from the two-and-a-half car garage into the house was already in place. However, the original owner must have used crutches to get around the house because neither bathroom was wheelchair accessible. The master bedroom bath was the only urgent remodeling job. The doorway was too narrow; fixtures were laid out inaccessibly and all was in sore need of updating. We decided not to tear up the hall bathroom, inaccessible though it was, because it had recently received a face-lift. This left me using the one off the master bedroom all the time.

The people we bought the house from would not be moving for a couple of months. This, along with our unbreakable apartment lease, meant we would not move until Halloween weekend. The house would be empty for six weeks allowing us to paint, redecorate on a minor scale—and—remodel the bathroom. I knew how to go about it and I would have enjoyed the process but mostly the job was literally out of reach. There was plenty of time to select a contractor and get the job done before moving day—or so we thought.

We interviewed contractors based on recommendations and chose a few from the yellow pages as well. Each of them was clearly told that the work must be completed before we moved in because I would not be able to use any bathroom in my house until it was. We selected a contractor whose quote fell within our budget range; he assured us the work would be completed on time so I would not be required to use a bedpan and bathe in the kitchen sink. We all laughed at that!

Well, the joke was on me. Things started out just fine; the workmen were conscientious, then the delays began. Due to the small room size, designing for accessibility was a matter of inches. Since positioning was key, I was asked to be on site to give my approval—then the work crew wouldn't show and a day of my time would be wasted. The phrase, "in two weeks" was heard about every two weeks.

December 20 was the actual completion date of the job meant to be finished by October 30!! Yes, the bedpan and I became well acquainted and I often did the dishes before taking a "bath." I felt the overall insensitivity to my situation to be inexcusable. The contractor knew what I needed, when and why. He *knew* what I was going through. Even writing this eight years after the fact makes me angry.

Why didn't we fire the contractor when things turned sour? Additional time would be lost in selecting a new contractor. We also found that one contractor does not want to step into the middle of another's work; in other words, no guarantees for what's been done—so we stuck it out.

Aside from the general lack of professionalism, I do not feel this contractor or others with whom I interacted are familiar with the various remodeling materials and technologies that improve housing access for people with disabilities. Understandably, it is difficult to keep up with everything that comes and goes on the market; I suppose this is why there are remodelers who specialize in working for people with disabilities. In my case, I had to find the adapted sink and toilet used in my bathroom.

The following are my recommendations for any remodeling contractor working for people with disabilities or older adults in need of renovating for accessibility purposes:

- Do not accept more than one or two jobs at a time; any more on the burner and nothing gets finished. In my case, I feel that the boss did little else than run around assuaging angry tempers. On one day, the carpenter told me he worked on five different jobs! How much could he possibly accomplish at any one site?

- Have a thorough knowledge of the materials and designs that ensure accessibility. Do not rely on the client to know what is best or appropriate for the need at hand. The person requiring the adaptations might still be adjusting to a mobility or sensory impairment and simply not be aware of the choices.

- All contracts provided by the home remodelers I have seen expect you to accept delays or late work as "unavoidable acts of God." They will not accept responsibility. Large construction projects generally exact a financial penalty for each day of work not completed on schedule. Conversely, a bonus is awarded for early completion. I would like to see these policies become part of individual remodeling contracts as well.

Barbara L. Allan

Director of the Access/Abilities Program for the Easter Seal Society of Washington, Barbara has been active for many years in the promotion of barrier-free design concepts and in producing both written and visual materials to support them. She is an associate member of the Washington State Governor's Committee on Disability Issues and Employment and is currently co-chair of its Subcommittee on Accessibility Awareness. In 1978, she initiated and co-authored *An Illustrated Handbook for Barrier Free Design—Washington State Rules and Regulations* (Easter Seal Society of Washington).

Often, the need for physical access remains remote or unrecognized until it becomes a personal issue. As a case in point, Barbara became aware of this "by accident." Following a spinal cord injury in the 1960s, and after having completed rehabilitation at a spinal cord injury center, she found herself "launched" into an environment fraught with barriers—previously unseen. Although she had gained certain physical strengths and skills through rehabilitation, she felt totally unprepared for the onslaught of physical barriers encountered. It was a harsh and frustrating experience—and this is her story:

> Looking for accessible housing when there seemed to be none was a formidable task. Stairs, steps, narrow doorways, inaccessible bathrooms—all combined to make a most discouraging picture.
>
> Having a background in interior design, I felt architects and designers should be educated on the need for architectural changes which could more readily accommodate people with disabilities. It seemed evident that most barriers could be eliminated by just small changes. A mere inch or two here and there could accomplish a great deal in the provision of access. Such changes in design would enable people to access buildings and facilities otherwise inaccessible.
>
> In an attempt to convey this message to architects and designers in particular, I received funding to produce a short film, "The Surest Test," portraying these frustrating barriers, hoping those in the design and construction industry might be favorably influenced. The Easter Seal Society of Washington supported this effort by funding an educational pamphlet developed to accompany the film—and subsequently offering me a staff position to establish a new program designed to educate and advocate accessibility. The offer, though unexpected, had appeal not only because it seemed important

to convey the message of accessibility design—but also because it was one of the (then) rare wheelchair accessible office spaces in which to work. It has recently been remodeled, thanks to the contributed efforts of the American Society of Interior Designers (ASID) local chapter, to be a model of accessibility design.

The Society's Access/Abilities program was established in 1972 specifically to educate and advocate accessibility design. Their first efforts incorporated the use of my film, "The Surest Test" (and its accompanying booklet). This film eventually gained national and even international exposure.

But for my personal life, the attempts to negotiate what might be termed a rather "hostile" environment—due to architectural barriers—was a frustrating and difficult experience. The search for accessible housing, accessing educational facilities, let alone the everyday necessities of shopping, transportation, parking, etc., were far from easy. Amenities such as accessing recreational and social activities and events seemed further down the list in terms of priorities.

In those early days, before there were any building code requirements or accessibility laws, and while trying to spread the message of accessibility, I frequently heard the comment, "but I don't see any disabled people out in the community." The unspoken assumption being—is there really a need? At that time there seemed to be little recognition of the fact that most people with disabilities, with the exception of a few bold and adventurous types, could not get out to be seen, due the vast array of architectural and transportation barriers existing at that time.

First and foremost after rehabilitation was finding accessible housing. The search was difficult but finally rewarding. A single-story ranch style house was found with a level site and no steps. The interior was open in plan and basically accessible for my functional ability at the time.

However, it later seemed desirable to do some remodeling to improve accessibility in both the kitchen and bathroom. An architect was selected and plans were developed with design decisions worked out well in advance between the architect and me. My desire was to make the kitchen remodel and the addition of a small sunroom and new patio and walkway models of accessibility. I wanted to demonstrate "universal design" by having the accessibility features be so integrated and aesthetically pleasing as to provide greater safety, convenience, and access for all users, and not appear special or different. Good design and functional access was the key focus here.

To undertake the modification of a residence for accessibility, even with specific design plans drawn up, I found, was to encounter contractors unfamiliar with such concepts and too prone to "do what they had always done"—instead of what was specified on the plans. It became apparent that contractor education on this subject was—and is—a major need.

Originally, the kitchen cabinetry was to incorporate modified modular components, to demonstrate how this could be easily and cost-effectively accomplished. The manufacturer had agreed to work it out using the architect's plans and design. Unfortunately, they later felt unable to carry this out and the cabinets had to be custom built—at a greater cost.

While the selected contractor had vigorously claimed to be able to carry out the plans, the results were less than desirable. The architect and I had carefully reviewed with the general contractor the unique features to be provided, but many features were overlooked or done incorrectly, necessitating re-doing—simply because of not being really understood or thought to be important.

Features, such as the sunroom sliding-door threshold, which the contractor assured us would be made flush for easy wheelchair access, he later said just could not be done. Electrical outlets, which were designated at specific heights for wheelchair reach-range, but which the electrician failed to see on the plans—were installed per the "usual." A built-in dining table whose mounting support had been wrongly placed had to be completely redone. Many features such as these were done incorrectly due to failure to consult the plans—and the subcontractors not understanding the access needs behind certain design features.

It became evident in this process that having accessibility features carefully worked out and drawn and specified on the plans, though very important, was not alone sufficient for a successful result. Even though time was spent going over the plans with the contractor and I received his assurance that he understood—the resulting numerous errors proved otherwise.

Although the kitchen and patio design won national recognition and award for accessibility design, the process indicated the need for better understanding of accessibility, and perhaps better communication between the owner and contractor.

As for the bathroom project, the subsequent contractor proved much more receptive and cognizant of the plans and specifications, and willing to consult frequently with me to clarify desired results. However, the plumbing contractor was less so, and, neglecting to consult the plans or me, installed the wall-hung water closet 1½" lower than specified. By the time I discovered it, the tile work and mirror had already been installed—which meant having to tear everything out to correct the height of the water closet. To the plumber, this height difference seemed insignificant. To me, the user, it was critical for wheelchair transferability.

The primary need in this remodeling process seems to be for greater awareness and sensitivity by the construction industry regarding the reasons behind accessibility design features and considerations, as well as clearer communication between owner and contractor, and/or architect and designer. Plans need to be clear and unique features perhaps highlighted and pointed out well in advance—to avoid costly errors.

The growing trend toward better understanding and awareness can only increase marketability for housing that is universally designed. Basic access, in terms of entry and circulation, plus flexibility of certain features allow for a wider range of users to be accommodated and furthers safety and convenience to all in the process.

Summary

These personal experiences give us a lot to think about. The professional must learn to listen carefully to the customer, whether that customer is disabled or not. When customers are direct in expressing their needs, we must accept what they are telling us. While a nondisabled person might tolerate and be willing to accept some unmet specifications ("mistakes"), a person with disabilities cannot because such mistakes would interfere with carrying out daily activities. It seems that there are a few individuals out there who do not represent this industry as professionally as it should be represented, and they make it difficult for the rest of us in this business. If you don't understand this market and are not willing to work at it and with your customer, then you shouldn't be in it! Customers should be Number One at all times, no matter what the circumstances—they pay our wages.

Terminology

Perhaps you have noticed that up to this point certain terms or phrases have been used (relating to disease or injury) that you might not be accustomed to using. These terms are probably not part of your usual construction vocabulary. If you are new to this market, this is something to expect, but these terms will soon become part of your working vocabulary.

As professionals, we need to have some awareness of fundamental human considerations and a working knowledge of various aspects of the diseases and disabilities of the individuals with whom we will be working. There is not enough room in *Accessible Housing* to explain all the terms in their entirety. I can, however, provide you with enough knowledge so that when a potential customer calls, you will be able to speak with some confidence and expertise on a given subject. This information will help you to better understand the disabilities of potential customers.

Some important terms to remember include:

- Manipulatory: Manual dexterity or use of upper extremities (hands).
- Nonambulatory: Unable to walk. Needs to use a wheelchair.
- Semi-ambulatory: Walks with assistive devices such as crutches, braces, canes, or a walker.
- Ambulant-disabled: Capable of slow or restrictive movement. Might have problems with coordination, strength, stability, or stamina.
- Equilibrium: State of balance.
- Osteo- and rheumatoid arthritis: Inflammation of joints.
- Ankylosing spondylitis: Arthritic condition of the spine.
- Allergy: A reaction to a substance.
- Hypertension: High blood pressure.
- Cardiac: Relating to the heart.
- Pulmonary: Relating to the lungs.
- Perception: The process by which information about the world/surroundings is received by the senses, analyzed, and made meaningful.
- Cognition: The mental process by which knowledge is acquired.
- Cognitive dysfunction: Impaired awareness with perception, reasoning, intuition, and/or memory.
- Sensory impairments: Those involving one or more of the five senses.
- Cerebrovascular accident: A stroke.

- Traumatic brain injury: Physical injury to the brain.
- Cerebral palsy: A developmental abnormality of the brain causing weakness and incoordination in the limbs.
- Peripheral nerve injury: Injury to any part of the nervous system lying outside the central nervous system (brain and spinal cord).
- Carpal tunnel syndrome: Compression of median nerve as it enters the wrist. Might cause pain and numbness in fingers.
- Muscular dystrophy: Disease that causes weakness and wasting away of muscles.

Spinal cord functions (neurological conditions):

- Multiple Sclerosis: A chronic, slowly progressive disease of the central nervous system.
- Amyotrophic Lateral Sclerosis: A disease of the nervous system in which motor neurons in the brain stem and spinal cord degenerate, leading to atrophy and paralysis of the voluntary muscles ("Lou Gehrig's disease").
- Parkinson's Disease: A progressive neurologic disease characterized by fine, slowly spreading tremors, muscular weakness and rigidity, and a peculiar gait.
- Quadriplegia: Paralysis of (usually) the trunk and both legs and arms.
- Paraplegia: Paralysis from the waist down, including legs.
- Partial Paralysis: Paralysis affecting only a certain part of the body.

It is your responsibility to follow through on the subject with an expert such as an occupational or physical therapist. Therapists are trained in anatomy and physiology, are very knowledgeable about bodily systems and disease processes, and work with patients who have either an acquired disability or a condition existing from birth. The world of physical medicine and rehabilitation includes therapists with physical, occupational, speech, industrial, and recreational specialties. Together, they form a multidisciplinary team to assess and evaluate an individual's level of function and determine appropriate treatments that support independent living skills and the ability to return to work.

The therapists work to help patients lead productive, independent, and rewarding lives by working to restore the patient's capacity for performing what physicians and therapists refer to as "Activities of Daily Living" (ADLs). ADLs include bathing, toileting, dressing, meal preparation, home maintenance, using personal and mass transit, shopping, and any task that we perform for our independence. Therapists help patients learn to carry out daily activities, either in an adapted way or by teaching them from the start.

So how can therapists help you in designing for accessibility? Quite simply, they can help you understand the abilities and physical requirements of your customers. By analyzing the home environment (i.e., studying the activities that your customers have to perform in their homes, kitchens, and bathrooms), therapists then can suggest either temporary or permanent solutions (a treatment plan) to help make the home environment easier to live in. A written treatment plan for the patient (might be based on physician's orders) will describe any treatments to be provided, the purpose of those treatments, and their anticipated outcomes. The plan is based on an evaluation of the patient's medical history, mobility, strength, general function level and cognitive abilities. As the patient continues treatment, he or she will be periodically evaluated for progress and the plan will be modified accordingly. Depending on the patient, a therapist might provide, design, or fabricate special equipment to aid the patient to enter the mainstream of everyday activities. This includes helping the patient with developmental skills and training in the use of equipment.

The therapist can tell you what features your customer requires and then leave it up to you to be creative. By working as a team, you and the therapist can determine how to make the home more functional for the customer. This doesn't mean you automatically start a room redesign project by knocking down walls. The project might require something simple, such as adding some equipment or reorienting existing fixtures and cabinets, individually tailoring the environment to meet specific needs. Even though some projects will be similar, you still need to consider each project separately; I can't stress this enough. Every situation and every customer (along with his or her family) will present a unique opportunity.

All the physical characteristics and terms described earlier share a common denominator—they concern sensory abilities and physical capacities. Senses (vision, hearing, smell, touch, and taste) and physical capacities (endurance, strength, and understanding) define the quality of our lives. Our homes present us with an opportunity to create an environment that meets and enhances every aspect of our abilities. When you are working with someone who has a disability or who wants to build with the future in mind, discuss a variety of courses and options. For example:

- People with medical problems or disabilities have varying medical precautions, and you need to ask about them. For example, some medications can cause sensitivity to sunlight or to different fabrics. Lighting and product color should be concerns in any design you develop.

- Physically, you want to know how the person gets around. It sounds obvious, but does the person use a wheelchair? Can this person use a wheelchair sometimes and walk at other times? Does walking require the use of some kind of assistive device or helper? And if someone has to help the person, does that mean that there needs to be room for two people (e.g., to walk down a corridor or walk through a doorway)?
- What positions (standing or sitting) can the person work in? Can this person kneel to access low storage space? For example, if a client had a bilateral amputation of both legs, he or she might not be able use this kind of storage.
- Find out about the customer's arm and hand use. A lot of people have the use of only one arm but can do everything that someone with both arms and hands can do. There are different adaptive devices that can be installed to improve the environment for your customer. Some people can use both hands but they might have limited strength or coordination. They might only be able to use the palms of their hands. Their fingers might not work, so you would want to look at what they can access with the palm of their hand. Also consider their endurance.
- Vision is important. Some people have low vision; they aren't blind but they have difficulty seeing small print. For people with low vision, lighting can be extremely important. This type of disability might not be visibly obvious, so it is something you need to ask about.
- Some people experience changes in their sensory abilities; for example, they might not feel the difference between hot and cold at all. Hopefully, they have someone in the home to test water temperature for them to prevent inadvertent scalding. Because this is an impairment that can't be visibly detected, it is up to you to ask. The type of plumbing fixtures you install could eliminate serious injuries to a person with this disability.
- Hearing limitations might or might not be obvious. You can ask about them. Is your customer sensitive to certain sounds? If so, you will need to be concerned about acoustics in response to this hypersensitivity.
- Other considerations include any safety precautions that need to be addressed. Does the person need a lot of nonskid materials in the bathroom, for instance? Should you mitigate sharp corners around tables or countertops?

- Space requires a lot of consideration, especially for someone who uses a lot of adaptive equipment. Perhaps your client has an electric wheelchair that is not used in the house. While a manual chair is preferred indoors, the electric wheelchair might require space for storage or electrical access for battery charging. Maybe your customer has walkers and different equipment in the bathroom that are needed only occasionally. Such equipment requires storage space.

Other factors to consider

Remember, a therapist can help a customer decide on the little things that matter. Depending on the problem, these could involve small changes that could have a big impact. Something as minor as positioning the person in a different way can make a task much easier. Sometimes positioning or changing tools can make a big difference. Sometimes just spacing a person's heavy activities throughout the day can help to determine whether a change in the design is required; perhaps just the routine needs changing. A therapist can help define these kinds of changes.

Be alert and be aware of some of the tools and different adaptive equipment on the market. You never know when you might need to recommend such devices or to purchase items to be used in conjunction with your design. These tools and adaptive equipment are known as home *health care products*. It would be wise to have catalogs on hand from companies that distribute these products, such as DMI (Duro-Med Industries, Inc.), who list over 100 items in their catalog.

Keep in mind that a standard handle of yesterday wasn't designed to accommodate special needs and one handle does not fit all applications and customers. Built-up handles or lighter-weight handles can be installed for someone who doesn't have a good grasp. Use a heavier handle for an individual who has lots of tremors. Handles in bright contrasting colors might be appropriate for people with visual problems. Using different sizes and shapes of handles can make things more accessible. One good rule of thumb is, if you can access a handle or a switch with the palm of your hand and the fingertips, or fine coordination is not required, then it's probably universally designed. For example, a wide-blade rocker switch can be accessed by an elbow or closed fist. Look for sound-activated switches.

There are products on the market that customers can use to extend their reach. These devices are normally called "reachers" or enabling tools, and they are available with vinyl, magnetic, and suction tips. They are perfect for reaching objects and help to avoid possible pain or injury caused by excessive bending and stretching. This sounds so simple, yet it could be something you could suggest to a customer to help save some renovation dollars.

Your customers might not realize that a padded mesh (Ultra Grip Liner and Grip Liner Coverings by Rubbermaid) placed on the countertop provides a non-slip gripping surface that can hold objects in place, a little trick you might want to suggest that can make a world of difference for someone who can only use one hand. Similarly, mounting a jar opener underneath a cupboard will enable a person to use only one hand to open jars. These are small things but either could make a useful and thoughtful "thank you" gift for your customers.

A client who was recently in a hospital or a rehab center might need adaptive equipment such as a tub seat in the bathroom. Figure 1-2 shows a prime example of such a product. This particular model

1-2 *Libra Model HA0200 is designed for independent bathing in the home setting, thus enhancing the quality of home care.* ARJO INC.

(by ARJO INC.) is powered by a 12V rechargeable power pack. This makes it ideal for any home care patient who needs assistance with bathing transfers, including those with rheumatoid arthritis, stroke patients, amputees, and others unable to successfully clear the tub height. In the raised position, bathers can independently transfer from a wheelchair, or sit down directly on the seat. Once seated, it is simple for bathers to rotate and place their legs in the water. They can then lower themselves to the bottom of the tub at the touch of a button for full immersion bathing. A product such as this might be a cost-effective alternative to replacing a bathtub with a more expensive barrier-free model.

Even with such products, installing grab bars is still a good idea so that customers can pull themselves across the seat if they should desire to do so. A hand-held shower, of course, is a nice option for your customers rather than sitting on a tub bench and having water shooting at them. A hand-held shower provides some control over waterspray direction. Perhaps getting off the toilet can be a real struggle. Installing economy toilet guard rails that use the toilet seat hinge bolts (Fig. 1-3) can provide the support the customer needs. Sometimes you just have to be creative.

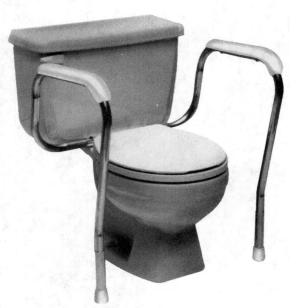

1-3 *DURO-MED Model 1804 is designed to provide support and easy maintenance.* DMI (DURO-MED Industries, Inc.)

Effective communication

As mentioned throughout this chapter, effective communication plays a major role in the success of your business and—most importantly—in how you handle and respond to your customer. If some of the material presented here seems redundant to you, you're probably right. The intent (and hope) is that every gray area becomes crystal clear: I want you to understand totally. With the help of Ken Smith, CKD, CBD, Director of Training for the National Kitchen & Bath Association (NKBA), this section highlights everything you have read so far and sets the stage for the rest of the book as well.

The highlights are broken down into two sets of terms that should make it easier for you to understand and visualize your role in this market. The first list contains terms that are considered unfavorable, if not outright unacceptable. They are, however, used on a regular basis. The second set lists terms that are more acceptable, less offensive, and often feature an expanded meaning or appreciation. Both lists include brief definitions of each term, its intention, and any advantages/disadvantages are noted as appropriate. Keep in mind that your customer's comfort is important, and use the tools in this section for better understanding when communicating with your customer.

Unacceptable terms:

- *Physically challenged*—many dislike the term and view it as a "made-up" term by those individuals who are not disabled in some way. Some view it as trite (superficial, stereotypical, and quasi) and even offensive.
- *Afflicted*—suggests deep psychological trauma, including a subdefinition of plague.
- *Invalid*—a word which says, when broken down, "in-valid." This is not a good label to attach to someone.
- *Cripple*—defamatory.
- *Defective*—defamatory.
- *Wheelchair bound*—unless chained to the wheelchair, the individual is not bound to or by the chair; quite the contrary, the chair provides freedom and mobility.
- *Handicap design*—"handicap" is used throughout society and in many federal documents. It is generally accepted and certainly understood, but it is considered harsh.
- *Compassionate design*—trite and presuming again, a term made up by someone not affected by a physical limitation.
- *Special design (for special people)*—same as above. Many find this somewhat offensive. They can appreciate the term

"special design" which, by itself, lacks substance, but they do not want to be considered "special people."

Preferred terminology:

- *Wheelchair user or wheelchair mobile*—denotes a positive action, someone striving for independence and "in charge."
- *Blind, deaf, and mute*—accepted as medical terms.
- *Impaired*—seems well accepted as a follow-up word to many other descriptive words, such as:

  ~ *"Mobility impaired"*

  ~ *"Hearing impaired"*

  ~ *"Visually impaired"*

  It indicates a limitation and need for compensation but often lacks enough information if used alone.
- *Physically limited*—a well-accepted term if used with an additional explanation to provide more information.
- *Lifespan design or lifetime design*—a good general term that requires specific definition. This can describe an environment in which residents can remain throughout a lifetime; an environment that will adapt to changing needs throughout the aging process, or one that will serve themselves, their children, and live-in parents with equal flexibility (multigenerational homes).
- *Barrier-free design*—indicates an open and barrier-free environment. This term is most often applied to those using wheelchairs or walkers.
- *Universal design*—well-known and widely used term indicating an environment usable by almost anyone entering the space.
- *Adaptable/adjustable design*—perhaps the most flexible and preferred term. Indicates an accessible environment, usually allowing for wheelchair clearance. Has adaptable features which will adjust to the user rather than require the user to adapt to the environment.

Don't worry if you can't remember everything in this chapter or the terms mentioned above. They will be used and discussed throughout the book. This first chapter is just an overview of what to expect if you should decide to go into this business, but it is a very important chapter. Refer to it as often as needed to keep you on the right path.

This book can help you to change your mindset in order to better understand and serve your customers. People with disabilities are just people, like you and me. Treat them with respect—treat them with dignity—treat them as you would like to be treated!

2

Focus on accessibility

When and if you decide to enter this market, you'll have some choices to make, including:

- Which market will you select for specialization—residential or commercial (multifamily)?
- Will you be involved in all aspects of universal design (i.e., barrier-free and adaptable/adjustable design and permanent modifications)?
- Will you consider building environmentally safe homes?

If you choose to tackle the commercial market, you'll be faced with unfamiliar regulations and standards which you are required to follow. In the residential market, you'll do whatever it takes to make the customer's home a comfortable living and working environment. But once you have decided on a solution (with the help of the customer and therapist, and depending on the complexity of the project), you will still need to run your plans past your local building department for approvals and permits.

The bottom line in all this is that the customer has priorities that need special attention, and your job is to satisfy those special needs. Your mission is to create or adjust the living environment so your customer can carry out daily activities, making sure you follow the requirements of the building codes.

Regulations and standards

As mentioned earlier, the commercial market, which also applies to multifamily housing (four units or more), has its own set of regulations and standards to follow. I suggest that you obtain a copy of those regulations and standards and become familiar with the specifications and guidelines. Unfortunately, the problem with the standards themselves is that some professionals treat them as ideal solutions, rather than the *minimal standards* they really are. The standards represent the minimal acceptable solution. In some cases, that is not the best or most creative solution to a design or construction problem. As a professional, you should treat existing regulations and standards as a starting point in the design of an accessible project.

Depending on what you are designing, you might be tempted to go under the minimum requirement (whether residential or commercial). It is not wise to let that happen for two reasons: first, the project will not pass inspection; second, you will not be helping the individual who has to live within this environment. If anything, you should exceed the minimum. Remember, it is your responsibility to make this project flow—to make it work to its full potential—for the individual with special needs.

Interestingly enough, standards are only voluntary minimum guidelines—they are not the law. A governing body might choose to adopt these guidelines into an enforceable code, but the standards carry no legal weight until that happens. Table 2-1 shows a comparison between regulations and standards in accessible construction. Table 2-2 shows regulations or laws that affect single-family and/or multifamily housing.

In short, there really are no laws regulating universal design (barrier-free and adaptable/adjustable design and permanent modifications) in private residential single-family homes. However, the laws that have been adopted in the commercial market and the associated voluntary standards provide helpful information to serve as a starting point in the design of universal projects, and there are local and state codes that impact residential construction. Building codes for accessibility might vary from state to state and even from state to city and from city to city within a state. These codes are often similar and they all address the same areas of concern. Many of the codes refer to ANSI (American National Standard Institute) Standard A117.1-1992, "Accessible and Usable Buildings and Facilities," a revision of ANSI A117.1-1986 (the standards are revised every five years). The main laws and standards in use are outlined. They are provided here by the National Kitchen & Bath Association (NKBA) from their publication, *Universal Kitchen Planning—Design That Adapts To People* (ISBN #1-887127-00-3), by Mary Jo Peterson, CKD, CBD.

Table 2-1. Regulations defining minimum accessibility and the building standards that apply to them

Regulations	Standards
Architectural Barriers Act of 1968 (ABA)	Uniform Federal Accessibility Standard (UFAS)
Section 504 of the Rehabilitation Act of 1973 (504)	Uniform Federal Accessibility Standard (UFAS)
Fair Housing Amendments Act of 1988 (FHAA)	Fair Housing Accessibility Guidelines, includes some components of ANSI 117.1
Americans with Disabilities Act of 1990 (ADA)	Americans with Disabilities Act Accessibility Guidelines (ADAAG), includes components of ANSI 117.1

Table 2-2. Building types and accessibility laws that govern their design and construction

	Laws		
Type of building	**Dwelling unit**	**Site**	**Common areas**
Private, single-family detached (site or factory built)	Zoning, building codes	Zoning	
Private, single-family detached, manufactured	Zoning, building codes, HUD	Zoning	
Rental, single-family, detached	Zoning, building codes	Zoning	
Private funds, rental, townhouse or multifamily of four units or less	Zoning, building codes	Zoning	ADA
Federal funds, townhouse or multifamily of four units or less	Zoning, building codes, ABA, 504	Zoning, ABA, 504	ADA
Private funds, multifamily of more than four units	Zoning, building codes, FHAA	Zoning, FHAA	FHAA, ADA
Federal funds, multifamily of more than four units	Zoning, building codes, ABA, 504, FHAA	Zoning, ABA, 504, FHAA	FHAA, ADA

Architectural Barriers Act

In 1968, the Architectural Barriers Act was passed to regulate buildings used or funded by the federal government. The Uniform Federal Accessibility Standards (UFAS) were published in 1984. The purpose of the UFAS was to set "uniform standards for the design, construction and alteration of buildings so that physically handicapped persons will have ready access to and use of them in accordance with the Architectural Barriers Act." The UFAS represented the most comprehensive standard to that date and was a good effort to minimize the differences among the federal standards and the access standards recommended for facilities that did not fall under the Architectural Barriers Act. The technical provisions of the UFAS were for the most part the same as the 1980 edition of American National Standard Institute ANSI A117.1, "Specifications for Making Buildings and Facilities Accessible to and Usable by Physically Handicapped People."

Fair Housing Amendments Act

In 1988, the Fair Housing Amendments Act was passed into law as an amendment to the Civil Rights Act of 1968. While the Civil Rights Act prohibited discrimination in the sale, rental, or financing of dwellings based on color, religion, sex, or national origin, the Fair Housing Amendments Act (FHAA) added people with disabilities and people with children to the list. In 1991, the Final Fair Housing Accessibility Guidelines were published to "provide builders and developers with technical guidance on how to comply with the specific accessibility requirements of the Fair Housing Amendments Act of 1988." This standard and law applies to multifamily construction where there are four or more units under one roof. While the requirements of the law are mandatory, these precise guidelines are not. "Builders and developers might choose to depart from the guidelines and seek alternate ways to demonstrate that they have met the requirements of the Fair Housing Act." The Act provides that "compliance with ANSI 117.1, or with the laws of a state or unit of general local government that has incorporated into such laws the accessibility requirements of the Act, shall be deemed to satisfy the accessibility requirements of the Act."

Americans with Disabilities Act

In 1990, the Americans with Disabilities Act (ADA) was passed into law, requiring nondiscrimination in many areas of life for people with disabilities. Title II of this Act relates to places of state and local governments (federal continues to be regulated by UFAS) and Title III relates to places of public accommodation and services operated by private enterprises. In 1991, the ADA Accessibility Guidelines (ADAAG) were produced to set "guidelines for accessibility to places of public accommodation and commercial facilities by individuals with disabilities."

The technical specifications are the same as those of the ANSI 117.1-1980 with a few exceptions and a section (4.1.1–4.1.7) dealing with how the requirements apply in different situations. At this time, ADAAG does not cover privately owned residential dwellings.

American National Standard for Accessible and Usable Building and Facilities

First issued in 1961, the current ANSI, American National Standard for Accessible and Usable Building and Facilities (A117.1), was revised in 1992. This standard was created as a model code "for adoption by government agencies and for organizations setting model codes to achieve uniformity in the technical design criteria in building codes and other regulations." It is also intended to be used by nongovernmental parties as technical design guidelines or requirements to make buildings and facilities accessible to and usable by persons with physical disabilities. It is in compliance with or is the basis for much of the information given in the other standards. In review, ANSI A117.1 is intended as a model code and technical design guideline, and it includes information relating to the kitchen (and the bathroom) among other things. [Author's note: remember, the "model code" referred to in this section is actually a voluntary consensus standard system and is not a code in use by code-enforcing municipalities unless specifically adopted.]

Section 504 of the Rehabilitation Act of 1973

The Rehabilitation Act was passed in 1973, but authorizing regulations were not issued until April 28, 1977. The Rehabilitation Act was modeled on the antidiscrimination language of the Civil Rights Act of 1964. It prohibits discrimination on the basis of disability in building and programs funded by the federal government.

The Reagan Administration adopted a narrow definition of the scope of the act, arguing that the regulations applied only to specific programs receiving federal funds. It is now applied to all programs and all aspects of agencies that receive federal funds. Thus, a building constructed on a private college campus funded by monies from a private benefactor would have to be accessible to individuals with disabilities if any part of a federally funded project was to be housed in the building. The Uniform Accessibility Standards (UFAS) apply to buildings under the jurisdiction of Section 504.

The material on Section 504 was provided by The Taunton Press through a book by Margaret Wylde, Ph.D., entitled *Building For A Lifetime, The Design and Construction of Fully Accessible Homes* (ISBN #1-56158-036-8, 1994).

The ADA: A sympathetic reassessment

Barbara L. Allan of the Easter Seal Society of Washington sent me an article she did for *The Seattle Daily Journal of Commerce* (February 8, 1995) that I found of interest and great value. I have included it in the hope that you find it just as valuable:

> As someone actively engaged in promoting and advocating the needs and benefits of barrier-free design for many years, I welcomed the ADA's impact on the built environment. By way of federal mandate, it brought widespread recognition of accessibility. It also brought some surprises—both good and bad.
>
> The ADA has given Washington reason to be proud. It is better prepared for the federal mandate than most states.
>
> Accessibility standards for new construction and remodeling have been part of the Washington State Building Code since 1976. It is largely for this reason that our state is gener-

ally recognized as a leader in the provision of accessibility to the built environment.

After all, design and construction standards that allow for our diverse population, which includes growing numbers of people with disabilities, make good sense. Designing and building to meet the needs of the real population—old, young, tall, short, able and less able—is a practical approach. This broad-based type of design to meet the widely ranging needs of the population is now called "universal design." It is a proactive approach to accessibility design, and it might eventually supplant the imposition of minimum standards.

The current ADA accessibility requirements recognize and incorporate minimum accessibility standards. Ideally, we can eventually get away from the labels and simply incorporate universal design elements into all building codes—to benefit all users.

Most of the issues surrounding the ADA, however, do not concern new construction, but requirements for removing *existing* barriers.

Whereas both ADA requirements and the Washington State Barrier Free Regulations apply to new construction and remodeling, the ADA's requirements for existing building and facilities go beyond state code and earlier accessibility efforts.

Under Title III of the Act, places of public accommodation (where goods and services are made available to the public by a private entity) are required to undertake barrier removal that is "readily achievable," which is defined as: "easily accomplishable and able to be carried out without much difficulty or expense."

From the standpoint of the end user, this has been a truly liberating advance.

Countless places of public accommodation (i.e., retail stores, hotels, theaters, restaurants, banks, etc.) have opened their doors to new customers who were formerly shut out by small barriers. Accessible parking places have arisen where none existed. Ramps have been added where only stairs had been, Braille signage and telecommunication display devices (TDDs) have become almost commonplace expectations.

The result has been that millions of people, previously denied access to goods and services, are now customers and clients.

And fortunately for those establishments, the State of Washington's building code had for several years already included most of the accessibility requirements that became a part of the ADA. Thus, buildings constructed since 1976 are less apt to need much barrier removal. As a result, businesses in this state have generally had to incur less difficulty and expense from ADA requirements for existing facilities.

In 1991, the State Building Code Council felt that the incorporation of accessibility requirements of the ADA (and the Federal Fair Housing Act) into the state barrier free regulations would benefit all concerned but particularly the building and construction industry. This inclusion results in plan review and enforcement procedures not available under federal civil rights laws.

Washington is the first state in the nation to submit its accessibility code requirements to the Department of Justice for certification of equivalency with the ADA. On December 6 it was granted preliminary certification. Following a 60-day comment period and two public hearings, it is expected to be the first state to receive ADA certification. [Author's note: Washington has received this ADA certification; it was included in state amendments to the 1994 UBC adopted on June 30, 1995.]

Certification indicates that the state code meets or exceeds the ADA minimum accessibility requirement. The benefit of certification is that in any ADA enforcement proceedings, it can serve as rebuttable evidence as to having met the Title III requirements.

There is, however, a down side of the ADA: confusion, misinterpretation and fear of litigation. These unnecessary side effects have been exploited by some at the expense of others.

The rush to comply with apparently sweeping requirements of the ADA—and to avoid the perceived threat of litigation—has obscured the actual requirements. Recognizing a market, sudden experts have arisen, with ADA seminars galore, to enlighten and inform the nervous building and design industry.

In spite of the admonition in the regulations that people with disabilities be consulted and included in this process, most of these seminars have been sadly lacking in this input. The result, rather than a more practical and commonsense approach to the requirements, has been the extremes of overkill-or-ignore.

The overkill approach has been to take the new construction standards and apply them to the barrier-removal requirements under Title III public accommodations, and often to Title II program access, as well. The Title II requirement for state and local government is directed to making their programs and services accessible, which might not include the need for architectural changes.

However, the assumption is frequently made that existing facilities must eventually be brought up to compliance with new construction standards. In most cases, this is neither accurate nor practical.

ADA survey checklists, based on new construction requirements, abound, with every detailed measurement included. Costly and often unnecessary ADA accessibility surveys are marketed as the only "safe" way to comply. And the crowning blow is that the mandate itself is frequently unfairly blamed for the unnecessary costs—and people with disabilities are done disservice in the process.

It is generally accepted that the new construction requirements under ADA require little or no additional costs.

However, barrier removal in existing facilities can cost a great deal if not properly understood. The Title III requirement for barrier-removal, in fact, does not require a site or facility survey. But it does require the "identification" of barriers needing to be removed. It requires the removal of those barriers which are "readily achievable," i.e., "easily accomplishable and able to be carried on without much difficulty or expense." This determination is made by the business, based on its size and the nature and cost relative to its financial resources for accomplishing such removal. If physical or structural changes are not readily achievable, then the law provides for alternative, nonstructural solutions for providing the goods and services.

The problem has been that most business owners are not aware of just what constitutes a barrier, or which ones need to be removed, despite the fact that the Department of Justice has given numerous examples and listed the basic priorities of barrier removal. Somewhat confused and edgy about the issue, businesses often hire the "experts" to provide a full-blown ADA accessibility survey, in order to comply with the perceived requirements.

The Department of Justice has provided much in the way of technical assistance, and this includes technical assistance manuals on both Title II and III, as well as technical assistance information through 1-800 phone lines. There are ADA checklists for existing facilities, which offer a commonsense approach based on the priority areas. In addition, there are local agencies serving people with disabilities that offer this information and expertise, and advocate cost-saving, practical approaches.

Given the new climate in Washington, D.C., and the scrutiny being given to unfunded federal mandates, the ADA appears to be a prime target for reassessment and possible revision. Business is crying foul on perceived unjust and burdensome requirements in general and unfunded mandates in particular.

Is there a reasonable means of resolving the legitimate concerns of both sides of this issue? I think there is a simple, commonsense approach to barrier removal under Title III public accommodations.

Here are the basics:

1 *Identify* the physical and communication barriers needing to be removed.
2 *Prioritize* the barriers in the order of their removal based on the financial ability of the business to accomplish the effort.
3 *Document* the process and the participation of any outside assistance, including qualified people with disabilities or organizations representing them.
4 *Remove* the identified barriers as prioritized and reassess further removal or improvements on an ongoing basis.

Rather than assume the need for a costly and detailed survey, businesses can have a simple "walk-through" by a qualified and experienced accessibility specialist to identify the key barriers.

Input or consultation from knowledgeable people with disabilities or organizations serving them can provide a more commonsense approach as well as reduce costs and save time. As an added benefit, the business would be meeting the federal mandate under Title III and certainly meeting the spirit and intent of the law—thereby demonstrating a "good faith" effort has been made.

Of course, the deadline for accomplishing the mandated barrier removal has long since passed (January 26, 1992). Any complaints filed against a business where no action has been taken would likely be more stringently dealt with over time.

Unfortunately many people fail to realize the larger benefits to business and society by complying with the ADA.

With improved physical access, people with disabilities can enter the workplace and be employed. They can purchase more goods and services and pay taxes. Businesses can expand their customer base, claim a tax deduction—and sometimes a tax credit—for removing barriers.

This law is intended to benefit not only people with disabilities directly, but allows for reduction of the costs of dependency. Independence allows individuals to be contributors to society rather than mere recipients of government services. Understood and applied, accessibility design is not costly or difficult to provide. Accessibility design and ADA compliance should be seen as a cost/benefit balance rather than a threat or a burden.

It is evident that the new Congress will be looking closely at all avenues for cutting taxes and reducing spending. One way to accomplish a significant reduction in spending would be to more accurately interpret and comply with the law as written, without lessening its actual aims and objectives.

The bottom line is that a building that incorporates accessibility requirements is safer and more convenient; it provides better access for the widest range of users—including those with disabilities; and it doesn't need to be complex or costly. It's unfortunate that it takes a federal law to initiate its implementation on the broader scale, and that its benefits are not more widely appreciated.

Summary

This brief overview on most of the major laws and guidelines regarding accessibility should help clarify how they could relate to future projects. Keep in mind that this is only an overview and that tremendous amounts of research and involvement on local, state, and national levels have led to these guidelines. It is not my intention to make you an expert on the subject of regulations and standards. However, I do want to make you aware that guidelines do exist and you need to work from and with them. Also, if you don't know, then ask—contact the appropriate agency for help with your particular situation. An old Nigerian proverb says it well: "Not to know is bad; not to wish to know is worse."

Understanding the terms

What do the terms "universal," "barrier-free," and "adaptable/adjustable design" mean to you? If you know their meanings, do you understand how to apply them to your work? Do these words mean essentially the same thing, or are they different in definition? What about an "environmentally safe home"? Up to this point have you been confused as to what the issues really are?

I have always used the term "barrier-free design." I'm sure there are other professionals who use the same term. An architect I know describes barrier-free design as an "architecture that does not inhibit access or use by all people." Is this also true of universal design? In simple terms, universal design can be defined as "the elimination of obstacles that would restrict anyone's freedom of movement throughout the home." The key words here are *anyone's freedom*. The key to successful designs and survival in this specialized market is ensuring that the end product is usable by people of varying size and abilities. In dealing with different individuals, you will face many challenges. In this section I try to define some terms with the help of other professionals who practice them in the field. However, barrier-free, accessible, universal, adaptable/adjustable—even though there are slight differences in definitions, it doesn't matter what you call your design. These terms all converge on two common goals: eliminating all obstacles that restrict freedom of movement throughout the home and ensuring the home is adaptable as the occupants' ages increase. Remember, the occupants of any barrier-free designs you build will want to remain independent as they age in their own environment.

Universal design

Linda Nitteberg, CKD, explains that universal design primarily concerns itself with the life of a building or the life of a facility. The hope is that if a building is properly designed with universal principles in mind, it will be easily accessible and usable for all individuals regardless of size, age, and personal requirements. This means that a short, young child will be able to access and maneuver in the environment as well as a tall, healthy, able-bodied standing adult. At the other end of the spectrum, an elderly, frail person who might be restricted to a wheelchair or a scooter will also be able to access and maneuver in the environment. Linda explains:

> For those who do not know what a scooter is, a scooter is a motorized vehicle that can take the shape of a tricycle or a cart with four wheels. You might have seen one at your state fair or grocery store or in use in outdoor settings. More and more they are being used indoors because of their swivel and/or lift seats. So universal design needs to include scooters just as well as wheelchairs.

Figure 2-1 shows examples of scooters. Your customers can go when and where they want, which means greater independence.

> The first thing we all should consider when we're designing for anybody is—safety—safety! Okay, that includes being aware of the dangers of falls, the dangers of burns, the possibility of something falling onto the cooktop or someone else in the kitchen. I like to install plenty of outlets to avoid the dangers of cords thrown all over the place. Anti-scald faucets are very important. Anti-scald faucets and pressure-balanced valves help protect the delicate skin of the young and the elderly.
>
> A second consideration of good design, according to Linda's school of design, is ease of maintenance. That means

2-1 *Electric (battery) powered scooters provide your customers with independence in the home as well as in the yard.* Provided by Electric Mobility Corporation

surfaces are cleanable. I love solid surface countertops. I like sealed burners. Self-cleaning ovens. Ovens with liners that come out and can be washed. And faucets with a good acrylic or powder coat finish.

The third thing I look for in design is functionality. A good work triangle. A work triangle where the traffic does not cross the path of the triangle. I like to keep the sink and the cooktop fairly close together, and items need to be stored where they're used, just like in any other kitchen.

Lastly, I like for a kitchen or bathroom to be attractive. Some people are really dropping the ball on this and making peoples' homes look like institutions. My philosophy is that universal design should be an expression of the customers' tastes and their lifestyle rather than an extension of the local hospital.

Lisa Moler Robey, CKD, CBD, and president of Harvey's Kitchens & Baths, offers the following comments:

Universal design is fun, commonsense design. The kitchen and bath do not have to look like a hospital unit, but can be beautiful and functional. In the kitchen, vary counter heights (at least two different heights) for all height users. Have some open space under counters for wheelchair access or a chair. At the kitchen sink or cooktop, use retractable doors with no floor in the cabinet, a removable sink front, or a fancy valance with a curtain that coordinates with window treatments in the room. Raise the dishwasher up so it is easy to load and unload and have storage under it. Have a pullout table or cart under the oven or beside it so there is landing area for hot items. Use full extension slides to make drawers and rollouts more accessible. The microwave should be installed 24"–48" to the bottom of it with a pullout counter near it. Refrigerators with bottom-mount freezers make the refrigerator more usable. Storage is best between 15"–48" high, so plan drawers, rollouts, and shelves to maximize this area. Use appliances with large easy-to-read controls and cooktop controls in the front.

In the bath, use showers without a curb and have a seating area and grab bars. Also use grab bars at the toilet or add blocking for them to be installed later. Adjustable height shower heads with massage spray adapt to all users. Use small 1" × 1" or 2" × 2" tiles on the floor for maximum slip resistance. For lavatories, use wall-hung sinks with shrouds, or vanity tops with wall supports, but always remember to have adequate storage elsewhere in the bath. Good examples of storage would be shallow base cabinets, open shelf base cabinets, and full height mirrored medicine cabinets. Adjustable mirrors are easily used by children or wheelchair users. There are products such as the Allegroh lav faucet (Hansgrohe Inc.) that has an effortless handle adjustment and a spout that rotates to form a fountain, which is great for children. It also connects to the water-powered Turbodent massaging mouth spray that makes dental hygiene easy, fun and safe—Turbodent does not require electricity for power (Figs. 2-2 and 2-3). Let's not forget to adjust the heights of switches and thermostats to be within reachable limits.

All of these things and many more make universal design fun and challenging. When designed universally from the beginning, the kitchen or bath will be safe, functional, and beautiful for everyone in the family.

Gary E. White, CID, CKD, & CBD, president of Whitmark Design, Inc. (dba Kitchen & Bath Design), is a pioneer in the field of safer de-

2-2
That's my idea of a drinking faucet—no cups.
Hansgrohe Inc.

2-3
If only it were this easy . . .
Hansgrohe Inc.

signs for kitchen and bath and is well known for his work with the
National SAFE KIDS Campaign. His "Safe Kids Bath" exhibit achieved
national media coverage after its debut at the "Design Ideal Center"
of The National Kitchen and Bath Industry Show in 1992. He is currently conducting a series of seminars for the Safe Bath Alliance. The
following are his comments on the subject of universal design:

> "Universal Design" means three things: accessibility, safety, and
> comfort. I have been teaching safe and accessible bathroom de-
> sign for the National Kitchen and Bath Association for four
> years. What I find most interesting on this subject is not the nuts
> and bolts of how to build more universal spaces. This informa-
> tion is easy enough to obtain from research and memorize.
> Anyone who cares to take the time to learn the applications can
> design and build safer, more comfortable and accessible spaces.
> All you need do is carefully read ANSI-A117.1 (now the guts of
> the Americans with Disabilities Act) to learn the necessary ba-
> sics. What I find intriguing and more challenging as a designer
> is the concept of the psychology of space.
>
> In my opinion space is more psychological than physical. I
> have learned this aesthetic lesson through years of remodeling

cramped awkward small kitchens and baths into spaces people swear are larger even though no walls were moved. I have learned that the careful orchestration of color, shape, texture, light, and composition can indeed make a space feel larger and more comfortable. As I studied universal design, I found that the psychology of space had a more thorough application than I had dreamed. It is, in fact, at the heart of true universal design.

Firstly, I learned about the relationship of safety and peace of mind. I studied my past work to discover what exactly it was that made small cramped spaces feel more comfortable and "larger." This is not the place to discuss at length the design principles behind this theory, but rather explain their results as it pertains to universal design. I learned that a relaxed and comfortable person was far less accident prone than one who is uptight. The more anxious, nervous, or frightened a person is, the more likely they are to have an accident. When we enter a space, our brain subconsciously surveys the area for potential danger. It reviews all the accidents you have had in the past pertaining to any perceived dangers in the space. It does this as a protection mechanism to help avoid accidents. Unfortunately, there is a backlash to this protective mechanism. When overloaded with warning, we get nervous, jittery, in a word, uptight.

This means that the middle-aged executive coming home from a bad day at the office after spending over an hour in bumper-to-bumper traffic who had one extra coffee in the afternoon is probably in as much or more danger, once home, than an individual with disabilities who had been home that day relaxing, especially if this home has been poorly designed for the psychology of space. To me, this is the essence of universal design, because it does indeed pertain to all of us.

Conversely, the more potential accidents the designer can iron out of the space plan, the more comfortable you make the space feel, the less the occupants are prone to have any accidents in the space. The less difficult and dangerous a space is, the less the brain has to do. It follows then that this less difficult and dangerous space will be more relaxing, more enjoyable. A relaxed atmosphere contributes to peace of mind, and it doesn't take a Harvard MBA to figure out that peace of mind is the essence of value.

The other aspect of the psychology of universal design I found most challenging is acceptance. All a designer needs to do is show middle-aged homeowners a grab bar and watch them run for the door. Everyone seems to feel that universal design is OK for the kids, the grandparents, or for disabled persons, but not for me, thanks. I believe it's some sort of human macho thing that we think that anything that looks like it makes life ergonomically easier, makes us look weaker.

I have found the best offense to overcome this objection is deceit. Good universal design is invisible, hidden, blended into the aesthetic of the design. The clever designer can find ways to make the necessary physical elements of universal design contribute to the theme of the design rather than looking like bolted on afterthoughts. If any universal element shows itself, look out, it's the "nursing home syndrome." If it looks like anything they have seen in a nursing home they don't want it. Nobody wants to be reminded of that ominous possibility, and we will live in an uncomfortable and dangerous environment rather than think about it.

Case in point: The SAFE KIDS Bath. In this bathroom I concocted a nautical theme for two young boys who live at the beach in Southern California. The tub platform was constructed to resemble a yacht. Ocean going boats usually have a rail running around them to prevent people from falling overboard. Therefore the railing of the yacht becomes the grab bar, but it's part of the design. This one is lit with fiber optic lighting; it glows and changes color, drawing even more attention to the one thing that most people are most reticent to accept. This is just one example of the many elements that are blended invisibly into this design. I won't take any more space here to discuss the individual elements. Suffice it to say that every aspect of safer design was integrated into this space. Can you spot any of them (Fig. 2-4)?

To this day, when I talk about universal design to a client and show them shots from my portfolio, I am most flattered when they ask, "So what's safe about this room?" What you don't see can't hurt you!!

For those of you who might have missed the other features in Fig. 2-4, they are as follows:

- The tub is a soft cushioning type bathtub—not porcelain or cast iron.
- The bathtub faucet is a pressure-balanced (temperature-limiting) valve, the same as the shower system.
- Located behind the glass blocks is the shower. The shower surround including the pan is made from solid material instead of tile—grout-free!

- The ceiling lights are small miniaturized recessed low-voltage halogens.
- The floor is finished in 9" × 9" (23 cm × 23 cm) vinyl tiles with embedded quartz crystals for durability and a no-wax wear layer).

2-4
With commonsense planning and today's exciting new safety products, you too can create a bathroom such as this. Gary White, CID, CKD, CBD, Kitchen & Bath Design, Newport Beach, CA

Adaptable/adjustable design

Adaptable/adjustable design "is that which can adapt a building to meet the unique needs of a particular occupant. Adaptive design takes into consideration the lives of the current users of a building, focusing on their present as well as future limitations," comments Linda Nitteberg, CKD.

The whole idea behind adaptable design is to preplan for the future so that features and products can be added or removed to adapt the environment to fit an individual's requirements. The process, which can be done in stages, doesn't require any major modifications to the dwelling either structurally or cosmetically; for example, bathroom walls fitted with ¾" (2 cm) plywood before the wallboard is installed so grab bars can be installed anywhere at any height later on. A removable vanity (base cabinet) will allow a wheelchair user easy access to a sink. Countertops and closet rods can be placed on adjustable supports so unskilled labor would be able to adjust them.

By preplanning, homeowners can make modifications in the future to meet needs due to changes in their physical or mental condition. In most cases, persons of all ages can benefit from these modifications.

According to the EPVA's *Adapt to Better Design*, adaptable design is not simply good design for persons who are disabled. Following is a list of advantages and benefits that apply to a number of different groups:

To builders/developers:

- Standardization of construction—with no need to build special "handicapped units."
- Increasing marketability—units have the appearance of conventional units.
- Adaptability to the needs of persons with various disabilities.

To owners/renters:

- Costs less to convert to a greater degree of accessibility should the occupant develop a disability at some point in the future.
- Affords people with a disability the freedom to visit friends and neighbors and, while visiting, to use the bathroom.
- Allows people to remain in their homes even with any disabling conditions that aging might cause (an important advantage considering the increasing average age of the U.S. population).

To property managers:

- Allows property managers to rent to a larger market. All units are usable by disabled and nondisabled equally.
- Improves tenant longevity.

As mentioned earlier, the word "handicapped" should be avoided in conversation unless being used in a phrase such as: "This person is handicapped when faced with a set of stairs when there is no ramp alongside." Don't be alarmed if you see such phrases as "handicapped units" in use. There are cities that indeed build units using this word in the title. This is just a title, and eventually these titles will probably be rephrased to eliminate the word "handicapped."

If you haven't already noticed, adaptable design can refer to adaptable housing, also known as multifamily housing built in the commercial market. The term "accessible unit" applies to the dwelling that meets the prescribed requirements for accessible housing. Adaptable/adjustable designs can apply to both the residential and the commercial markets.

Adaptable housing

For those individuals who plan to enter the commercial market, the following information supplied by the HUD is very helpful:

> An adaptable housing unit is an accessible dwelling unit with adaptable features that eliminate the "special" appearance and/or meet the needs of the individual user by adding or adjusting elements. An adaptable housing unit includes all of the accessibility features required by ANSI and UFAS (such as wider doors, clear floor space, and accessible routes) and allows a choice of certain adjustable features or fixed accessible features.

When adaptive design is properly implemented, an accessible unit looks no different from a standard unit. Adaptability solves the problem of making accessible housing attractive and marketable to people who do not need or want some of the accessible features that look different or might be inconvenient, while making it possible for the adaptable feature, such as clear knee space and grab bars, to be available when a tenant requires them.

Misconceptions about adaptable housing

As the concept of adaptable housing has been refined, some housing providers as well as consumers have developed misconceptions about the idea. Some building industry people have viewed an adaptable unit as a standard unit that would be remodeled if a disabled person wanted to move in and required certain accessible features. This remodeling would widen doors, add an accessible entrance, remodel kitchens and bathrooms, and provide accessible storage. Owners who have made this interpretation have called for a 60- to 90-day waiting period. However, in today's mobile society, it is unrealistic to subject a tenant to a wait of two to three months for an apartment.

Truly adaptable units can be adjusted or adapted without renovation or structural changes because the basic accessible features like door widths and a ground level entrance are already there. Nonstructural adaptations might include changing counter and sink heights; removing a cabinet to reveal a knee space under the work surface, kitchen sink, and bathroom lavatory; and attaching grab bars where needed. These changes can be made without delaying occupancy by the new tenant. The building maintenance staff, tenant, or owner should be able to make these simple kinds of adjustments in a few hours.

Some people with disabilities and disability organizations fear that the adaptable housing unit will not be as usable for a wheelchair user as a fixed accessible unit. Their thinking is that the adapted units will be less accessible because of their designs or because of the reluctance of owners and managers to make adequate adaptations. When adaptable dwellings are built correctly, they have the same features as those required in fixed accessible units, but the standards allow some of the features to be temporarily hidden by a cabinet or omitted for marketing to people who don't need them. An adaptable unit is an accessible unit with features that can be tailored to the specific needs of the tenant.

Benefits of adaptable housing

Adaptable housing benefits both providers and consumers of such housing. Developers, owners, and managers of multifamily housing benefit when they build adaptable units because the units can be rented easily to both able-bodied and disabled individuals. This aspect alone should expand the market for these accessible units and eliminate the need to compromise on rents or provide other incentives for leasing them to able-bodied tenants. The manager or owner who installs adaptable units should be able to meet the needs of any prospective tenant.

Some landlords have already recognized the potential marketing advantage of offering adjustable counter heights to short people or pointing out the ease and safety of moving valuable furniture through the wide doors. Some managers (and tenants) have taken advantage of the maneuvering space in bathrooms by placing bookshelves, open shelving, or other furniture in these usually austere spaces. One survey reports that able-bodied tenants are very fond of these larger bathrooms. Adaptability features can be turned into selling points that improve the units' marketability.

Tenant longevity has long been recognized as an advantage to landlords. Fewer turnovers mean less clean-up and reconditioning, fewer vacant days, and higher profits. People with disabilities who find and adjust an adaptable house to meet their particular needs are likely to stay. Adaptable housing can also be expected to increase tenant longevity because able-bodied tenants who acquire a permanent or temporary disability (due to age or any other cause) are less likely to have to move to more accommodating facilities.

The growing population of older people is a potentially large market for appropriate housing. Many older people do not wish to be placed in "special" housing but recognize they might need some "assistance." Because adaptable housing does not look special, its adaptability allows many older individuals to remain in their homes longer than they might in nonaccessible units. Where services are provided as part of a housing program, adaptable features can reduce the demand on personnel and make it easier and less expensive to provide appropriate help when needed.

Manufacturers can also benefit from the development of adaptable housing and are vital in its successful growth. Adaptable housing design creates a new market for existing products and creates new opportunities for innovative new products that are adjustable or designed to meet a range of needs.

People with disabilities and their companions and service providers will all benefit from the adjustable features of adaptable housing. People with severe disabilities often live with able-bodied spouses or attendants who perform specific household tasks, such as cooking, that the individual with disabilities cannot do for him/herself. In an adaptable house, able-bodied and disabled individuals can live together and the adaptable features will fit both. For example, the kitchen can remain set up for use by a standing person, and the rest of the home, including the bathroom, can be accessible to the resident with disabilities.

Adaptable housing, if produced in adequate numbers and types of units, will benefit the community by putting a supply of accessible units on the market in all price ranges and locations. Since adaptable units are attractive and usable by everyone, it can be anticipated that they will be popular with most people, including those with disabilities, and will be fully occupied.

For the adaptable housing concept to succeed, it is vital that enough units be built to meet the demands of the community (which includes individuals with disabilities). This number needs to be much greater that the small number of fixed accessible units that have been required. An increase in the number of adaptable units benefits all people who need improved access with no disadvantage to others. Mass production, improved marketability, and further refinement of methods should prevent costs from becoming a disadvantage to owners.

Codes and regulations for accessibility generally apply to public facilities and multifamily housing, but the concept of adaptability can be a positive marketing tool for all types of housing. Individuals who are older or have disabilities are not only renters but also home buyers. It is generally accepted that there are over 49 million people with disabilities in the U.S. and they are from every socioeconomic strata. Add to these numbers the older population; people with spinal cord injuries; individuals who are deaf or hard of hearing; people with arthritis, heart disease, hypertension, and partial paralysis; and children, and a significant potential market emerges.

With increased experience with the adaptable housing concept and growing participation of product manufacturers and better market information, the building industry might find that most houses can be made accessible at little or no increase in cost. One key to low-cost accessibility is simple, inexpensive methods for providing adaptable features. *Accessible Housing* outlines ideas throughout that you could use in both new and existing construction.

Permanent modifications

Permanent modifications are not adjustable and are not easily removed or changed back to their original condition. Normally these modifications address individuals with major physical needs. A good example of this type of modification would be a ceiling-mounted self-transfer lift system that would extend from the bedroom to around the bathroom. Often the modification will have a negative effect on the look and feel of a home and might hurt its resale value. If you find yourself involved in a major modification, try to blend it into the aesthetics of the home. Use attractive features and products; for example, contrasting colored lever-type door handles that harmonize with the door or plastic grab bars colored to coordinate with the surface on which they will be installed (contrasting colors help those who are vision impaired).

Environmentally safe home

An environmentally safe home is a home built with environmentally safe products. Product choices can make a difference in the levels of indoor air pollution. According to the American Lung Association, Minneapolis Affiliate, and the success in 1993 through 1995 of their HEALTH HOUSE:

> The stakes are high.
>
> Today, incidences of indoor air pollution are multiplying so quickly the Environmental Protection Agency lists it as the fourth-largest environmental threat to Americans.
>
> Indoor contaminants ranging from formaldehyde and carbon monoxide to dust mites and radon are resulting in a growing frequency of eye, nose, and throat irritations; allergic reactions; chronic headaches; and asthma. In fact, a Mayo Clinic study conducted from 1964 to 1983 found that asthma

rates of children had doubled and, in some cases, tripled. And the Centers for Disease Control announced that the national rate of asthma deaths in the 1980s increased by 46 percent.

As professionals, we must choose intelligently the products we use and educate ourselves as well as our customers in order to protect their health. In chapter 8 I will discuss in more detail how you can make the home a safe environment for your customers.

Chapter 3 includes some necessary tools (books, videos, organizations) to expand upon the information provided in this book to help you enter this market with a positive attitude. I strongly recommend that you start filling your library with information on the subject, but don't let these books just sit on the shelves. If you want to succeed in this business, take the time to read the information!

3

Who can help?

How do you feel about the accessible housing market now that you have read the first two chapters? Is it a market worth considering? As you can see in chapter 1, the market has always been there. It's possible that we professionals have been so involved in "comfortable" projects that we haven't popped our heads above the sawdust to see what is going on around us; or perhaps we have been aware of this market but chose to sidestep it because it would not be comfortable or because we perceived difficulties in approaching its special needs. Perhaps it's time to blow away the sawdust and educate ourselves about this market.

I strongly suggest you reread the section in chapter 1 titled "Hear it Firsthand." Those individuals who shared their personal experiences had good reason for speaking out. The market is here, and if you are going to jump into it, don't make the same mistakes that their contractors made. Educate yourself, do your homework, be honest, work with your customer, and most of all: live by your word.

The purpose of *Accessible Housing* is to help educate you and steer you in the right direction. However, keep in mind that it takes many years of varied experiences to understand this market. This book won't have all the answers, but it does offer the tools you'll need to find the answers, including consultants, information, and organizations. It is your responsibility to follow through to find the answers or the services you need to help you put a project together. If you don't know—ask, and if you still don't know—don't do it! The best thing you can do for yourself is to admit that you might not know everything. Keep asking until both you and your customer are comfortable and satisfied with the information or service you've been seeking.

This chapter, as well as others in this book, provides some of the tools that will help you to better understand this market. Appendix A provides addresses for further inquiries. Some information and services are free, some organizations request a donation, and others have set fees. Fill your library with information that will keep you abreast of the subject of special needs, and hire those services that will help you stay on top of this market.

Agencies and organizations

Many agencies and organizations have orchestrated and contributed to the laws that govern barrier-free design standards. Their ongoing support for the cause can be better understood through the information, services, and seminars they provide. Some have gone so far as to do the work as well. Their constant involvement is paving the path to a better understanding of this market, and there is no better way to understand this market than to get involved in these organizations through local chapters, which could be located in (or near) your hometown. Get involved, provide support when you can, and use the information and services that are available. A number of these agencies and organizations are mentioned in the following pages.

National Easter Seal Society

As one of the largest and oldest nonprofit charitable organizations serving people with disabilities, the National Easter Seal Society offers a wealth of information: brochures, books, and video and audio cassettes can be found in their Catalog of Resources. The catalog is broken down into the following product categories:

- Americans with Disabilities Act (ADA)
- Attitude Awareness
- Education
- Housing
- Volunteerism

The Easter Seal Society's mission is to help people with disabilities achieve independence. Their catalog was developed to help business, disability-related organizations, and federal, state, and local government to implement the ADA successfully. Products offered in the catalog address the ADA legislation, attitude awareness training, and issues related to employment, transportation, and housing.

Founded in 1919, Easter Seals has established a leadership role in the following areas:

- Provision of quality rehabilitation programs to meet the diverse needs of people with disabilities and their families
- Promotion of assistive technology that is leading the way to independence for people with disabilities

- Passage and implementation of critical legislation and government programs affecting the lives of people with disabilities
- Development and distribution of public education campaigns to encourage positive attitudes toward people with disabilities

They have been a major player in the nationwide accessibility movement. In 1958, the National Easter Seal Society, in partnership with the President's Committee on Employment of the Handicapped, was instrumental in laying the groundwork for this movement through the awarding of a research grant to the University of Illinois to establish minimum standards for making buildings and facilities accessible to people with disabilities. The resulting research findings were submitted to the American National Standards Association (now the American National Standards Institute—ANSI), and published in 1961 as the first standards on accessibility, "Making Buildings & Facilities Accessible to and Usable by the Physically Handicapped," ANSI A117.1-1961.

Following its publication, this standard was widely circulated by the National Easter Seal Society through a national campaign targeting architects in an effort to promote voluntary acceptance and utilization of the standards. Despite this national education program, voluntary utilization was found to be less than effective. Several states attempted to implement that standard, either through legislation or adoption into building codes, but success was limited. As a standard—and not a code—its scope was limited. Enforcement and compliance were also limited. It became evident that much remained to be accomplished in the implementation of accessibility design standards.

In 1965, a National Commission was established to study the issue of eliminating architectural barriers. The Commission reported its findings in 1967 in *Design for All Americans*. Recommendations from this report resulted in passage of the Architectural Barriers Act of 1968 (PL [Public Law] 90-480), which required adoption of the ANSI standard (A117.1) in federally funded buildings.

For further information, contact:

National Easter Seal Society
230 West Monroe St., Ste. 1800
Chicago, IL 60606-4802
312-551-7141

The Easter Seal Society of Washington

An affiliate of the National Easter Seal Society, the Easter Seal Society of Washington became involved in helping to promote the ANSI Standard in Washington State and to foster its use. Subsequently, the state adopted the ANSI Standard through legislation passed in 1967 (RCW [Revised Code of Washington] 70.92), which required all state-funded buildings of public accommodation to incorporate this standard. In 1971, the Act was amended to include privately funded buildings of public accommodation as well.

In 1972, in response to a growing awareness of the need to educate and advocate for accessibility in the built environment, the Easter Seal Society of Washington established the Access/Abilities program. The major objective of this program was to work with the building and design community to promote a better understanding of the need for more accessible building design and construction.

Following the adoption of the ANSI Standard in Washington State, it was found that the law was not well implemented or enforced. It was subsequently recognized that the accessibility requirements should be written in code language and incorporated into the (then) proposed Washington State Building Code Act. Initially, the State Building Code Act (RCW 19.27) adopted the ANSI Standard, A117.1. However, with the collaborative efforts and support of the Easter Seal Society of Washington, the Washington Association of Building Officials, and other organizations representing people with disabilities, efforts were made to have legislation introduced to amend the Washington State Building Code Act and to draft specific regulations for barrier-free design to replace the ANSI Standard as part of the state building code.

In 1975, this legislation was introduced as well as legislation mandating the Washington State Building Code Advisory Council to draft and promulgate such regulations. Following passage of the legislation and a year of intensive research and development based on the most recent national standards, "Rules and Regulations Setting Barrier-Free Design Standards" were adopted by the Council and became effective on October 1, 1976.

This effort was strongly supported by the Easter Seal Society of Washington as a major commitment toward the provision of greater independence for people with disabilities. The passage of this legislation would provide greater accessibility to the built environment, and therefore, access to housing, employment, education, recreation, and so on.

Initially, the Society had focused on education and advocacy in the area of accessibility design. However, support for the incorporation of barrier-free design requirements into the state building code soon developed into a major thrust for the Society. Barbara Allan, Director of the Access/Abilities Program, was appointed as a member of the first State Building Code Advisory Council, and chaired its technical advisory committee, which was responsible for drafting the barrier-free regulations.

The Society's Access/Abilities program soon became a contact point and a major source of information regarding the code requirements and development. Its staff was directly involved in the initial statewide training program for building departments across the state on the new state building code requirements, which included the barrier-free requirements.

The Society also participated in ongoing accessibility training for state and national building and design-related organizations toward the general furthering of understanding and promotion of accessibility design needs and benefits.

Following passage of both state and federal legislation in the area of accessibility requirements, such as the 504 requirements under the Rehabilitation Act of 1973, the Federal Fair Housing Amendments Act of 1988, and the Americans with Disabilities Act of 1990, the Access/Abilities program functioned not only as an educational and promotional avenue but also as a provider of technical assistance to architects and designers, building departments, and others seeking to implement and better understand the growing and changing requirements.

In its efforts to enhance and promote better understanding of the benefits of accessibility design and the real user needs behind it, the Society offers the services of the Access/Abilities program through the provision of seminars, workshops, and presentations to a wide variety of audiences. They have also developed various publications, such as *An Illustrated Handbook of the Washington State Barrier-Free Regulations*. This document is widely used and now in its sixth edition (1995) under a slightly different title. Barbara Allan initiated and co-authored this book in 1978.

The Introduction to the 1989 edition says it well: "In this era of 'normalization' and 'mainstreaming,' people with differing degrees of mobility and disability are seeking the opportunity to exercise their right to develop their talents and become as self-sufficient and independent as possible in their contribution toward, and participation in, society."

The goal of this handbook is to facilitate opportunities and solutions. If regulations are properly implemented, people who have been previously denied access will be further integrated into society. Limitations based on ignorance will be replaced with solutions based upon understanding and information. The current (1995) version of this document, *Accessible Design for All—An Illustrated Handbook: The Washington State Regulations* (sequel to *An Illustrated Handbook for Barrier-Free Design, Washington State Rules and Regulations*) should do much to further that understanding.

The Society has added a special Housing Assistance and Modification program, which assists in making minor modifications to existing housing (e.g., the removal of barriers in individual living environments). It helps in the identification of accessible housing and provides technical assistance to enable persons with disabilities or age-related limitations to remain in their homes with greater safety and convenience. Staff can assist with the evaluation of access needs and provide design recommendations, barrier removal, and barrier-free consultation. In view of the increasing need for these services, the Society has recently expanded its accessibility services with the addition of a construction division.

For more information, contact:

Easter Seal Society of Washington
State Office
521 2nd Ave. West
Seattle, WA 98119
800-678-5708

Easter Seals Construction

Easter Seals Construction is a division of the Easter Seal Society of Washington. Created in April 1994, it attempts to fill the void between very large construction companies that charge large prices to accomplish accessibility modifications and small firms that generally know very little about the rules that govern such modifications.

In addition to general construction expertise, the division is staffed by individuals who are knowledgeable in the special needs of people with disabilities. They have direct access to a vast array of referral information with the Society. From time to time they find themselves involved in correcting projects done by inexperienced contractors. Through observation and correction, Easter Seals Construction has become aware that professionals have many obstacles to overcome before they can understand the true meaning of accessibility.

The following list targets ignorance and methods of construction—two areas where mistakes are commonly found. These areas are frequently associated in the special needs market. The purpose of this list is not to point a finger but merely to illustrate those areas that need improvement. If you find yourself starting to veer off the path, take the time to evaluate this list again. This will help you to stay on track and survive in this very rewarding market.

Ignorance:
- Lack of knowledge of accessibility needs
- Insensitivity

- Apathy
- Inertia

Methods of construction:
  Crawl space vs. slab
  - Crawl space = step up to entry
  - Slab = level entry

  Garage access to house
  - Step up to entry
  - Use of spring-loaded hinges on fire doors

  Exterior door thresholds
  - ¾" (19 mm) to 1½" (38 mm) obstacle for swinging doors and sliding glass doors

  Interior doors
  - Normally less than 36" (91 cm) openings
  - Generally no maneuvering room on the latch side of the door

  Hallways
  - Normally 36" (91 cm) wide (or less)

  Countertops
  - Normally 36" (91 cm) high
  - Overhead cabinet heights

  Closets
  - Rods too high
  - Only floor-level storage

  Electrical
  - Switch heights
  - Receptacle heights
  - Thermostat heights

  Plumbing
  - Toilet frequently placed between tub and vanity, making installation of grab bars almost impossible.
  - Grab bar backing should be installed in all houses during construction.

Overall, the Easter Seal Society, through its efforts at the national level as well as those of the Washington State Society, has been a leader in helping to create better access to the built environment and thus to enhance opportunities for people with disabilities to both contribute to and participate in life and their communities.

To learn more, contact:

Easter Seals Construction
4301 South Pine, Ste. 57
Tacoma, WA 98409
206-472-0041

HUD User

Sponsored by the U.S. Department of Housing and Urban Development's Office of Policy Development and Research (PD&R), HUD User is a research information service and clearinghouse for people who are working toward improving housing and strengthening community development. HUD User collects, develops, and distributes housing-related information that can help you be more efficient and effective. Some of HUD User's collection of research includes materials about:

- Building technology
- Community development block grants
- Demographic trends
- Fair housing
- Housing for the elderly and people with disabilities
- Lead-base paint abatement
- Manufactured housing
- Public housing
- Regulator barriers to affordable housing

Some of the resources and services offered by HUD User include:

- Referrals drawn from their network of contacts in housing and community development. They can provide the names of agencies or organizations to contact for more information.
- Blueprints of energy-efficient and cost-effective housing designs available in full-sized working drawings.
- Audiovisual programs including videotapes, slides, and accompanying materials designed as training resources, "how-to" guides, and curricula. The programs cover a wide range of subjects.
- *Recent Research Results*, a free monthly current-awareness bulletin that features information on HUD research activities, policies, programs, and publications. Copies of this bulletin are sent to all registered users.

HUD User is also a source for information on adaptable housing. Ever since provisions for accessible housing have been included in building codes and standards, the building industry and people with disabilities have been dissatisfied with most fixed accessible housing units mandated by state and federal laws. Among the complaints are inappropriate design details, inadequate space for families, clinical appearance, high vacancy rates, limited numbers, and poor location. Adaptable housing, a little-understood design approach, appears to be one solution for many of these problems. It holds the promise of more universally usable housing in the future at little or no extra cost.

What is it? Adaptable housing is accessible housing that does not look different from other housing but that has features which, in only minutes, can be adjusted, added, or removed as needed to suit the occupants whether they are disabled, older, or nondisabled. By creating housing that can fit any occupant, the adaptable design approach opens up the possibility for mass-produced, attractive, and universally usable housing in all sizes, price ranges, and locations.

Adaptable housing has many potential benefits both for disabled people who need accessible housing and for the developers, builders, and managers of housing. As adaptable housing becomes widely available, disabled people will have a greater choice of housing locations both to live in and to visit. Developers and builders will find it is less expensive to build more units of the same kind. Owners and managers will be able to rent to a larger market.

For the past 23 years, the concept of adaptable housing has been continuously developing into a method for residential design. Adaptable housing features are now specified in the national and federal standards for accessibility, which have been adopted into many state and local building codes.

As the adaptable housing concept becomes more widespread, the demand for information on designing and building adaptable units increases. HUD's manual, *Adaptable Housing: A Technical Manual for Implementing Adaptable Dwelling Unit Specifications for HUD*, provides this information and promotes the further development of adaptable housing in the United States.

The manual is divided into three chapters:

- Chapter 1 provides background information on the development of adaptable design, defines and explains adaptable housing, clarifies some misconceptions, and describes the benefits of adaptable housing.
- Chapter 2 contains technical information. It explains and illustrates some suggested methods for providing adaptable features, shows examples of their use in model kitchens and bathrooms, and gives cost comparisons for these methods.
- Chapter 3 describes the role of manufactured products in adaptable design, gives examples of some products that are helpful in creating adaptable housing and lists their sources, and discusses the need for new products.

Even if you are using this manual in addition to other recommended information mentioned throughout this book, it is important that you refer to current codes in force in your area for all required dimensions, sizes, forces, loads, and arrangements of elements. You must rely solely upon the standards, common practice, and approval of local jurisdictions for compliance with laws, regulations, and life safety requirements.

For more information, contact:

HUD User
P.O. Box 6091
Rockville, MD 20850
800-245-2691

American Lung Association, Minneapolis Affiliate

The American Lung Association has been fighting lung disease for over 90 years. With assistance from the medical community and the American Thoracic Society, they provide education, community services, advocacy, and research. They offer a variety of health education programs about lung disease and its prevention, and their activities are supported by the public and volunteers and are supplemented by donations to the Christmas Seals Campaign and other voluntary contributions.

The Minneapolis Affiliate offers consulting services through their "Healthy Building Consulting Group." They have also authored a workbook titled *The Health House Workbook: A Consumer Guide to Healthier Homes*. Those who are considering building an environmentally safe home need to look at this book. It provides practical, straightforward information on how to build a healthier, more energy-efficient house. The information has been researched and developed from guidelines established by the American Lung Association, Minneapolis Affiliate, and its panel of building science consultants and housing specialists.

The workbook includes such topics as:
- Identifying pollution sources in the home
- Understanding a home's mechanical system
- Selecting a builder
- Choosing building products for a better indoor environment

A special "building blocks" section offers information on how specific environmentally safe features can be incorporated into the home. The workbook also makes recommendations on interior design, mechanical systems, lighting, and ways to reduce health risks from poor indoor air quality.

To learn more, contact:

Health House Project
American Lung Association/MPLS
1829 Portland Ave.
Minneapolis, MN 55404
612-871-7332

Eastern Paralyzed Veterans Association (EPVA)

The Eastern Paralyzed Veterans Association is a chapter of the Paralyzed Veterans of America. This association is a private, nonprofit corporation. Membership is open to veterans who have incurred a spinal cord injury or who have a disease of the spinal cord. Since 1946 the EPVA has operated programs designed to enable members, as well as other persons with disabilities, to lead full and productive lives. During this time they have put together resource information (print and videos) that covers a wide range of subject matter. Write for their "resource information" catalog and add to your library from the wealth of available information.

Three easy-to-understand videotapes are available that can give you a better understanding and outlook into this market. The videos clearly portray the market and the requirements of the ADA in accurate and straightforward terms and will prove helpful for anyone involved in or planning to enter the accessibility market.

(The descriptions below are derived from the videos themselves.)

"A Change In Perspective"

Able-bodied people need to view people with disabilities, like those with spinal cord injuries, in a different way. They need to adopt a point-of-view that is not obstructed by a wheelchair; in other words, a change in perspective. Too often the special needs of people with physical disabilities are overlooked and that creates problems, but sometimes looking at a problem from a different point of view will provide the solution. A change in perspective can yield significant benefits.

This video introduces you to five people who lead productive lives because they stress ability over disability. The 30-minute video examines the physical and social issues connected with spinal cord injury and smashes outdated attitudes about persons with disabilities. "There's a lot more to life than just standing up."

"Understanding the Americans with Disabilities Act"

This video was developed to answer the most commonly asked questions about the ADA. It is not a substitute for the *ADA Handbook* but merely summarizes the law and shows how individuals can benefit from it. The video was taped at a variety of businesses, and minor modifications at these establishments are illustrated to show how they comply with ADA. It also points out that these modifications don't have to be expensive. The video is a good introduction to the *ADA Handbook*.

"Accessibility"

What is it? To most people, the word "accessibility" suggests convenience, approachability, and proximity. For wheelchair users, accessibility has a more complex meaning. For those who are mobility impaired, accessibility can make a difference between freedom and a life that's restricted. "Accessibility" guides you through a building from the perspective of a wheelchair user. Accessible design features shown make a site and building accessible to the mobility-, sight-, and hearing-impaired. Specific dimensions are superimposed graphically as each accessible element is covered. General information about ADA is also provided in the video, and some common myths about accessible construction are analyzed.

Accessibility is a necessity when it comes to disabled individuals living to their potential in life. Viewing this video can help put things into perspective for a better understanding so you can help your customers achieve the freedom to pursue the same goals in life as their able-bodied peers. Nothing more—nothing less!

These three videos are available through Video Management Services at 800-489-8436. For more information, contact:

Eastern Paralyzed Veterans Association
75-20 Astoria Boulevard
Jackson Heights, NY 11370-1177
718-803-3782

Center for Accessible Housing

The Center for Accessible Housing is a nonprofit organization and is recognized as the national leader in research, training, and information dissemination for accessible housing, universal design, and life-span housing. The Center conducts research, collaborates with manufacturers, and provides training and technical assistance that helps government, industry, and individuals create living spaces and products that enable people with disabilities to lead independent lives. They also promote strategies to make accessible and universally usable features commonplace, easily achievable, and low cost in all housing. The following projects illustrate the Center's mission:

- Training—The Center provides training directly to people with disabilities and disability advocates, designers, professionals in the building industry, housing providers, and design students at the postsecondary level. Training focuses on housing issues from the perspective of these various constituent groups. Topics for training include: owner/tenant/landlord rights and responsibilities under the Fair Housing Amendments Act; accessible home modifications; universal and adaptable design in housing; accessibility on difficult sites; and code compliance under the

Uniform Federal Accessibility Standard and Americans with Disabilities Act Accessibility Guidelines. The Center developed both the training format and the materials for the unique Fair Housing Trainings.

- Materials Development—The Center has an impressive portfolio of graphic, text, and audiovisual products developed on topics relevant to accessible and universal design in housing. Materials include books, monographs, how-to manuals, TechPaks on specific design/construction problems, slide/tape presentations, and bibliographies. They also publish a newsletter that is mailed to over 3,500 individuals in the Center's professional and design advisory networks.
- Housing Design Technical Assistance—The Center operates an information and referral service on issues related to housing design, construction, modification, and assistive technology for the home. This service includes on-line technical assistance with specific design or construction problems. The technical assistance specialists can provide a range of services, including product research, plan review, and design oversight on new construction and home modifications.
- Stock Floor Plans—A large number of requests for assistance are for floor plans of accessible housing. In response to these requests, the Center has developed "stock" plans covering a wide range of square footages, housing types (single-family, multifamily, co-housing), and styles. A catalogue of six plans is available from the Center. An order form for complete plan sets is included in their catalogue. Plans sell for $20 per set (Fig. 3-1).
- Evaluation Studies—The Center evaluates products and appliances, particularly those important for home-management activities, as well as housing systems. Consumer input is used to identify the products and systems evaluated, and consumers participate in the evaluations. The findings have been put into booklets that are of value to your customer as well as yourself. As of this writing, the topics that are available are *Door Hardware, Household Vacuum Cleaners,* and *Microwave Ovens*. The price is $4.50 per booklet, but check on quantity prices as well because other topics might be available by the time you read this book.

The Center is part of North Carolina State University's (NCSU) School of Design. The Center has multimedia graphic production capability with computer work stations, video equipment, and full on-line

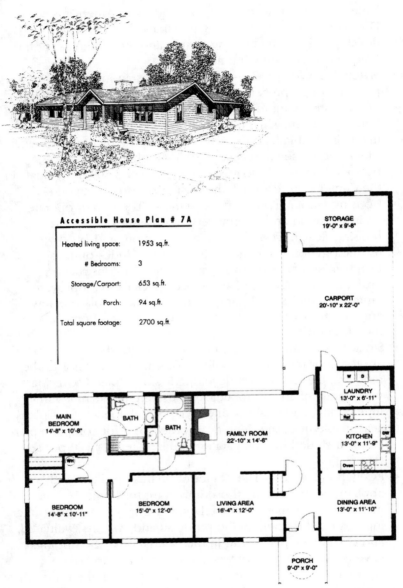

Accessible House Plan # 7A

Heated living space:	1953 sq.ft.
# Bedrooms:	3
Storage/Carport:	653 sq.ft.
Porch:	94 sq.ft.
Total square footage:	2700 sq.ft.

STORAGE
19'-0" x 9'-8"

CARPORT
20'-10" x 22'-0"

LAUNDRY
13'-0" x 6'-11"

KITCHEN
13'-0" x 11'-9"

MAIN
BEDROOM
14'-8" x 10'-8"

BATH

BATH

FAMILY ROOM
22'-10" x 14'-6"

BEDROOM
14'-8" x 10'-11"

BEDROOM
15'-0" x 12'-0"

LIVING AREA
16'-4" x 12'-0"

DINING AREA
13'-0" x 11'-10"

PORCH
9'-0" x 9'-0"

3-1 *Features of this house: Separate living and dining rooms and a large family room with fireplace allow this 3-bedroom, 2-bath plan to accommodate a family of four easily. A large utility room allows easy access from the carport to the kitchen. A generous covered front porch affords convenient access to a formal entrance hall. Optional layouts for the bathrooms accommodate roll-in showers, 3' x 3' showers, or conventional tub/shower units with transfer seats.*

Accessible House Plan #7A. Center for Accessible Housing

electronic interfacing among its collaborating organizations. They also have the most extensive collection in the U.S. of resource materials on accessible and universal design as it applies to housing for people with disabilities. The library is a unique collection of 6,000 volumes of literature and instructional materials; a graphic library of illustrations of accessible features, including housing designs; and a collection of 20,000 slides showing problems and solutions for accessible environments.

To receive more information about universal design, design solutions, or products, contact:

Center for Accessible Housing, School of Design
North Carolina State University
Box 8613
Raleigh, NC 27695-8613
800-647-6777

Americans with Disabilities Act (ADA) Handbook

The *ADA Handbook* represents one part of the overall effort by the Equal Employment Opportunity Commission (EEOC) and the Department of Justice (DOJ) to provide information and assistance on the ADA to people with disabilities, businesses, and the public. It is intended to serve as a basic resource document on the ADA. The *Handbook* contains annotated regulations for Titles I, II, and III; resources for obtaining additional assistance; and an appendix, which contains supplementary information related to the implementation of the ADA.

While supplies last, the *Handbook* is free. Other related materials as well as the *Handbook* can be obtained by calling 1-800-514-0301. This document is a "must" for your library.

You can purchase the *ADA Accessibility Guidelines* through:

Architectural and Transportation Barriers Compliance Board
1331 F St., NW
Ste. 1000
Washington, DC 20004
800-872-2253

American National Standards Institute

The American National Standards Institute (ANSI) is a nonprofit, privately funded membership organization that promotes the use and development of voluntary standards and conformity assessment activities as a means of advancing the national economy; benefiting the public health, safety, welfare and environment; enhancing U.S. competitiveness; and facilitating domestic and international trade, commerce and communications. It is a federation of organizations that coordinates the development of U.S. voluntary national standards and is the U.S. member to the nontreaty international standard bodies.

ANSI serves a diverse membership of 1,300 member companies, 250 professional societies and trade associations, 30 government agencies—both regulators and nonregulators, 20 institutions such as libraries and universities, and a variety of consumer and labor interests. (This information was reprinted with permission from the American National Standards Institute.)

ANSI does not write standards; rather, it serves as a catalyst for standards development by its diverse membership. They do not write laws either. The ANSI standards are guidelines that government agencies may adopt (in part or in whole) for use in setting codes. They may also be used by nongovernmental parties as technical design guidelines. For information on membership, contact:

American National Standards Institute
11 West 42nd St.
New York, NY 10036
212-642-4900

To pick up a copy of the *American National Standard for Accessible and Usable Buildings and Facilities* (ANSI A117.1), contact one of the following model code organizations in your area:

Building Officials and Code Administrators International (BOCA)
4051 West Flossmoor Rd.
Country Club Hills, IL 60478-5795
708-799-2300
BOCA publishes the National Building Codes

International Conference of Building Officials (ICBO)
5360 South Workman Mill Rd.
Whittier, CA 90601
310-699-0541
ICBO publishes the Uniform Building Codes

Southern Building Code Congress International (SBCCI)
900 Montclair Road
Birmingham, AL 35213
205-591-1853
SBCCI publishes the Standard Building Codes

Be aware that model codes and standards adopted at the local level establish the minimum design and construction requirements in the community. To better understand what codes are and how they work, pick up a copy of *Intro to Building Codes* from:

National Conference of States on Building Codes and Standards, Inc. (NCSBCS)
505 Huntmar Park Dr., Ste. 210
Herndon, VA 22070
703-437-0100

Trade associations

As I mentioned before, joining an organization in your community can do you a world of good. There are also trade associations you can join and become active in. Trade associations exist to help professionals succeed in their businesses. You will have to decide which associations best fit your profession—of course, it wouldn't hurt to join more than one. When you become a member, you receive products and/or services at reduced cost as one of the benefits of membership. Some associations even provide the opportunity to work toward certification in a particular field (for example, kitchens, baths, or remodeling). Even though the information, products, and services they offer are vitally important, you will find it is even more valuable just to be able to talk and share information with other members who have the same concerns you do. Other professionals are individuals like you with similar experiences, and might just have answers you need. It only makes sense to help fellow professionals—you never know when you'll need a favor returned!

Associations also bring members together to work as a team on worthwhile projects within the community. For example, the "Rampathon" project was done in '95 in my hometown. Members of the Spokane Home Builders Association, the Apprenticeship programs, and the Remodelers Council came together and donated time and materials to construct a wheelchair ramp for a local resident. This event gave the members:

- A chance to work together
- An opportunity to share building ideas
- A chance to give to the community in a worthwhile project
- Publicity

I firmly believe that what you give, you get back—you just have to commit to the cause. As you can see in Figs. 3-2 and 3-3, joining an association can enhance member success and excellence, promote professionalism and ethical business practices, and

3-2 *Putting the handrail at the correct height is critical when building a ramp.* C.R.S., Inc.

3-3 *This is what it's all about—team effort!* C.R.S., Inc.

provide leadership and direction within the industry and in your community.

An association that can help in all these areas is a worthwhile investment of your time. Check out one of the following trade associations.

National Association of Homebuilders (NAHB) Research Center

The NAHB Research Center was established in 1964 as a wholly owned, nonprofit subsidiary of the National Association of Home Builders (NAHB). The Research Center serves the research needs of the home building industry, its related industries and professions, and public sector agencies in the housing field. Major areas of activity include:

- Study of new technologies and analysis of financial, regulatory, and land-use issues
- Development of techniques for energy and resource conservation
- Promotion of methods for increasing the nation's supply of affordable housing
- Market research
- Construction of a research home to demonstrate innovations and foster their adoption
- Certification of products used in home building

Their Total Quality Construction program promotes the latest and most up-to-date techniques that builders across the nation are using to improve quality and still maintain profit margins. Services include:

- Seminars
- Proprietary builder training
- Focus groups
- Newsletters
- Professional services
- Publications

The NAHB Research Center has a complete library of useful information. Start by getting their list of publications, the *Directory of Accessible Building Products: 1995.*

As discussed in the introduction, the nation's overall population is aging, and this trend will continue. Many older persons who do not have specific disabilities experience reduced mobility, which affects their ability to perform simple tasks in the home. The onset of limited mobility usually comes gradually, and persons currently without such problems cannot assume that they will never experience them in the future. In view of the significant likelihood that accessibility features will be desired either in the present or the future, home builders should give full consideration to building in such features during initial construction. *The Directory of Accessible Building Products: 1995* contains descriptions and illustrations of over 180 commercially available products. It can provide help in planning and designing for people with disabilities and age-related limitations in their own environment whether that includes building new homes or remodeling existing ones.

The NAHB also offers a video, "It's All In The Planning," which features the Adaptable, Fire-Safe Demonstration House built by the NAHB Research Center in 1990. It is one of the most realistic videos on the market, demonstrating an adaptable home in a residential setting. The house was designed by a modular home manufacturer and has ample curbside appeal for mainstreaming into the housing market. Except for the sprinkler system (a local code requirement) and an elevator that was installed for demonstration purposes, the total cost of the house exceeded that of a standard model by only 2 percent for that time period.

The word "adaptable" signifies that not all possible changes and modifications to improve safety and accessibility were actually built into the home. Instead, some were installed, and the house was designed to make other changes and modifications for the accommodation of disability less costly if they should be required. The house is, therefore, both a present-day home and one that is suitable for lifetime living. This approach could be widely adopted in new home construction (Fig. 3-4).

3-4 *From the very beginning, this was easily accessible from the outside. The house is constructed on a 2 percent grade sufficient to carry water away from the foundation but not too steep for a wheelchair.*
NAHB Research Center

To better understand this concept of design, the video was divided into the following sections:
- It's All In The Planning
- Getting Around
- The Kitchen
- Single Floor Living
- Fire Safety
- Growing Need

The video demonstrates how a standard house plan can easily be modified to accommodate a wide variety of needs, often at little or no expense. The key is all in the planning. This is an excellent video to help you get a better understanding of and a feeling for the way things should be—this one is a must for your library!

You can contact:

NAHB Research Center
400 Prince George's Boulevard
Upper Marlboro, MD 20772-8731
301-249-4000

National Kitchen & Bath Association (NKBA)

The National Kitchen and Bath Association serves and represents firms and individuals involved in all aspects of the residential kitchen and bathroom industry. Their mission is to enhance member success and excellence, promote professionalism and ethical business practices, and provide leadership and direction within the industry. Joining such an organization can give you the support needed to achieve all the increased profits, status, and recognition you deserve as a kitchen and bathroom professional.

The NKBA can help you build your business through:
- *Networking*—Increase your own understanding of how to be successful by sharing the experience and knowledge of other professionals. Local, regional and national activities help you establish a vast array of industry contacts.
- *Information*—Get the complete industry news you need, when you need it, on market trends, vital research, legislative, and business issues.
- *Education*—Acquire focused, industry-specific instruction in kitchen and bathroom design, presentation and drawing skills, sales and project management techniques. All courses are taught by leading experts and practicing professionals.
- *Promotion*—Take advantage of ongoing programs to guide consumers to NKBA members through national advertising,

member publicity in newspapers and magazines, design
contests, "idea" publications for your customers, and more.

- *Certification*—Increase the level of your professional status
  with the prestigious Certified Kitchen Designer (CKD) and/or
  Certified Bathroom Designer (CBD) accreditations.
- *Confidence*—Enjoy the recognition you will receive as an
  involved, active leader in the industry who has achieved the
  highest standards of skill and quality. This confidence in your
  professional ability is, in turn, shared by your customers.

The NKBA's Services and Supplies Catalog is packed full of products such as:

- Business management tools
- Drawing/planning and presentation supplies
- Hiring and training aids
- Marketing and public relations supplies
- CKD and CBD Society materials

Unfortunately, two-thirds of the products offered in the catalog
are available only to NKBA members. You might need to join the
NKBA to get those handy tools.

For further information, contact:

National Kitchen & Bath Association
687 Willow Grove Street
Hackettstown, NJ 07849
908-852-0033

Design assistance and ideas

It is sound business sense to ask questions when you need answers
and to hire subcontractors if you are unfamiliar with or not licensed
to perform a particular phase of a project. Similarly, when moving
into an area such as the accessible housing market, which might be
foreign to you, it makes good business sense to seek the proper help.
There is no better way to understand this market and to succeed in it
than to hire the proper professionals so you can get assistance when
and where you need it in order to satisfy the customer.

The following companies specialize in this market. Even though
they are selling products or services, they are still in this business to
help you. If you do not truly understand this market, the one who
will suffer is the customer. So ask for help when and where you need
it. Fill your library full of information and contact the following companies to see what types of service they can offer your business.

EASY STREET ENVIRONMENTS

One thing you can do that will help you truly understand this market is to visit a rehabilitation environment and experience it firsthand. One such program is EASY STREET ENVIRONMENTS, offered at Northwest Hospital in Seattle, Washington. It is a custom-designed life-size replica of a city where patients can practice the skills and basic activities of daily living necessary to reenter the community after sustaining a disabling condition. Areas of activity in the community might include a grocery store, movie theater, car, restaurant, bank, city bus, laundry, and a home with a bedroom, dining room, and kitchen. A stroll through the community might seem simple to a nondisabled person; however, to the patients newly facing life with a disability, it simulates numerous barriers they are likely to encounter in real life once they leave the hospital (Fig. 3-5).

Patients learn to overcome obstacles such as turnstiles, uneven surfaces, steps, getting in and out of a car or bus, opening and closing heavy doors, and grocery shopping. Even negotiating across thick

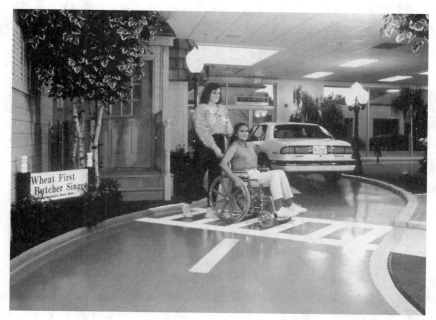

3-5 *New Hanover Regional Medical Center, Wilmington, NC. On the street, patients work on safely propelling a wheelchair, testing endurance by crossing the street, observing the different stages of a traffic light, and interacting with the public.* EASY STREET ENVIRONMENTS, Habitat, Inc., Tempe, AZ

pile carpeting can be a challenge for individuals relying on walkers or wheelchairs for mobility. EASY STREET ENVIRONMENTS provides patients the opportunity to relearn daily living skills in a safe environment to help them regain their independence and confidence in everyday tasks. This type of comprehensive rehabilitation environment is an ideal setting for patients pursuing their goals of functional independence, and it provides you with an ideal setting in which to observe and identify common obstacles that persons with disabilities will encounter in their everyday lives (Fig. 3-6).

The concept originated in 1984 at Phoenix Memorial Hospital by David A. Guynes of GUYNES DESIGN, Inc. He understood that rehabilitation requires persistence, sensitivity, and a treatment space that encourages mobility, skills in communication and cognition, safety awareness, socialization, and most of all, confidence in living independently at the highest level possible.

EASY STREET ENVIRONMENTS operates facilities across the United States and Canada; check to see if one is near you. Make an

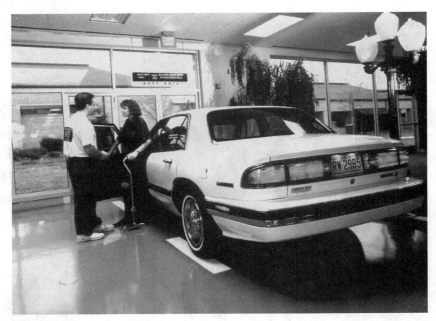

3-6 *New Hanover Regional Medical Center, Wilmington, NC. Patients may work on transferring in and out of a car, loading and unloading the trunk, and operating the foot controls, steering wheel, and turn signals. Activities may also include reading a map, calculating mileage, and planning a trip.* EASY STREET ENVIRONMENTS, Habitat, Inc., Tempe, AZ

appointment to see it for yourself—the patients you see there will be the customers you will be working for. If you are unable to locate a facility in your area, contact Habitat, Inc. They will provide you with a list of facilities so you can make an appointment.

EASY STREET ENVIRONMENTS' rehabilitation programs are designed to help patients with functional impairments affecting mobility, communication, activities of daily living (ADLs), cognitive skills, and social interaction resulting from injury or illness. This includes individuals recovering from:

- Strokes
- Head injuries
- Spinal cord injuries
- Neurological disorders
- Arthritis
- Orthopedic injuries
- Amputations
- Post neurological surgery
- Post orthopedic surgery
- Parkinson's disease
- Neuromuscular disorders

Imagine watching an individual who can't move his or her fingers successfully close a twist-tie on a loaf of bread after 15 minutes. This is a big accomplishment for any individual with this type of disability. The next time you casually close a loaf of bread, think about the person who has to struggle to learn how to do it and how you can improve this person's life through your designs.

A picture is worth a thousand words—but a site is worth a thousand pictures! For more information, contact:

Habitat, Inc.
6031 South Maple Ave.
Tempe, AZ 85283
602-345-8442

Northwest Hospital
1550 North 115th St.
MS H020A
Seattle, WA 98133
206-368-1096

GUYNES DESIGN, Inc.
1555 East Jackson
Phoenix, AZ 85034
800-264-0390

GUYNES DESIGN, Inc.

The following information has been included with the assistance of Patricia A. Moore, founder of MOORE Design Associates. Today she is president of GUYNES DESIGN, Inc. (GDI), which merged with MOORE Design Associates in 1991. Pat, a renowned specialist in aging and the needs of elders, and a designer involved in universal design, is also co-author of *Disguised: A True Story.*

Pat's husband, David A. Guynes, fractured his back in a fall from a cliff when he was 15 years old. He became an architect and brought his experiences in conquering injury and gaining function into a new form of rehabilitation medicine. The company he founded in 1981 specializes in real-life environments (within the hospital setting) where patients and their families can regain skills lost to injury or illness.

GDI develops and designs healthcare facilities specializing in physical medicine and rehabilitation, including projects with emphases on geriatric, industrial, and pediatric rehabilitation. They are in the forefront of developing unique products and services for use by therapists and persons with disabilities (Fig. 3-7).

Some of GDI's projects include:

- DRIVESYMS, a unique driver assessment and training program using actual cars, trucks, vans, and buses. Using a laser disc player, the system provides scenes encountered daily by drivers and uses a computer-based program for skill determination and evaluation. The vehicle is placed in a setting that can include elements of streets, sidewalks, and parking lots for maximum realism and motivation.
- INDEPENDENCE SQUARE, an "Activities of Daily Living" environment designed and engineered to be part of an in-patient or out-patient rehab setting. This approach allows patients and their families to prepare for home and community life activities in a safe and controlled simulation within a healthcare setting. Each environment is designed and developed with a clinical program team comprised of faculty members, GDI staff, and consultants. The resulting criteria support a unique project, providing the precise programs and services that will benefit the facility's community.
- OUR TOWN, where the focus is on the rehabilitation needs of elders. Specifically addressed are ambulation training, cognitive assessments, and physical conditioning, which promote independent lifestyles for elders recovering from the effects of stroke, joint surgery, or cardiac care (Fig. 3-8).

- PATHWAYS, an advanced ambulation and mobility course featuring curbs, curb cuts, ramps, and steps combined with surfaces that simulate a variety of environments and settings. Cracked and broken pavement, loose gravel, leaves, stones, sand, and even water can be utilized to create every aspect of the ambulation challenge. The placement of crosswalk signals, bus stop and pedestrian signs in conjunction with doors, entryways, benches, and other environmental icons enhance the effectiveness of the course.

- PATIENT ROOM FURNITURE (custom designed healthcare furnishings), REHAB 1,2,3 (pediatric environments), The ROAD to RECOVERY (donor recognition system), SOUND SYMS (cognitive assessment and evaluation systems), SPACE MANAGEMENT SYSTEMS (healthcare storage and retrieval units), and WORKSYMS (work hardening equipment and environments) are other areas in which GDI is involved.

3-7 *INDEPENDENCE SQUARE Rehab Center at Kessler Institute for Rehabilitation, East Orange, NJ. An accessible apartment is featured in this rehab unit with a complement of interchangeable appliances and furnishings so that patients can determine what will best assist them in their own homes.* GUYNES DESIGN, Inc.

3-8 *INDEPENDENCE SQUARE Rehab Center at GENESIS Outpatient Center, Jacksonville, FL. This expansive environment includes a home life center featuring a front porch with ramp and stairs for evaluation and skill-building of patients and their families. Local builders and suppliers benefit from the opportunity to work with therapists and patients to assess new products and materials and to train in the necessary design and home building supports required by people with accessibility issues.* GUYNES DESIGN, Inc.

For further information or to visit one of the hospitals and nursing centers utilizing the ADL environments created by GUYNES DESIGN, contact:

GUYNES DESIGN, Inc.
1555 East Jackson
Phoenix, AZ 85034
800-264-0390

Welcome, H.O.M.E., Inc.

Welcome, H.O.M.E. (House of Modification Examples), Inc., has designed an aesthetically pleasing, functional, barrier-free "demonstrator home" with accompanying bed and breakfast suites. It is their intention to demonstrate how a home's environment can be user-friendly to persons living with a variety of physical limitations (as well as unique challenges), but its design can benefit people of all ages, sizes, and shapes. When it is completed (targeting late 1996), you can be a guest there and can discover over 123 ideas that make this an easy, safe, comfortable environment (Fig. 3-9).

Welcome, H.O.M.E. realizes that not everyone will be able to actually visit, so they have products and services that will help bring the ideas to you:

- They have compiled an informational packet titled *Come As You Are* to enable as many people as possible to learn about the design concepts and the providers of the products and services that have come together to create this home.
- Welcome, H.O.M.E. is a state of Wisconsin representative to the National Center for Accessible Housing. They continue to update and keep abreast of products and services, which they can offer you in an in-person presentation.

The situations of people with disabilities are often unique. While Welcome, H.O.M.E. has attempted to introduce enough ideas to arouse your curiosity and challenge your creativity through the information they offer, they also realize that the design of their project might not meet everyone's specific needs—but it's a good starting point! Take a little vacation and check it out for yourself:

Welcome, H.O.M.E., Inc.
P.O. Box 586
Newburg, WI 53060
414-675-2525

American Standard

American Standard has assembled a handy 47-page booklet titled, *American Standard ADA Design Guide* (order number SA94134). This publication features complete specifications for its products as well as their recommended installation height. The booklet covers:

- Design guidelines for the Americans with Disabilities Act
- Designing a barrier-free washroom
- A selection guide for toilets, bathtubs, urinals, and lavatories
- Kitchen sinks
- Pressalit barrier-free products
- Faucets

For more information, contact:

American Standard Literature Department
P.O. Box 639
Hanover, MD 21076
800-948-1185

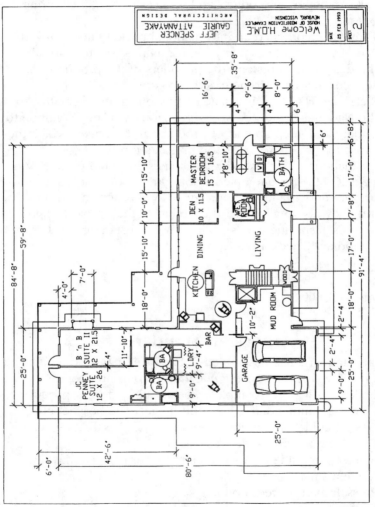

3-9 *A well-thought-out plan.* Welcome, House of Modification Examples, Inc. (Welcome, H.O.M.E.)/Jeff Spencer A.I.A. Architect

GE Appliances

GE Appliances published a 30-page booklet titled *Real Life Design* (Pub. No. 24-C264) about a kitchen that was designed by Mary Jo Peterson, CKD, CBD. As mentioned earlier, the term "universal design" is just one of the many descriptive terms in use throughout the industry. GE believes that a better phrase, one that contains more description, is "Real Life Design." As they put it:

> Real Life Design is simply good design. It can be appreciated by everybody because it makes so much sense in everybody's life. It takes into account that most people don't fit a stereotypical norm. Baby boomers in huge numbers are finding out that they aren't as spry or sure-sighted as they used to be. Along with the usual problems faced by an aging population, Real Life Design also acknowledges a wide range of physical and mental abilities and impairments. It even acknowledges that a great many of our most worthy citizens are children!

> Real Life Design says, for example, that an individual in a wheelchair should be able to peel potatoes comfortably at a sink that is height adjustable. But so should a person who stands over 6 feet tall. A grandmother using a walker should be able to literally pull the shelves of a wall cabinet down toward her with one hand. But this kind of access is equally convenient for her 9-year-old granddaughter.

The booklet is beautifully done and filled with full-page color photos that point out the featured designs. It is full of information, contains a question-and-answer section, and has a list of agencies and organizations. This booklet should definitely be added to your library.

To obtain your copy, contact:

Dri-View Manufacturing (GE Company)
4700 Allmond Ave.
Louisville, KY 40209

or call the GE Answer Center for general product information or questions at 800-626-2000.

Whirlpool Home Appliances

Every person has some type of physical or mental limitation that makes certain tasks more difficult to accomplish than others. All too often people forget to take these limitations into consideration when designing a kitchen or laundry area. The result can be choices that turn simple day-to-day tasks into difficult chores. For that reason, Whirlpool put together a 23-page guide titled *Kitchen and Laundry*

Guide for Builders and Remodelers: The Less Challenging Home (Form No. MSC-61).

This guide is designed to help you rethink your approach to planning a kitchen or laundry area. From affordable modifications of existing rooms to attractive new room designs, this guide shows how careful planning and proper selection and installation of appliances can make tasks easier for homeowners. A big plus for this guide is the emphasis on the appliances. The color photos illustrate proper installation and use of the appliances, and the photos picture a wide variety of individuals using them. This guide delivers a hands-on approach that you need to successfully design a kitchen or laundry room for your customers.

Whirlpool offers other informational products that are worth looking into; for instance, their video, "Universal Design Kitchen," features a selection of appliances and materials to help make kitchens barrier-free and adaptable for use by children, parents, and grandparents.

Gathering detailed information before you begin any project will help you create a more effective environment for the customer. These products can be obtained from:

Whirlpool Corp.
2000 North State Rt. 63
Benton Harbor, MI 49022-2692
800-253-1301

Concepts Kitchens and Baths

Linda Nitteberg, CKD, has been in business since 1982 and has been involved in the Northern California Chapter of NKBA since that time. She is a regular speaker at design classes in the CKD program and is a member of NARI (National Association of the Remodeling Industry), a professional remodeling group, where she provides design assistance on special projects. Linda brings a unique mixture of expertise to the topic of accessible and adaptive design.

Since 1975, when she served as a facilitator for the White House Conference on this issue, she has been an advocate for the rights of disabled individuals. At that time, she was a graduate student in rehabilitation counseling and was designing for friends who used wheelchairs.

In addition to being a general contractor, a business owner, and a designer, Linda has dealt firsthand with life in a wheelchair. One of her greatest pleasures is teaching classes to people with disabilities. Because of her personal experience, she can share information that you or I would never be able to understand. To tap into Linda's unique expertise, contact her:

Linda Nitteberg, CKD
CK&B
1661 Glenroy Dr., #101
San Jose, CA 95124
408-264-2284

Mary Jo Peterson, CKD, CBD, Design Consultant

Mary Jo Peterson is a certified kitchen/bath designer and an educator with specific expertise in universal design that incorporates the needs of people of varying sizes and abilities, including those with disabilities and those who are aging. She focuses her design practice on residential and commercial building projects in New England and provides consulting support to major home builders and remodelers nationwide.

An author and teacher of the NKBA training program on universal design, Mary Jo is a member of the NKBA Speakers Board and gives presentations on accessible design issues. She is also a member of the Advisory Board of the Association for Safe and Accessible Products (ASAP) and has completed numerous writing and speaking assignments in its behalf.

Mary Jo has written two books, *Universal Kitchen Planning: Design that Adapts to People* and *Universal Bath Planning: Design that Adapts to People*, both published by the NKBA. She has worked with national product manufacturers on staff training and design of spaces and products incorporating universal concepts. As mentioned previously, she has designed a universal kitchen for GE Appliances and contributed to related literature and training for GE staff and customers.

Currently serving on a number of cross-agency committees, Mary Jo works at integrating universal design into home and product design. This work has involved her with state and federal government agencies and advocacy groups as well as professional organizations such as the NAHB, NARI, the American Institute of Architects (AIA), and NKBA. She actively promotes change and education toward universal design.

To contact her:

Mary Jo Peterson, CKD, CBD
Design Consultant
3 Sunset Cove Rd.
Brookfield, CT 06804
203-775-4763

LifeStyle HomeDesign Services

Those builders and remodelers who work from home plans know how important it is to make sure that the plans you use are correct in design before beginning the job. It is also important to follow those plans, especially in this market. Barbara Allan (see chapter 1) emphasized this as she described her experiences on her own project, where the plans were not followed or completely understood by the professional hired to do the work. Be sure the person you hire to put your plans together has the experience required by this special needs market. Don't forget to mention what area (city, county, and state) you are building in so provisions can be incorporated in the drawings to meet any applicable codes for energy, earthquakes, or hurricanes. It is also important to know all the necessary dimensions before putting any plans together. An inch added to the height of a toilet, for instance, can make a big difference to the individual who has to use it. The homework you do now can save you from costly future mistakes.

Brad Johnson, C.P.B.D. (Certified Professional Building Designer), of LifeStyle has 18 years in residential design. He has worked with builders to produce designs to appeal to the public in a "fast tract" subdivision setting and also created unique one-of-a-kind custom plans for individual clients that best fit their needs and lifestyle. He has designed new plans as well as modified existing plans to fit the needs of the customer. The following examples of his plans should give you a few ideas of features required by the owner that were incorporated into the design:

Plan A (Fig. 3-10). This design was created "from scratch." The main emphasis that the owner wanted to achieve was an openness at the entry to living/family space. With its wide halls, minimum 4'6" (137 cm), even more openness was acquired. All door and opening widths were maintained at 3'0" (91 cm) to allow for easy access to any room in the home. Access to the master bedroom is directly off the living room.

The bathrooms required the minimum 5'0" (152 cm) clear radius for easy maneuverability of a wheelchair. Ample space was provided at the side(s) of the toilets to allow for "slide" access. The master bath shower is a "roll in" type.

The kitchen cabinet layout was left off the working drawings. The owner contracted with a custom kitchen and bath design firm to supply the design for accessible fixtures and appliances. The interior dimension was given for the area, which was then designed into the floor plan.

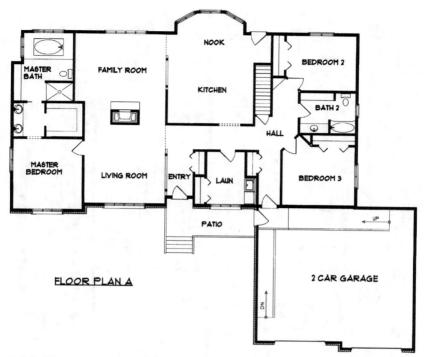

3-10 *The two ramps in the garage are unique.* LifeStyle HomeDesign Services

A ramp was installed, with a minimum slope of 1' (30 cm) rise per 12' (366 cm) run from the garage to the main living area. The length of run for the ramp from the garage to the basement was too short to accomplish the minimum slope requirements, so in this area a ramp was designed with the minimum slope possible and an escalating platform was installed to carry the owner to the basement floor. Future plans include a deck and ramp to be installed at the back door.

Plan B (Fig. 3-11). This plan was derived from an existing design but the changes were too extensive for comparison with the original. The house is on a slab foundation with a maximum of 2" (5 cm) vertical distance from living floor height to any exterior finished floor height (i.e., garage, patio, and stoops). A "rolled curb" can be used in place of a ramp, thus eliminating the use of any more exterior space.

A "rolled curb" is the rounded edge of a slab or foundation, similar to a street curb. It normally refers to the slab that protrudes directly in front of the threshold of an exterior

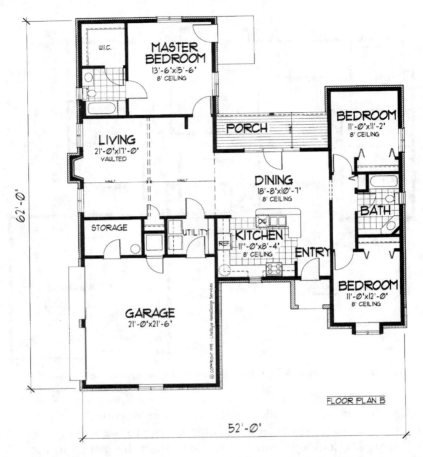

3-11 *Notice all the open space—there is very little hall space.* LifeStyle HomeDesign Services

door. When this type of application has been formed, it allows a wheelchair user to roll easily in and out of a door (see Fig. 3-12).

Hall spaces were eliminated to rooms and areas that a wheelchair user would be using a majority of the time. The hall bath is located across from the larger opening to keep any traveling down a hall in the wheelchair to a minimum. The hall is at a comfortable width of 3'8" (112 cm) for the occasional access needed. [Author's note: ANSI A117.1-92 requires a 4' space in front of a door if the door can be pushed and a 5' space if the door must be pulled. In Fig. 3-11, the bathroom door is offset from the living room doorway, so

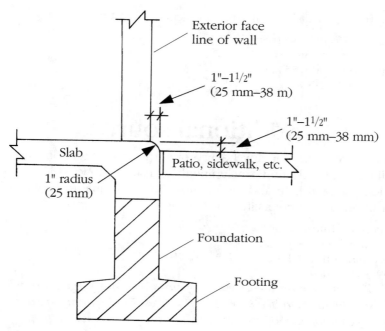

Exterior face
line of wall

1"–1¹/₂"
(25 mm–38 m)

1"–1¹/₂"
(25 mm–38 mm)

Slab

Patio, sidewalk, etc.

1" radius
(25 mm)

Foundation

Footing

3-12 *Rolled curb detail.* C.R.S., Inc.

there isn't a clear 3'8" in front of the bathroom door. This could be resolved by either repositioning or enlarging the living room doorway so it aligns with the bathroom door. Additionally, one bedroom door, the entry (front) door, and the exit from the utility into the garage all lack 18" (46 cm) clearance on the latch sides of the doors (ANSI guideline). Again, solutions are quite simple—the hallway could be extended to the front of the closet in the bedroom, the utility door could open outward into the garage, and the front door could be repositioned closer to the bedroom wall. Standards and codes are constantly undergoing revision, but strive to keep current. Remember also that there are no residential accessibility guidelines or codes for less than four dwelling units. Since commercial guidelines are the best we have at the present time, follow them.]

The kitchen was laid out with openness to the entertaining areas. The opening between cabinet runs is 4' (122 cm). The master suite offers the 5' (152 cm) clear turning radius and the closet features a 3' (91 cm) wide door. The closet offers ample space for maneuverability. The doors to all habitable rooms are 3' (91 cm).

To learn more about what they can do, write:

LifeStyle HomeDesign Services
275 Market St., Ste. 512
Minneapolis, MN 55405
612-347-0777

Additional sources

Besides what has already been brought to your attention, there are still many organizations, including those listed below, which can provide additional help and information. Take the time to contact them for information on specific topics of interest.

Accent on Information
P.O. Box 700
Bloomington, IL 61702
309-378-2961
   A computer retrieval system of products and services to help the physically disabled live more effective lives. Publications are available on selected topics. Source for information on product suppliers.

Adaptive Environments
374 Congress St., Ste. 301
Boston, MA 02210
617-695-1225
   Offers Consumer's Guide to Home Adaptation *for $12. This publication features information on the step-by-step process of home adaptation for persons with disabilities and includes six to eight pages of products and assistance resources.*

American Amputee Foundation
Box 250218, Hillcrest Stn.
Little Rock, AR 72225
501-666-2523
   National information, inquiry, and referral service for people who have had a limb amputated. Sponsors nationwide give-a-limb program.

American Foundation for the Blind
1110 Plaza, Ste. 300
New York, NY 10001
800-232-5463 or 212-502-7600
   Produce talking books and tapes. Can provide written evaluations on computer products.

Amputees in Motion, International (AIM)
P.O. Box 2703
Escondido, CA 92033
619-454-9300

Primarily a support group but can provide information and assistance about appropriate modifications to homes and recreational facilities to accommodate the disabled.

Arthritis Foundation, Inc.
1314 Spring Street NW
Atlanta, GA 30309
800-283-7800

Supports research to find a cure for and prevent arthritis. Offers free information on arthritis and ways people can cope with the disease. Also has material on the availability of local community services (e.g., support groups, classes, exercise classes).

Association for Safe and Accessible Products
1511 K Street NW, Ste. 600
Washington, DC 20005
202-347-8200

Gathers and disseminates information on safe and accessible products, promotes and publicizes the benefits of such products, creates and identifies opportunities for increased utilization of them, and serves as a resource to the marketplace and the public sector.

Brain Injury Association, Inc.
1776 Massachusetts Avenue, NW
Washington, DC 20036-1904
800-444-6443

National advocacy organization providing services to persons with brain injuries and their families. Provides a catalog of educational materials covering topics specific to brain injury.

Canine Companions for Independence
P.O. Box 446
Santa Rosa, CA 95402-0446
800-572-BARK (2275)

Information on dogs trained to assist people (in hearing/social areas) of all disabilities except blindness.

Center for Assistive Technology
University at Buffalo
515 Kimball Tower
Buffalo, NY 14214
800-628-2281

Provides information, referrals, and a number of direct services to persons with disabilities. Focus is on assistive, technological, and home environmental modifications for older (60+) persons with disabilities.

Center for Inclusive Design and Environmental Access (IDeA)
School of Architecture and Planning
State University of New York at Buffalo
390 Hayes Hall
Buffalo, NY 14214
716-829-3485

Conducts research on architectural issues related to design for people with disabilities. Provides technical and design assistance both for new construction and on home modifications for people with disabilities.

Disabled American Veterans National Service Headquarters
807 Maine Ave. SW
Washington, DC 20024
202-554-3501

Nationwide network of services available to disabled veterans, their families, and their survivors. Provide counseling services on veterans' benefits and services, assist in filing and pursuing claims, provide disaster relief to disabled veterans who need help, and participate in pre-separation programs conducted by the armed forces.

Fair Housing Information Clearinghouse
P.O. Box 9146
McLean, VA 22102
800-343-3442 or TTY 800-290-1617

Fair housing guidelines. Can answer questions of a technical nature on accessibility.

Gazette International Networking Institute
4207 Lindell Blvd., #110
St. Louis, MO 63108
314-534-0475

Information on housing, equipment, and independent living for people with polio, spinal injuries, ventilators, and neuromuscular disease.

Independent Living Research Utilization Program
2323 South Shepard St., Ste. 1000
Houston, TX 77019
713-520-0232

Provides information and technical assistance pertaining to independent living and disability rights. Can provide information on how to contact local community-based living centers.

National Center for Disability Services
201 I.U. Willets Rd.
Albertson, NY 11507-9850
516-747-5400

Provides educational, vocational, and research services for persons with disabilities.

National Council on Independent Living
2111 Wilson Blvd., Ste. 405
Arlington, VA 22201
703-525-3406

Provides technical assistance to independent living centers located throughout the U.S.

National Federation of the Blind
1800 Johnson St.
Baltimore, MD 21230
410-659-9314

Will make some legal referrals and advocacy. Can provide publications on employment issues, technical assistance, and access to a computer bulletin board. Sells aids and devices. Has large exhibit at annual conferences on available adaptive equipment.

National Institute for Rehabilitation Engineering
P.O. Box T
Hewitt, NJ 07421
800-736-2216 or 201-853-6585

Specializes in helping people who have severe, unusual, or multiple physical limitations. A team composed of electronic engineers, physicists, psychologists, optometrists, and other volunteers reviews the person's capabilities, disabilities, and task-performance goals to recommend and implement programs that will increase the person's performance. People will not be denied services because of an inability to pay. Includes geriatric rehabilitation.

PAM (Physically Impaired Association of Michigan) Assistance Center
601 West Maple
Lansing, MI 48906
800-274-7426

Information on adaptive devices.

Research and Training Center on Independent Living
University of Kansas, Room 4089 Dole
Lawrence, KS 66045
913-864-4095 or FAX 913-864-5063
  Training, consulting, and publications library for independent living by people with multiple/severe physical limitations.
United Cerebral Palsy Associations, Inc.
1660 L St., NW
Washington, DC 20036
212-481-6300 or 202-776-0406
  Provides information and referral services to individuals with cerebral palsy and other disabilities.

Although every effort was made to ensure this list is up to date, there is the possibility that by the time this book is published, telephone numbers might have changed, different area codes could be in effect, or the organization might have moved to a new location. If you find any of this information has changed, you might try checking with another organization to see if they can provide you with more current information.

If you have made it through the first three chapters and still feel good about this special needs market, then you should find the rest of the book enjoyable. These first three chapters were designed to be "eye openers" to help you find out if you have what it takes to understand this market and be able to go into it. Reading *Accessible Housing* can make a difference in your life and in the lives of your customers if you choose to go into this business, or it can help you succeed in the business you might already be running. You can make a difference!

4

Marketing in the barrier-free environment

Many of us go into business because we enjoy what we do. That's clearly a bonus, but the real purpose of being in business is to make money—not the amount that only takes us from one job to the next, but enough so that we can add to our savings or retirement accounts at the end of each job. However, to achieve this goal, it is essential to generate the greatest possible profit margin on every job sold, and the only way to do that is to thoroughly understand the market and produce the best-quality job in the least amount of time.

This can become a reality if you perfect what you do best and don't spread yourself too thin. Perhaps you can specialize in only one facet of the construction industry. For example, kitchens and bathrooms seem to go hand in hand. As a remodeler, you could start a division that would handle special needs projects in these areas. Realistically, however, even in as large a market as barrier-free construction, only 15 to 20 percent of your business will be directly related to it. Of course, these numbers are not carved in stone. With the right market and the proper advertising budget, these percentages could change dramatically—and in your favor.

With the understanding of customer needs you gained in earlier chapters, and the tools given in this chapter, you should be able to reach those customers, close more sales, and yield a higher profit margin. Even though you will be helping the cause through service to the special needs market, don't lose sight that you are in business to make money. As harsh as it sounds, that is reality.

Making yourself known

To identify the potential customer and help the potential customer learn who you are, you have to step forward and get your face and/or company known to the general public. Customers today are very smart shoppers. They might not be in the position to do the work themselves, but because they know their injury or disability, they have done their homework.

On your initial appointment with the customer, it is important to determine what this person really wants and needs. Doing so will give you the best opportunity to sell yourself. Sometimes it is best just to listen. Give customers a chance to express what is really on their minds and hear them out. Then guide them toward their ideal project—but do not try to sell them something they don't need. Remember, the customer needs someone who will be a professional at all times—and yet be friendly.

Keep an open mind and watch for opportunities to suggest options. While your customers might have done their homework, they might not be up on the latest in products or ideas. Make your suggestions in such a way as not to confuse the issue or lose sight of the customers' main goal—freedom within their own environment. Besides, you might be following the guidelines laid out for you by therapists. It will be your job to blend your expertise and those special requests into a united project that will be both pleasing and comfortable for the customer. It is possible that the customer is overloaded and confused as to what is happening. It will be up to you to put the customer at ease. Learn from your experiences with past customers; it most definitely will help you with future potential customers. Being more understanding and sympathetic to customer needs can indeed help you close a sale.

A code of ethics helps professionals keep their focus on why they are in the business, and it assures customers that their needs are important. If you haven't already got one, I suggest you mull over your past and write your own code, one that you can live up to. It would even be a good idea to have it printed so you can include it in packages to be presented to potential customers. It wouldn't hurt for you to look at it occasionally—just to remind yourself why you are in business. If you are at a loss for words, how about something like this:

We measure our success by the satisfaction of our customers. We strive daily to deliver the finest product, and we are committed to:

- Honesty and integrity in all our interactions with customers, potential customers, subcontractors, suppliers, and employees

- Treating each customer, potential customer, subcontractor, supplier, and employee courteously and in a professional manner—with respect and dignity
- Giving each project the very best effort—both in thought and in action—this company has to offer
- Estimating each project at a fair price, neither inflating prices during times that are especially busy nor bidding unrealistically low prices in an attempt to mislead customers
- Addressing each concern of the customer, no matter how small it seems
- Resolving in a timely and professional manner any problems involving one of our projects

Promotion

Promotion is a very important element of being in business and should not be taken for granted. In order to survive in any business, promotion is a necessity. Because the market is wide open and also new to other professionals, it is extremely important that you start to promote yourself now. Only you can sell yourself, but you need a clear vision of both you and your goals, and you will need the proper tools. Consider how to promote yourself. Are you a contractor who:

- Builds new homes occasionally?
- Specializes in kitchens and baths only?
- Has a showroom and specializes in kitchens and baths only?
- Remodels, but does not specialize in any one field?
- Is involved in new construction and occasionally does remodeling projects?
- Has a quick-fix-it or handyman division?

No matter how you classify yourself, the business principles will be the same. Depending on the direction you choose, your overhead might be higher or you might have to hire sales people, purchase specialized tools and equipment, or carry inventory.

A good way to start is with a business card to present to potential customers. The design and layout of a business card can reveal a lot about an individual and a business, and this is important because once that business card is handed out, you have no idea into whose hands it might fall. Make that first impression count! Business cards should be clean, well-organized, easy to read, and they should deliver a message. Company names should be clearly visible at a quick glance.

The business cards in Fig. 4-1 are appealing. Two of the three companies have showrooms; should the showrooms have been indi-

4-1A *Great Logo!* Gary White, CID, CKD, CBD, Kitchen & Bath Design, Newport Beach, CA

4-1B *Very clean!* Harvey's Kitchens & Baths

4-1C *This card uses a reversed image for the International Symbol.* Concepts Kitchens and Baths

cated on their business cards? The first card (A) displays the type of work done by this specific company and the certifications indicate they are well qualified in the design department. The second card (B) indicates that the company specializes in a particular market. The third card (C) again indicates a specialized market. It shows something the other two cards do not: how long the company has been in business. Even more important, it uses the international symbol of accessibility.

Because the symbol can be found at accessible parking spaces, areas of refuge (rescue assistance), passenger loading zones, and toilet and bathing facilities, the general public can identify with it immediately. Using the symbol on a business card makes it easy for an individual to identify that this professional could be involved in some types of accessible projects, so it is very important to use this symbol on your business cards as well as in advertising. The accessibility symbols in Fig. 4-2 are two versions you could incorporate into your promotional material. Business cards using these are easy for the customer to comprehend.

4-2A
Reversed image. Americans with Disabilities Act Accessibility Guidelines (ADAAG), 7/26/91, as published in the Federal Register

4-2B
Standard image. ADAAG, 7/26/91, as published in the Federal Register

You should also consider assembling a portfolio or presentation package. Before you can do this, however, you will want to do some or all of the following:

- Get involved with local chapters of national contractor/remodeler associations.
- Support charitable organizations.
- Enter contests through trade publications and associations.
- Obtain testimony from satisfied customers.
- Start a newsletter.
- Display your business at local home and garden shows.
- Work with occupational therapists and rehabilitation services at hospitals and clinics.
- Pass business cards out at heath-care equipment stores.
- Give presentations to third-party referral sources that work with seniors or those with disabilities.

Your professional accomplishments are of interest to your community as well as to the trade, so when you land a unique or unusual project, contact the editor of the home improvement section of your local newspaper as well as the editors of trade publications. You might have a story and it never hurts to get your name in print. Article reprints are also a great addition to your portfolio. Take pride in your work and toot your own horn—loudly!

Your portfolio should include the following:

- A brief history of your company
- A detailed map of your location
- Your code of ethics
- Articles about awards you have received
- Any magazine and newspaper articles featuring you, your company, and/or your projects
- Testimony from satisfied customers
- Before and after photos of unusual projects
- Newsletter
- Your business card
- A postcard so customers can keep in touch
- A list of services you offer or products you sell, possibly in an attractive brochure format such as the one shown in Fig. 4-3
- A customer home analysis
- A customer service program (Fig. 4-4)
- An access loan program (if available in your area—consult local banks)
- Information about tax benefits (accessible/adaptable/adjustable modifications—consult your accountant)

Creative Living Solutions

Enhancing Your Home To Meet Your Current Needs

EH LS

Extended Home Living Services, Inc.℠

4-3
Good example of the front cover of a tri-fold brochure offering services or products.
Extended Home Living Services, Inc., Northbrook, IL

Portfolios can be expensive, but the trade-off in increased sales will make them worth every penny. At your next home improvement show, you will be one step ahead of your competition with a professional package to hand to potential customers.

Options available

Contractors who are considering specializing in universal design might want to explore some other options. The following should be considered if you are a well-established professional and have the capital to take the risks involved.

Showroom

If you already specialize in kitchen and bath projects and the majority of your construction business is related to just that, then you should consider a full and total commitment to that market. The best way to do this is to open a showroom, which allows you to bring in customers to view set-up models. This simplifies analyzing their needs, and the visual, tactile arrangement helps customers reach solid

Extended Home Living Services, Inc.®

EXTENDED HOME SERVICES'
CLIENT SERVICE PROGRAM

◊ The company will develop an understanding of the clients' and their caregivers' specific needs including recommendations from their physicians and therapists.

◊ We will develop an itemized proposal through on-site assessment that clearly addresses accessibility modifications or alternative options.

◊ A determination will be made if architectual renderings will be required, and if so, outline anticipated fees.

◊ Extended Home Living Services will provide information regarding potential funding resources and assist when advocacy is required.

◊ The client and their caregivers will be contacted for a review of the proposal, cost, and payment schedule.

◊ Upon proposal acceptance, construction plans will be reviewed with the family and plan review will continue throughout the course of the project.

◊ We will continue throughout the coming years to stay apprised of any changes in the clients' needs and act accordingly.

3445 Carol Lane • Northbrook, Illinois 60062 • (708) 824-1999 • Fax (708) 298-0930

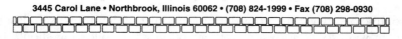

4-4 *An important sales tool that professionals should live up to. You will need to come up with your own.* Extended Home Living Services, Inc., Northbrook, IL

decisions. A showroom also provides an opportunity to display and sell accessory items that customers need to see installed and allows you to incorporate universal and barrier-free designs into the displays. Finally, a showroom gives you a meeting space so once a month you can conduct a seminar for customers to help them better understand their environment and to bring them up to speed on the newest products being offered in this special needs market.

The biggest advantage to a showroom is that it helps to transform you from a small independent contractor to a legitimate credible business in the consumer's mind. When considering a showroom, consider the following points:

- Plan on at least 1,200 square feet with 80 percent of that space devoted to displays. For showrooms that are 2,600 square feet or larger, plan to devote at least two-thirds to display. The amount of square footage you choose should be based on location and the lowest price you can get per square foot.
- Make sure the building is totally accessible—inside (including bathrooms) as well as outside.
- Ascertain that there is ample parking.
- Make sure the building is close to a main arterial road, for easy access and possible foot traffic.
- Ensure the building is completely visible at night.
- Plan a showroom with great eye appeal both inside as well as outside (especially for those who window-shop at night). Figure 4-5 shows a display by Gary White, CID, CKD, CBD, Kitchen & Bath Design. Inspired by the California disasters, this complete working kitchen is called "The Fault Line." It is a volcanically inspired eruption of fire that changes color before your eyes through the use of layered lighting effects, fiber optics, and a computer-driven scenic sequencer. The irregularly broken edges of the fault seem to come apart, glowing and changing color. Decorated with charred foliage, fractured glass, and local sandstone, it brings a smile to all no matter what their recent experience has been. The lava-like effects are simply spectacular at night!
- Consider putting at least one display involving universal or barrier-free design close to the storefront so the display can be seen from the outside. (If you have to put a wheelchair and a mannequin in the setting to get the message across— then that's what should be done.)
- Keep regular business hours (e.g., 10 a.m. to 5 p.m., Monday through Saturday).

Do not rely on the showroom to attract all your customers; that is the purpose of advertising and salespeople. Rather, the showroom gives your company credibility, name exposure, and a place to discuss products (as they are displayed).

It is possible that you will have peak seasons (especially around holidays or in the spring) for standard projects. This, of course, de-

4-5 *The showroom display was inspired by the California disasters.* Gary White, CID, CKD, CBD, Kitchen & Bath Design, Newport Beach, CA—Photo by Larry Faulke

pends on your geographical area, the traffic flow, location, length of season, and type of advertising. As for the special needs market, you can expect it to be pretty much a year-round business. Of course, this depends on your sales force and how clever you are with your advertising.

To keep the showroom afloat, consider using two full-time salespeople on straight commission. However, during your peak season, two to six salespeople might be more appropriate; realistically assess your peak season.

Because it is difficult during the off months for a sales force on straight commission, you might have to lower the number of salespeople and concentrate on sales being made on a more regular basis.

You are bound to have ups and downs in sales, but the combination of standard and universal design could make things a little more steady throughout the year. Devote at least 5 percent of your gross sales to showroom cost, and try to maintain a 30 percent gross profit, which nets approximately 15 percent profit. A showroom can set you apart from the competition—but it does not guarantee success. Design and build the very best project for your customers and hopefully everything else will take care of itself. Don't compromise quality, service, or customer satisfaction. Instill this philosophy in your employee training, be sure your sales force and subcontractors (if you use any) understand this, and don't forget to practice it daily yourself.

Handyman service

Perhaps you have a lucrative full-line remodeling company with a handyman division already in operation. Have you ever considered taking that division and applying the energy toward adaptable/adjustable modifications? This could be an operation with a very large potential market, and it could be quite profitable. For example, this handyman division could deal with the installation of:

- Handrails
- Grab bars
- Clip-on deluxe safety tub bars
- Ramps
- Phone jacks
- Extra lighting

These small tasks might not seem worth the energy, but to a customer, achieving a professional-looking installation of these items can be a total nightmare. These customers have reached the point in their lives when they have to admit to themselves that they are not capable of doing the work. So they hire out. The work will get done—somebody is going to do it—it might as well be you! Small items such as these that can make a world of difference in the customer's freedom.

Starting a division such as this can keep one or two men busy and will allow you to stay focused on the larger projects. If you are a builder, you can start a remodeling company in the same fashion as a handyman service. Just stay channeled—maybe only handling projects dealing with universal or barrier-free designs.

Advertising

Advertising costs can easily eat up profits, especially if potential leads do not turn into signed contracts; therefore, make every ad count. It is always a good idea to start small and work your way up, depending on what you can afford and what your work force can handle. You might have to go through a trial-and-error process first, but take care not to oversell yourself. Of course, listing yourself in the yellow pages of the phone book does work; it also establishes your name in the eyes of the community. Where should you advertise? If you specialize in kitchens, for example, list your main ad under Kitchen Remodeling and take your free listing under Bathroom Remodeling. If you are a remodeler, list your main ad under Contractors—Remodel & Repair and your free listing under Kitchen or Bathroom Remodeling. And here is a thought—if your local phone book has a category titled Disabled Persons Assistance, give this section a try. In addition to the phone book, there are other forms of advertising that should be considered.

Billboards

One form of advertising that I found worked great is the mini billboard. In a one-month period, I averaged about 20 calls a day. Unfortunately, I didn't have the sales force to keep all the appointments so I found myself referring potential customers to other contractors in the area. In my situation, the billboard hurt me more than it helped, but I had to try it and it was very effective in generating inquiries.

Because the person viewing your billboard will probably be in a moving vehicle, it is important that your telephone number be the first thing seen. The second thing should be what you do (using the International Symbol definitely helps), and the third is the name of your company. Be sure to use a white background behind the telephone number to make it stand out for easy reading. I recommend using a billboard during the beginning of the season; make sure you will be able to handle all the calls.

Community papers

Have you ever seen those small free papers full of want ads as you leave your local grocery store? You've probably picked up a few yourself as you passed through the door. Have you ever thought about advertising in one of those papers? These community papers can be a great source for advertising.

The ads are quite inexpensive, so taking out a full-page ad won't break you, and I found a full-page ad placed at the beginning of the season brought great results. Of course, in order to maintain name awareness, I ran a small ad for years before placing a full-page ad.

If you are placing a smaller ad, try one that reads across two or three columns and is at least 2 inches (5 cm) high. This makes it easier for the reader to spot. Also, adding color to the border (if color is an option) helps the reader identify your ad over the competition. A little trick that works when placing a border around an ad is to use a double border: a thick outer line and a thin inner line. The inside line should only be about 5 to 10 percent of the thickness of the outside border, and round the corners instead of having square ones. This layout makes your ad different enough that it seems to jump off the page. This is just what you want it to do—make direct eye contact with the reader.

Newspapers

I have never advertised in a newspaper, but others in the field recommend placing an ad in the front page (or main) section of your paper. Consider using the Saturday paper instead of the Sunday issue, which is usually so large that a small ad can become lost. Besides, it is easier for the reader to scan a Saturday paper. Reading the Sunday paper can be an all-day process!

The main goal of your ad is to get noticed by the reader. Therefore, it follows that you will want to place as large an ad as you can afford. The more white space in your ad, the more it will stand out from all the others (Figs. 4-6 and 4-7). Your ad can appear larger if you do not use borders because the surrounding margins become part of the ad.

Do not interchange what I recommend for a community paper with what was recommended for daily newspapers. The two types of papers are entirely different in format and content, and the recommendations included here are for those specific applications.

Franchises

At the present time, franchise opportunities in the kitchen and bath markets are not available. Research for this book revealed that a couple of firms began franchise operations but were unsuccessful. Perhaps by the time the book is in your hands, the opportunity will again exist. A franchise gives you the option to go into business for yourself even without experience in construction. Perhaps you just want to change your occupation within the construction field and specialize. If so, a franchise can teach you how to market and sell, how to get a project built using qualified contractors from your area, and how to manage the business.

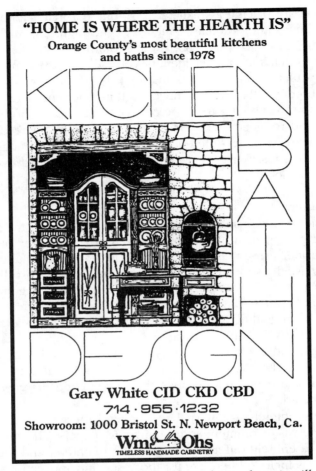

4-6 *Even though the ad appears busy, there is still a lot of white area to balance it out.* Gary White, CID, CKD, CBD, Kitchen & Bath Design, Newport Beach, CA

If you choose to buy into a franchise, be sure they will provide assistance in the following areas:

- *Marketing* You should receive guidance about advertising in the yellow pages as well as in the local newspaper, the creation of publicity releases, the assembly of your own portfolio or presentation package, and help in understanding the marketing benefits from any available national marketing programs. Will the franchiser (franchise corporate office) supply all the tools necessary for a complete media campaign to generate sales leads?

- *Sales* The franchiser should provide you with video and classroom training to sharpen your sales presentations so you can convert leads into successful sales.
- *Construction* You need to understand standard designs that have been developed within the structure of the franchise. Either you or your lead carpenter should receive field training in quick installation techniques that maintain quality at the same time. You will also want assistance in design both for aesthetics and functionality and help in learning to work with local contractors as subcontractors and government agencies.
- *Administration* You need a supply of business forms for bidding, contracts, and statements, as well as the software that allows you to enter the information onto these forms through a computer. Make sure you have a clear understanding of how to manage cash flow, purchasing, materials, and, most important, setting a high gross profit.

Find out if you have control over plans you design for the customer or whether the plans need approval from the franchiser before you apply for any building permits. You also need a clear understanding of the type of warranty offered through the franchise and who backs that warranty.

4-7 *Notice the unusual shape, along with the four inside borders. This ad really stands out.* Harvey's Kitchens & Baths

If you are not already aware of this, a franchise costs money. Royalties, anywhere from 4 to 8 percent, must be paid by the franchisee on gross sales receipts. Franchise fees could run between $15,000 and $40,000, depending on the geographical area or territory you are purchasing. You will be required to have working capital on hand in the neighborhood of $25,000 to $80,000, and this start-up cost might or might not include the franchise fee. However, there could be "mini" franchises offered with fees that start at $16,500 and slide upward, based on territory size. These types of franchises are only available in smaller "third-tier" markets that are not part of a larger metropolitan area and only in new markets where there are no other franchisees. Check out the financial arrangements very carefully. Also check that you do not have to pay royalties for anything else.

The franchise organization is in business to make sure its franchisees succeed in building their businesses. That is how they stay afloat. You become joined at the hip as a married couple until you sell or close the business. But as I mentioned before, two companies tried getting franchises afloat but were unsuccessful. If the opportunity should arise to buy into a franchise, keep in mind that the corporation normally approves your application. Be extremely careful and seek legal counsel before signing any contracts.

Selling

From the moment you answer that first inquiry call, you are selling yourself. How you answer the phone and meet your appointment on time right down to your appearance and how you handle yourself in front of potential customers determines whether they will hire you. Customers make up their minds about hiring a contractor within the first ten minutes of the appointment. A good first impression is essential!

Be courteous and well-informed at all times. You do not win any points—or contracts—by being rude. When a customer asks you a question, be confident and answer it like a professional. Customers can detect a phony. If they ask a question and you don't know the answer, admit it and then offer to do some research and get back to them with your findings. Of course, make sure you follow through on your promise. Be a well-rounded professional at all times: selling yourself sells the job.

I have enclosed my own list of "dos and don'ts" for meeting with potential customers. I recommend you study and practice them before going on any appointment.

Appointment dos and don'ts

- Be on time—if you're going to be late, call the customer.
- Dress code:
  - ~Shirt and tie are not necessary.
  - ~Work clothes are fine provided they are not full of dust and don't smell. Work clothes show customers you are a hands-on individual.
  - ~Work boots are okay, but make sure you do not track foreign material into the customer's home.
  - ~Hair should be presentable (combed).
- Never use profane language, no matter who is around.
- Don't voluntarily bring up politics and religion.
- Never argue.
- Listen well; use your ears, not your mouth.
- Handle disagreement diplomatically.
- Customers are not impressed with a "know-it-all."
- Putting down other professionals is not only unprofessional conduct, but customers are not interested.
- If you don't know, admit it.
- Learn to say "no," for whatever reason; can you realistically handle this project?
- Think twice before trying to force a sale.

Most of all, treat a customer as you would like to be treated, and practice all of the above whether you are on an appointment or on the job.

You probably already know that a customer is not always right. In cases like this, it is better to listen with your ears, not with your mouth. If you have not yet read Dale Carnegie's book, *How to Win Friends and Influence People* (Pocket Books, ISBN 0-671-41299-X), and/or Les Giblin's book, *How You Can Have Confidence & Power in Dealing With People* (Wilshire Book Company, ISBN 0-87980-072-0), you should! These two powerful books can help you to understand and deal with people, and they are especially helpful in promoting effective communications. Do yourself a favor and read one—or both—of these books. It will be the best commitment you could make to your career.

The next time the phone rings, think professionalism. Have confidence and be well-informed. Be on your best behavior at all times. You'll be surprised at how simple courtesy can influence the people around you—employees, subcontractors, customers, and yourself. Contractors don't just swing hammers any more; they're people-oriented professionals!

Public relations tools

As mentioned earlier in this chapter, a portfolio or presentation package is one of the most effective sales tools you could ever assemble. This package will help you stand head and shoulders above the competition in the customer's eyes.

Selling yourself might not be enough, especially since money (generally a lot, depending on the project) is involved. There are other tools that are helpful in getting sales leads to call you. You make them up yourself or, if you belong to an association, the association might provide them.

- If you are interested in getting your company name out in a selected zip code area, a door hanger might be the answer. A door hanger provides great space for a business card but don't forget to add a line that is as simple as "Call for your estimate today."
- Color brochures can present your qualifications and professional status. They are perfect for use in dealing with prospective customers, as handouts, or in direct-mailing promotions. The only thing remaining is to have your name, address, and phone number imprinted.
- Ad reprints used in national consumer magazines by associations can get the message out. The reverse side is left blank for personalized imprinting. These can be an excellent handout at a home improvement show.
- Purchase booklets that are put out by organizations where you can add your company's name and address. Booklets should have a purpose for the customer; for example, *Keep Your Home Safe & Secure* published by the Burglary Prevention Council. This 10-page booklet covers tips to safeguard a home—residential security devices and general measures that can be taken. Because of the market you will be dealing in, this could be a perfect selling tool. For quantity prices, contact:

Burglary Prevention Council
221 North LaSalle St., Ste. 3500
Chicago, IL 60601-1520

If you belong to an association, be sure to contact them for information about ready materials and other tools that could be of use.

Closing sales

There is no "magic formula" for closing a sale. There are just so many variables from the time you first see a customer until you present the bid that there is no guarantee that they will choose you, even when you have invested a lot of time or they are regular customers. Following the steps outlined in this chapter can improve your odds. Specializing in your field and perfecting your skills can help you as well. Consider reading Zig Ziglar's book *Secrets of Closing the Sale* (Fleming H. Revell Company, ISBN 0-8007-1213-7).

With a showroom and a sales force of two, you need to close four out of every ten leads. You will be cheating yourself if you do not sell 35 to 40 percent of your leads. It would be nice to close every lead you bid, but in reality you wouldn't have enough manpower to handle all those jobs comfortably, especially if you want to maintain high quality.

Remember that it is never easy to be successful, and success is one of those things that just can't be guaranteed. Here are some guidelines to increase your chances for success:

Integrity: Without this, you shouldn't be in business.

Attitude: Treat customers, prospective customers, suppliers, and employees with courtesy and fairness.

Priorities: Your customer is important; without the customer, you would not be in business!

Courtesy: Always be polite in your business relationships.

Standards: Maintain high standards both in products supplied and in quality of work.

Perfection: Keep reaching for it.

Advertise: If you don't, why bother with anything else?

Concede: Never win an argument with a customer. Never try to.

Home improvements can be a hard sell. Educate yourself, learn new techniques, experiment with alternative products, and be creative with your advertising and sales approaches. *Accessible Housing* helps you learn and use the necessary tools to close more sales satisfactorily. It is up to you to make those tools work for you. Only you can increase the odds, so good luck on selling your next project—be a winner!

Subcontractors

Finding talented and reliable subcontractors can be an exhausting trial-and-error process, especially with more than 40 different types of specialty contractors or subcontractors in the industry. Choosing the right subcontractor for a specific job is a decision only you can make. Building and maintaining relationships with subcontractors (once you have found subcontractors you are comfortable working with) can be a very difficult, but rewarding, experience.

Whatever your reasons for hiring subcontractors, keep in mind that they are professionals with individual personalities working to run and manage successful companies. Like many general contractors, they rely on a support network of quality subcontractors to produce much of their work. Your judicious use of subcontractors could make or break your project and might work to your overall advantage. Subcontractors can help you to meet state licensing requirements (when appropriate) and can speed production.

To get the best out of your subcontractor relationships, follow these guidelines:

- Hire and work with the same subcontractors.
- Give subcontractors the opportunity to bid their part of the project.
- Don't let their price cause you to shop for a lower-priced subcontractor.
- Communicate with subcontractors, asking for their opinions and/or input.
- Give adequate notice of scheduled work or delays and immediately advise them of any changes.
- Provide accurate plans for them to work from.
- Arrange for materials you are supplying to arrive on time for their work.
- Provide good working conditions on the job site.
- Offer general direction (to meet job specifications) as needed, but let the subcontractors do their own work.
- Arrange for a qualified worker (not the customer) to be on hand to answer subcontractors' questions or to tackle any problems that should arise.
- Most important, pay promptly—money talks!

Quality

To ensure that you receive the quality work that your customers deserve, build and strengthen your relationships with subcontractors. Quality relationships produce respect and performance; quality work requires fewer callbacks.

Giving subcontractors the opportunity to bid their portion of the work allows them to scope the job and head off any potential problems that might otherwise not be discovered, problems that could affect your bid. Nothing is more embarrassing than to approach a customer with a mistake and then ask for additional funds to cover it. By rights, this is your problem—not the customer's—depending on how the general conditions of your contract are written.

When subcontractors participate in the bidding process, they reaffirm that the job will run smoothly and profitably. Working with the same subcontractors for about 20 years, I have developed relationships with them to overcome customers' budget constraints. These relationships have permitted us to rebid jobs, coming up with alternative plans of action that won both the customers' approval and met their budgets while at the same time meeting codes. While this didn't happen often, it was reassuring to feel that I could go to subcontractors and be confident they would work with me. When a job was underbid, our give-and-take relationship helped us to work out compromises we could both accept.

Loyalty

In return for their loyalty, you need to support your subcontractors; they, in turn, will support you. Most subcontractors work for other general contractors as well as their own customers (consumers), so their schedule could be as tight as yours. Although you might have a strong working relationship, you might not always be able to hire a particular subcontractor for a particular job. Because you might have to hire another subcontractor, it doesn't hurt to establish working relationships with more than one of the same trade.

Your preferred subcontractor could recommend an equally qualified subcontractor for your particular job. Remember, a job could arise when you will need both subcontractors, and their previous relationship could be a big help.

Finally, your payment track record can reinforce the subcontractor's loyalty to you, especially during a busy construction season.

Good neighbor policy

Treat subcontractors as you would like to be treated and work to build a personal relationship with them. Keep in mind that they can be a good source of leads. Don't be afraid to ask them to send business your way and be sure to do the same for them.

It might be helpful to attend meetings or join an association for subcontractors. This can provide an informal opportunity to meet and get to know other subcontractors in your area.

The bottom line is that you need them as much as they need you. By working as a team, you'll produce the highest quality work possible, ensure the customer's happiness (repeat business!), keep your overall production costs down, and increase profits.

Costs

Keep yourself abreast of the costs of products that you purchase from your suppliers. If you have a computer, update this information on a monthly basis. Before you pay your invoices, check them over and enter any changes. If you do not have a computer, then make up a materials list for each supplier and review the prices on a regular basis.

This process allows you to keep current; if you run into a time crunch, at least you will have the prices at your fingertips for quick bid calculations. It really helps to know your prices. Many suppliers give 1,000 board feet prices instead of linear feet. They will make the conversion for you but it would be a good idea if you knew the formula.

- A board foot is defined as a piece one inch thick (nominal) by one foot wide (nominal) by one foot long (actual) or its equivalent. A good example would be a 2" × 6", which also equals one board foot for each foot of length.
- Board footage is calculated by multiplying the nominal thickness in inches (T) by the nominal width in inches (W) by the actual length in feet (L) and dividing by 12. The formula is:

$$\frac{T \times W \times L}{12} = \text{Board Feet}$$

Sample problem

What is the cost per piece for a 1" × 12" × 6' when the cost is 0.415 per 1,000 board feet? What is the cost per lineal foot?

Solution

- 1" × 12" × 6' divided by 12 equals 6 board feet.
- 0.415 × 6 equals $2.49 per piece.
- $2.49 divided by 6 equals 0.42 per lineal foot.

If you are required by your municipality to obtain any permits, they will ask for drawings of what you plan to build (especially for an addition or a major undertaking that involves the structure). The drawings or plans should include a site plan—a drawing of the entire property. The site plan should show how the new project relates to the house and other structures as well as to the property, and it should include elevations or side views. You might also need to provide detailed framing plans. The plans will probably need to be prepared by an architect and might have to reflect a seal of approval from an engineer for supporting members (e.g., when you are building over the side of a hill, depending on how high the structure will be).

If detailed plans are required, be sure to include their costs in your bid. Before actually hiring architectural or engineering services, have a signed contract for the project first. Keep in mind that if customers sign a contract on their own property, they have the right to cancel that contract within three working days. If the contract is signed at your place of business, you are fairly safe. In any case, I would wait a good four to five days before doing anything.

What you can do on your own, however, is to make simple plan view drawings (looking down from above). This helps when selling to a potential customer and gives you a worksheet to use when compiling your bid. Additionally, it provides the information you need to pass on to an architect or engineer if their services should be required.

Itemizing

I firmly believe (because of my track record) that itemized bids are easier to sell to a customer than an estimate. An itemized bid helps a customer decide because it shows in black and white where their dollars and cents will be spent. The bid also serves you in two ways:

- If the customer decides that the bid is too high, you will be able to curb the bid by either redesigning the project or downscaling the quality of the product. This means, of course, that compromises are necessary on both sides. Maybe the customer can downsize the project. Maybe you can lower your profit margin and/or labor (but don't lower your price just to get the job). This can be done easily with itemized bid sheets.
- If you get the job, the itemized bid sheets can serve as a materials list and a worksheet.

I know that a lot of professionals would rather not show how they arrived at the bottom line price—but the customer is hiring you and has a right to see where the money is going. If you are worried about the customer taking your bid sheet and shopping around, forget it. This happens and you can't stop it. However, if drawings are involved, request a retainer before releasing them. If you have followed everything so far up to this point, you don't need to worry. Just sell that job. I know from experience that giving customers itemized bids can tip the scale in your favor. Customers today want to know where and how their dollars will be spent. They want details. And, quite frankly, that's the type of customer you want to work for.

Because an estimate is only an educated guess, I don't use them. If you feel a customer is shopping around, either over the phone or in person, give a ballpark verbal estimate. You will know immediately whether or not you can do business.

Do you have good itemized bid sheets? Figure 4-8 shows the itemized bid sheets I developed and used in the field. Itemized bid sheets clearly spell out the many materials and products you will use on your projects. These sheets help you to organize your thoughts as you itemize the requirements of the job and calculate expenses. If you would like to obtain these forms for your own use as well as other business forms, an order form for the Helping Hands™ Packet can be found in appendix B.

If you are like me, you don't want to spring expensive surprises on a customer just because you estimated a job—try using the itemized method!

Markup

The purpose of using an itemized bid is that it helps you determine the direct job costs related to a particular project. Many contractors go out of business because they don't know the five basic direct job (hard) costs:

- Labor
- Materials
- Subcontractors
- Debris
- Plans and permits

Once you have determined your direct job costs, you need to apply an adequate markup to the bid or proposal. There is no easy answer to how high your markup should be; but in reality, the markup you determine helps set your goal for a comfortable net profit. Unfortunately, the competition can dictate your markup. However, if you are a creative salesperson, you will sell that contract over a low-ball bidder.

Many contractors work with a 70 percent markup. Multiplying your overall hard costs by 1.70 yields the overall contract price you'll present to the customer. You might want to include taxes in the hard costs, but consult your accountant regarding the legality involved in this practice before applying your markup to taxes. There are also some ethical considerations. Not all jobs need or require a huge markup, but some do. It all goes back to determining what the market will bear and your track record for closing sales.

A 70 percent markup could put you right out of the ballpark, so you need to find the correct markup for the market in your area. First, you need to distinguish between markup and gross profit margin. We have already established that a markup is the percentage applied to the overall hard costs to arrive at a total dollar figure (contract price).

CONTRACTOR'S ITEMIZED BID SHEET

CUSTOMER'S NAME _____   BILLING ADDRESS _____

JOB ADDRESS _____   JOB DESCRIPTION _____

WORK PHONE _____   RESIDENT PHONE _____

ARCHITECT _____ ADDRESS _____ PHONE _____

ESTIMATOR _____ APPOINTMENT DATE _____ BID DATE _____

This is an itemized bid, not an estimate sheet. An estimate is an approximate bid, which reflects only educated guesses. The result can be the consumer paying hundreds over that price. An itemized bid reflects all material costs, labor, taxes and permit fees. This gives you, the consumer, a new confidence in the prices quoted you for construction, and/or remodeling.

MATERIAL LIST

Lumber

1 x 2	@	$
1 x 4	@	$
1 x 6	@	$
1 x 8	@	$
1 x 10	@	$
1 x 12	@	$
2 x 2	@	$
2 x 4	@	$
2 x 4	@	$
2 x 4	@	$
2 x 6	@	$
2 x 6	@	$
2 x 6	@	$
2 x 8	@	$
2 x 10	@	$
2 x 12	@	$
4 x 4	@	$
4 x 6	@	$
4 x 8	@	$
LAMINATE BEAMS	@	$
LAMINATE BEAMS	@	$
MISC.	@	$
MISC.	@	$
MISC.	@	$
MISC.	@	$

Treated

2 x 4	@	$
2 x 6	@	$
2 x 8	@	$
4 x 4	@	$
6 x 6	@	$

Cedar

1 x 2	@	$
1 x 3	@	$
1 x 4	@	$
1 x 6	@	$
1 x 8	@	$
1 x 10	@	$
1 x 12	@	$
2 x 2	@	$
2 x 4	@	$
2 x 6	@	$
2 x 8	@	$
2 x 10	@	$
2 x 12	@	$
MISC.	@	$
MISC.	@	$

Painting

PAINT INTERIOR	@	$
PRIMER INTERIOR	@	$
PAINT EXTERIOR	@	$
PRIMER EXTERIOR	@	$
STAIN	@	$
SEALER	@	$
FINISH COAT	@	$

MISC.	@	$
MISC.	@	$

Drywall

MUD JOINT/TOPPING	@	$
½" SHEET ROCK	@	$
½" WP SHEET ROCK	@	$
⅝" TYPE X SHEET ROCK	@	$
CORNER BEADS	@	$
MISC.	@	$
MISC.	@	$

Plywood/Siding

⅜" SOFFIT MATERIAL	@	$
½" CDX	@	$
½" WAFERBOARD	@	$
⅝" WAFERBOARD	@	$
⅝" T-1-11	@	$
¾" CDX	@	$
¾" P BOARD UNDERLAYMENT	@	$
¾" AC PLYWOOD EXTERIOR	@	$
¾" TG PLYWD UNDERLAYMENT	@	$
PANELING	@	$
TREAD MATERIAL	@	$
LAP SIDING	@	$
MASONITE SIDING	@	$
ALUMINUM SIDING	@	$
STEEL SIDING	@	$
VINYL SIDING	@	$
SHAKES (GROOVED)	PER SQ	$
MISC.	@	$
MISC.	@	$
MISC.	@	$

Insulation

1½"	@	$
3½" R-11	@	$
6" R-19	@	$
R-30	@	$
TUFF-R CELOTEX ¾"	@	$
TUFF-R CELOTEX 1"	@	$
SILL	@	$
MISC.	@	$
MISC.	@	$

Hardware

NAIL, SCREW, STUDSHOTS		$
SHIMS, STAPLES, PLASTIC		$
HINGES/BALL BEARING	@	$
DOOR CLOSURES	@	$
HANDLES	@	$
HANDLES	@	$
HANDLES	@	$
DEAD BOLT	@	$
THRESHOLD	@	$
PIPE/DUCTWORK	@	$
JOIST HANGERS	@	$
JOIST HANGERS	@	$
JOIST HANGERS	@	$
BOLTS	@	$

Unless otherwise specified, as contractor, I will only use new products. All materials will be of top commercial quality, as will all my workmanship.

Creative Remodeling Services, Inc. © 1986 Leon A. Frechette

4-8A *Page 1, Contractor's Itemized Bid Sheet.* C.R.S., Inc.

CONTRACTOR'S ITEMIZED BID SHEET — PAGE 2

Bid guarantee — Remember... this is an itemized bid, and you can have confidence in the prices we quote you...

WASHERS _____ @ ____ $ ____
MISC. _____ @ ____ $ ____
MISC. _____ @ ____ $ ____
MISC. _____ @ ____ $ ____
MISC. _____ @ ____ $ ____
MISC. _____ @ ____ $ ____

Adhesive
CONTACT CEMENT ____ @ ____ $ ____
ADHESIVE _____ @ ____ $ ____
ADHESIVE _____ @ ____ $ ____
ADHESIVE _____ @ ____ $ ____
CAULKING _____ @ ____ $ ____
CAULKING _____ @ ____ $ ____
MISC. _____ @ ____ $ ____
MISC. _____ @ ____ $ ____

Doors
WOOD _____ @ ____ $ ____
_____ @ ____ $ ____
_____ @ ____ $ ____
_____ @ ____ $ ____
METAL _____ @ ____ $ ____
_____ @ ____ $ ____
BI-FOLD _____ @ ____ $ ____
_____ @ ____ $ ____
_____ @ ____ $ ____
_____ @ ____ $ ____
POCKET DOOR ____ @ ____ $ ____
_____ @ ____ $ ____
_____ @ ____ $ ____
SCREEN DOOR ____ @ ____ $ ____
PRE HUNG _____ @ ____ $ ____
_____ @ ____ $ ____
_____ @ ____ $ ____
_____ @ ____ $ ____
_____ @ ____ $ ____
MISC. _____ @ ____ $ ____
MISC. _____ @ ____ $ ____

Frames
POCKET DOOR ____ @ ____ $ ____
WOOD _____ @ ____ $ ____
METAL _____ @ ____ $ ____
MISC. _____ @ ____ $ ____
MISC. _____ @ ____ $ ____

Closet Parts
SHELF _____ @ ____ $ ____
RODS _____ @ ____ $ ____
POLE END _____ @ ____ $ ____
SHELF SUPPORT ____ @ ____ $ ____
MISC. _____ @ ____ $ ____
MISC. _____ @ ____ $ ____

Molding
CASING _____ @ ____ $ ____
JAMBS _____ @ ____ $ ____
BASE _____ @ ____ $ ____
MISC. _____ @ ____ $ ____
MISC. _____ @ ____ $ ____

Bathroom Parts
MIRROR _____ @ ____ $ ____
MEDICINE CABINETS ____ @ ____ $ ____
SHOWER DOOR ____ @ ____ $ ____
SHOWER ENCLOSURE ____ @ ____ $ ____
TOWEL BAR _____ @ ____ $ ____
RINGS _____ @ ____ $ ____
TISSUE HANGER/CLAMP ____ @ ____ $ ____
MISC. _____ @ ____ $ ____
MISC. _____ @ ____ $ ____

Concrete
CONCRETE _____ PER YARD @ ____ $ ____
CONCRETE FOOTINGS ____ PER YD. @ ____ $ ____
CONCRETE WALLS ____ PER YD. @ ____ $ ____
" DRIVEWAYS ____ PER YD. @ ____ $ ____
" SIDEWALKS ____ PER YD. @ ____ $ ____

CONCRETE STEPS ____ PER YD @ ____ $ ____
" FLAT WORK ____ PER YD. @ ____ $ ____
" MISC. ____ PER YD. @ ____ $ ____
REINFORCING STEEL ____ @ ____ $ ____
FILL _____ PER YD. @ ____ $ ____
PETE GRAVEL ____ PER YD. @ ____ $ ____
EXPANSION STRIPS ____ @ ____ $ ____
QUICK POUR _____ @ ____ $ ____
CONCRETE BLOCKS ____ @ ____ $ ____
BRICKS _____ @ ____ $ ____
MORTAR _____ @ ____ $ ____
MISC. _____ @ ____ $ ____
MISC. _____ @ ____ $ ____

Roofing
ASPHALT CEMENT ____ @ ____ $ ____
FLASHING _____ @ ____ $ ____
FELT PAPER _____ @ ____ $ ____
KRAFT PAPER ____ @ ____ $ ____
3-TAB _____ PER SQ @ ____ $ ____
CEDAR SHAKES ____ PER SQ @ ____ $ ____
DRIP EDGE _____ @ ____ $ ____
TRUSSES _____ @ ____ $ ____
TRUSSES _____ @ ____ $ ____
TRUSSES _____ @ ____ $ ____
MISC. _____ @ ____ $ ____
MISC. _____ @ ____ $ ____
MISC. _____ @ ____ $ ____
MISC. _____ @ ____ $ ____
MISC. _____ @ ____ $ ____

Vents
SOFFIT _____ @ ____ $ ____
GABLE _____ @ ____ $ ____
ROOF _____ @ ____ $ ____
JOIST/WALL _____ @ ____ $ ____
MISC. _____ @ ____ $ ____
MISC. _____ @ ____ $ ____

Tile
CERAMIC _____ PER SQ FT ____ $ ____
BULL NOSE _____ @ ____ $ ____
OUTSIDE CORNERS ____ @ ____ $ ____
QUARRY _____ PER SQ FT ____ $ ____
GLUE _____ @ ____ $ ____
GROUT _____ @ ____ $ ____
MISC. _____ @ ____ $ ____
MISC. _____ @ ____ $ ____

Flooring
HARDWOOD _____ PER SQ FT ____ $ ____
FLOOR COVERING ____ PER YD ____ $ ____
FLOOR TREAD _____ @ ____ $ ____
SEAMING KIT _____ @ ____ $ ____
CARPET _____ PER YD @ ____ $ ____
PAD _____ PER YD @ ____ $ ____
METAL _____ @ ____ $ ____
RUBBER BASE ____ PER FT @ ____ $ ____
MISC. _____ @ ____ $ ____
MISC. _____ @ ____ $ ____

Counter Material
PB COUNTER TOP ____ @ ____ $ ____
BELVCO EDGE _____ @ ____ $ ____
PRE-MADE LAMINATE TOP ____ LIN FT ____ $ ____
OAK EDGE LAMINATE TOP ____ LIN FT ____ $ ____
LAMINATE _____ SQ FT ____ $ ____
MISC. _____ @ ____ $ ____
MISC. _____ @ ____ $ ____

Glazing
TAPE _____ @ ____ $ ____
MOLDINGS _____ @ ____ $ ____
GLASS _____ @ ____ $ ____
MISC. _____ @ ____ $ ____
MISC. _____ @ ____ $ ____

Windows/Accessories
WINDOW WELL METAL ____ @ ____ $ ____

Creative Remodeling Services, Inc. © 1986 Leon A. Frechette

4-8B *Page 2, Contractor's Itemized Bid Sheet.* C.R.S., Inc.

CONTRACTOR'S ITEMIZED BID SHEET   PAGE 3

WINDOW WELL CONCRETE _____ @ _____ $ _____ . _____
TRIM _____ @ _____ $ _____ . _____
WINDOWS _____ @ _____ $ _____ . _____
_____ @ _____ $ _____ . _____
_____ @ _____ $ _____ . _____
_____ @ _____ $ _____ . _____
_____ @ _____ $ _____ . _____
_____ @ _____ $ _____ . _____
_____ @ _____ $ _____ . _____
_____ @ _____ $ _____ . _____
_____ @ _____ $ _____ . _____
_____ @ _____ $ _____ . _____
_____ @ _____ $ _____ . _____
MISC. _____ @ _____ $ _____ . _____
MISC. _____ @ _____ $ _____ . _____

Fireplace
MANTELS _____ @ _____ $ _____ . _____
FIREPLACE _____ @ _____ $ _____ . _____
CHIMNEYS _____ @ _____ $ _____ . _____
PIPE _____ @ _____ $ _____ . _____
PIPE _____ @ _____ $ _____ . _____
MISC. _____ @ _____ $ _____ . _____
MISC. _____ @ _____ $ _____ . _____
MISC. _____ @ _____ $ _____ . _____
MISC. _____ @ _____ $ _____ . _____

Ironworks
HAND RAIL _____ @ _____ $ _____ . _____
RAILING _____ @ _____ $ _____ . _____
SADDLES _____ @ _____ $ _____ . _____
SUPPORTS _____ @ _____ $ _____ . _____
MISC. _____ @ _____ $ _____ . _____
MISC. _____ @ _____ $ _____ . _____

Rental
TOOLS _____ @ _____ $ _____ . _____
MISC. _____ @ _____ $ _____ . _____
MISC. _____ @ _____ $ _____ . _____
MISC. _____ @ _____ $ _____ . _____
MISC. _____ @ _____ $ _____ . _____
MISC. _____ @ _____ $ _____ . _____
MISC. _____ @ _____ $ _____ . _____
MISC. _____ @ _____ $ _____ . _____
MISC. _____ @ _____ $ _____ . _____

Appliances
MISC. _____ $ _____ . _____
MISC. _____ $ _____ . _____
MISC. _____ $ _____ . _____
MISC. _____ $ _____ . _____
MISC. _____ $ _____ . _____

Cabinets
TRIM _____ $ _____ . _____
CABINETS _____ $ _____ . _____
_____ $ _____ . _____
_____ $ _____ . _____
_____ $ _____ . _____
_____ $ _____ . _____
_____ $ _____ . _____
_____ $ _____ . _____
_____ $ _____ . _____
_____ $ _____ . _____
_____ $ _____ . _____
_____ $ _____ . _____
_____ $ _____ . _____
_____ $ _____ . _____
_____ $ _____ . _____
_____ $ _____ . _____
_____ $ _____ . _____
_____ $ _____ . _____
_____ $ _____ . _____
_____ $ _____ . _____
_____ $ _____ . _____
_____ $ _____ . _____
_____ $ _____ . _____
_____ $ _____ . _____
_____ $ _____ . _____
_____ $ _____ . _____
MISC. _____ $ _____ . _____
MISC. _____ $ _____ . _____

Extras or Misc. Items
_____ $ _____ . _____
_____ $ _____ . _____

SUB TOTALS
_____ $ _____ . _____
_____ $ _____ . _____
CARPET _____ $ _____ . _____
WINDOWS _____ $ _____ . _____
APPLIANCES _____ $ _____ . _____
REMAINING MATERIALS _____ $ _____ . _____

SUB-CONTRACTOR'S ITEMIZED BID SHEET

As contractor, I have the right to use my own sub-contractors for completion of jobs as needed. The following labor charges may or may not include materials. You may have confidence in the fact that I, as contractor, will not only stand behind said sub-contractors, but will also guarantee their work as my own.

Excavating
EXCAVATE _____ $ _____ . _____
GRADING & FILLING _____ $ _____ . _____
MISC. _____ $ _____ . _____

Concrete
CURBS _____ $ _____ . _____
DRIVEWAYS _____ $ _____ . _____
FLOORS/FLATWORK _____ $ _____ . _____
FORMS _____ $ _____ . _____
LIGHTWEIGHT _____ $ _____ . _____
STEPS _____ $ _____ . _____
WALKS _____ $ _____ . _____
PUMP _____ $ _____ . _____
MISC. _____ $ _____ . _____

Masonary
CHIMNEYS & FIREPLACE _____ $ _____ . _____
COMMON BRICK _____ $ _____ . _____
CONCRETE BLOCK _____ $ _____ . _____
FACE BRICK _____ $ _____ . _____
TILE _____ $ _____ . _____

MANTELS _____ $ _____ . _____
STONEWORK _____ $ _____ . _____
MISC. _____ $ _____ . _____

Sanitation
SEWER _____ $ _____ . _____
PLUMBING _____ $ _____ . _____
MISC. _____ $ _____ . _____

Electrical
WIRING _____ $ _____ . _____
MISC. _____ $ _____ . _____

Air Conditioning
DUCTS/MECHANICAL _____ $ _____ . _____
EQUIPMENT _____ $ _____ . _____
MISC. _____ $ _____ . _____

Heating
GAS/ELECTRIC _____ $ _____ . _____
MISC. _____ $ _____ . _____

Lath & Plastering
DRY WALL _____ $ _____ . _____
EXTERIOR _____ $ _____ . _____

Creative Remodeling Services, Inc. © 1986 Leon A. Frechette

4-8C *Page 3, Contractor's Itemized Bid Sheet.* C.R.S., Inc.

SUB-CONTRACTOR'S ITEMIZED BID SHEET   PAGE 4

INTERIOR	$	
MISC.	$	
MISC.	$	
Ceiling		
ACOUSTIC	$	
MISC.	$	
Glazing		
MIRRORS	$	
MISC. GLASS	$	
PLATE GLASS	$	
MISC.	$	
Mill Work		
CABINETS	$	
COUNTER TOPS	$	
DOORS	$	
MISC.	$	
Doors		
CUSTOM	$	
COMMERCIAL	$	
RESIDENTIAL	$	
GARAGE OPENERS	$	
MISC.	$	
Tile		
CERAMIC TILE	$	
QUARRY TILE	$	
MISC.	$	
Floors		
CARPET	$	
FLOOR COVERING	$	
HARDWOOD	$	
MISC.	$	
Painting & Decorating		
PAINTER/STAINER	$	
WALL PAPER	$	
MISC.	$	
Roof		
COMPOSITION	$	
STEEL	$	
HOT ROOF	$	
TILE	$	
TRUSSES	$	
MISC.	$	

Metal Work		
ORNAMENTAL IRON	$	
SHEET METAL	$	
STRUCTURAL STEEL	$	
MISC.	$	
MISC.	$	
Siding		
ALUMINUM	$	
STEEL	$	
VINYL	$	
INSULATION	$	
MISC.	$	
MISC.	$	
Miscellaneous		
AWNINGS	$	
CLEANING WINDOW, ETC.	$	
INSULATION/SOUNDPROOFING	$	
MOVERS	$	
REFRIGERATORS/FREEZERS	$	
REMOVING DEBRIS	$	
WINDOW SHADES	$	
MISC.	$	
Fire Prevention		
FIRE EXTINGUISHERS	$	
FIRE SPRINKLERS	$	
MISC.	$	
Landscaping		
FENCE	$	
LAWN	$	
SHRUBBERY	$	
SPRINKLER SYSTEM	$	
MISC.	$	
Extras		
	$	
	$	
	$	
SUB-TOTAL	$	
*CONTRACTORS ____ %	$	
SUB-CONTRACTORS TOTAL	$	

*The percentage we place on the sub-contractors is for contracting and guaranteeing their work.

This is the total breakdown on your itemized bid.

PROFIT MARGINS

			$	
			$	
CARPET	@	%	$	
WINDOWS	@	%	$	
APPLIANCES	@	%	$	
MATERIALS	@	%	$	
LABOR			$	
SUB-CONTRACTORS			$	
DEBRIS			$	
			$	
SUB-TOTAL			$	

BLDG. PERMIT	$	
PLAN CHECK	$	
ENGINEERING FEE	$	
ARCHITECT	$	
SURVEY	$	
	$	
	$	
2nd SUB-TOTAL	$	
TAX___ %	$	
COMPLETE BID	$	

This bid reflects the quoted prices on materials as of your bid date, and therefore have their own time limits per companies involved.

If this bid is not within your budget, please call and we will re-evaluate your needs, and work out a compromising bid.   Thank you.

GENERAL CONDITIONS ON THE REVERSE SIDE.   Creative Remodeling Services, Inc. © 1986 Leon A. Frechette

4-8D *Page 4, Contractor's Itemized Bid Sheet.* C.R.S., Inc.

That same dollar figure divided by the dollar amount of the markup will give you the gross profit margin. Out of the gross profit margin you will pay your overhead, and what is left over is your net profit, so it is important to keep your overhead down in order to yield a higher net profit. Overhead consists of expenses such as:

- Advertising
- Tools and equipment
- Rent
- Vehicles
- Administration
- Sales force

As I mentioned before, if you have a showroom, 5 percent of your gross sales need to be devoted to those costs. Keep in mind this is only part of the total overhead. I would recommend counting on at least 20 to 25+ percent of the gross volume to cover the total cost of your overhead. Be aware that as your company increases, so will your overhead costs—it's a continuous upward spiral.

Let's assume that it will take 22 percent to cover your overhead costs, and you are maintaining a 30 percent gross profit margin. Subtracting 22 from 30 leaves you with an 8 percent net profit.

For clarification, here are a couple of examples of different markups and gross profit margins using the same job costs:

1 $ 9,000 (Hard costs)
  +3,600 (40 percent markup)
$12,600 (Contract price)
$ 3,600 ÷ $12,600 = 29 percent (markup divided by contract price = gross profit margin).
Gross profit margin (29) less percent overhead cost (22) equals net profit percent (7).

2 $ 9,000 (Hard costs)
  +6,300 (70 percent markup)
$15,300 (Contract price)
$ 6,300 ÷ $15,300 = 41 percent (markup divided by contract price = gross profit margin).
Gross profit margin (41) less percent overhead cost (22) equals percent of net profit (19).

Keep in mind that if you underestimate the job, make a mistake, have an accident, require more labor and materials than are budgeted, run into the unexpected—all of these can eat into your profits! Be sure to spell out in black and white on your contract exactly what you are going to do. Leave no room for misunderstanding or misinterpretation. Using itemized bid sheets helps to eliminate errors during the bidding process, and don't be afraid to add into the bid a contingency figure (15 percent or higher) to cover the unexpected, changes, or overruns. Cover all your bases!

Contracts

Perhaps you use generic business forms purchased at your local stationery store and have never taken the time to come up with a legally binding contract. The most important thing you can do for yourself and your customer is to have an excellent working contract. A contract that spells out the terms and conditions of the project should be drafted in such a way as to protect the rights of the customer as well as yourself. Unfortunately, because of the "sue happy" society we live in, the days of the handshake are long gone and you have to rely on legal documents to do business today. By making the contract benefit both you and your customers, you help put them at ease when they do have to sign the contract.

When designing your contract, be sure to consult with an attorney who specializes in contract law. There are a few precautions you need to take when presenting the contact to your customer:

- *Date, name, and address* Make sure that the date is correct, and check the spelling of the names involved in the contract. If the customer is married, list both names. If the address where the project is to be done differs from the billing address, it too should be noted on the contract.
- *Contents of the project* The project should be explained completely in writing. This includes materials, permit, and labor costs involved. If you are not able to get the entire body of the project detailed on the contract then continue on as many sheets of paper as it takes. Be sure that they are referenced back to the contract to be united as one document. Also, let your customer have the contract for a couple of days so they can read it in their own comfort zone. If they do not understand something, rewrite it so they do understand it.
- *Dates of work* By all means allow yourself enough time to do the project; however, you need to include starting and completion dates for the project into the contract.
- *Payment schedule* The contract must show the amount agreed upon by you and the customer. I would recommend that a payment schedule be written into the contract. Agree on a deposit up front and then divide the remaining balance into three equal payments: the first payment due at the two-thirds mark, and the final payment held by the customer for at least three days after you complete the project, final inspections (if

required) have been made, and the approvals have been received. This suggested payment schedule is merely a rule of thumb and might not apply in your state. The payment schedule is based on the size of the project as well. Payment schedules might differ in the commercial market from the residential. Be sure that the payment schedule you and the customer agree upon complies with local and state laws.

- *General Conditions* This is the fine print found on the back side of the contract. These conditions cover the legal rights, warranties, rules, and regulations concerning the job. Again, be sure they protect both parties. Figure 4-9 shows the general conditions that are found on the backside of the Itemized Bid Sheets, Contract/Agreement, and the Extra Work and/or Change Order forms contained in the Helping Hands Packet. This should give you an idea of the 17 articles that make up the general conditions I offer. One article that is missing is attorney fees. Even though it has not been included, you can add it to the front of the contract by saying: "In any legal action on this contract, the prevailing party shall be entitled to reasonable attorney fees and costs." Depending on your state, you could win a case but not be entitled to attorney fees without the proper wording in the contract. Let's hope that day never comes!
- *Signature and date* After the customer understands the contract, the general conditions, and the body of the contract, and your contractor's license number has been added (if required in your state), then have the two identical contracts signed (don't forget to sign both yourself). Retain one copy for your records.

One last thought Make sure you follow through and put extra work or changes into a legal document and have the document signed by the customer. Treat change orders the same as a contract—don't wait until the end of the job to straighten this all out. You might lose—it's your word against the customer. Protect yourself and the customer and put everything legally into writing.

These first four chapters should help you decide whether or not you are making the right choice. The remainder of *Accessible Housing* focuses on the mechanical tools necessary to do the actual work. Again, no matter what is being shown or recommended, be sure to consult your local building department. A lot of products are shown in the following chapters; contact those manufacturers for information on their products. The more you stay abreast of these products, the easier it will be for you to solve a problem for your customer in a reasonable time. Do your homework—it will save you in the long run!

GENERAL CONDITIONS

Article 1. The Contract includes The Agreement and its General Conditions, together with the Drawings and/or Specifications. Two or more copies of each, as required, shall be signed by the parties and one signed copy of each retained by each party.

The intent of these documents is to provide for all labor, materials, appliances and services of every kind necessary for the proper execution of the project, and the terms and conditions of payment therefor.

The documents are to be considered as one, and whatever is called for by any one of the documents shall be as binding as if called for by all.

Article 2. Except as otherwise noted, Contractor shall provide and pay for all materials, labor, tools, and other items necessary to complete the project.

Unless otherwise specified, all materials shall be new and of top commercial quality. All workmanship shall be of commercial quality.

All workmen and subcontractors shall be skilled in their trades.

Article 3. Permits and licenses necessary for the completion of the project shall be secured and their costs advanced by the Contractor, appearing in the Specifications as additional costs to be paid by Owner as part of the total contract sum. Contractor shall comply with all laws and regulations bearing on the conduct of work, and shall notify Owner if the Drawings and/or Specifications are a variance therewith.

Article 4. Contractor shall adequately protect the work, adjacent property of Owner, and the public, but shall be responsible only for damage or injury due to his act or neglect.

Article 5. Contractor shall permit and facilitate observation of the work by public authorities at all times and by the Owner and/or his agents **at such times as will not interfere unduly with completion of the work, nor subject Contractor to undue risks of injury to Owner.**

Article 6. Owner may order changes in the work, **the Contract Sum being adjusted accordingly.** All such orders and adjustments shall be in writing. Claims by Contractor for extra cost not shown in the Estimate/Bid must be made in writing to Owner before execution of the involved work.

Article 7. Contractor shall re-execute any work that fails to conform to the requirements of the contract and that appears during the course of the work, and shall remedy material defects due to faulty materials or workmanship which appear within a period of **ONE YEAR** from the date of completion of the contract. The provisions of this article apply to work done by direct employees of Contractor and to work done by subcontractors. In reference to concrete work, warranty shall cover faulty materials, or workmanship. Cracks in concrete should be reviewed as most are caused by weather conditons. Damages due to any imporper use or failure to properly maintain by Owner after completion of the work by Contractor are expressly exempted from this limited warranty of Contractor. **Correction and repair of such defects will be subject to additional charges by Contractor.**

Article 8. Should the Contractor neglect to execute the work properly or fail to perform any provisons of the contract. Owner after 3 days notice to Contractor, and Contractor's security, if any, may terminate this Agreement.

Article 9. Should the work be stopped by any public authority for a period of thirty days or more, through no fault of Contractor, or should the work be stopped through act or neglect of Owner for a period of 3 days, or should Owner fail to pay Contractor any payment within 3 days after it is due, then Contractor may, upon 3 days written notice to Owner, stop work or terminate the contract and recover from Owner payment for all work executed and any loss sustained plus reasonable profit and damages.

Article 10. Payments shall be made as provided in the Agreement. The making and acceptance by Contractor of the final payment shall constitute a waiver of all claims by Owner against Contractor, other than those arising from unsettled liens or from faulty work appearing within **ONE YEAR,** as contained in Article 7 for the General Conditions, and of all claims by Contractor except for any previously made and remaining unsettled. **Payments otherwise due may be withheld on account of defective work not remedied or liens of Contractor's labor or suppliers filed against Owner's property.**

Article 11. The final payment shall not be due until the Contractor has delivered to Owner a release of any liens arising out of this contract, or receipts in full covering all labor and materials for which a lien could be filed, or a bond satisfactory to the Owner indemnifying Owner against any such lien.

Article 12. Owner has the right to have other contracts in connection with the work, if Contractor has not provided subcontracts for affected phases of the project, then Contractor shall properly cooperate with any such additional contractor.

Article 13. Time shall be of the essence in this Agreement.

Article 14. If Contractor is delayed at any time in the progress of the work by changes ordered in the work by the Owner, by labor disputes, fire, unusual delays in transportation, unavoidable casualty, or other causes beyond Contractor's control, then the time for Contractor performance shall be extended for such reasonable time as Owner's and Contractor' Attorney's may together agree.

Article 15. Areas of Owner's premises in which Contractor is to work must be cleared by Owner of Owner's personal property in order to avoid possible damage. Owner may hire Contractors to remove such personal property, but Owner expressly agrees that Contractor will not be liable for any damage to such personal property during any such clearing. Contractor becoming an agent of Owner during such phase of operation. Owner shall have the right to direct such clearing operation. Owner agrees that this right to direct Contractor's work shall end upon completion of clearing operation.

Article 16. Contractor agrees that only top grade materials are to be used in performing this Agreement. The parties agree that all salvage resulting from work under this contract is to be retained by Contractor unless other agreements are contained in the written specifications.

Article 17. Owner and Contractor agree that the Specifications prepared in conjunction with this contract reflects necessary labor and materials based on preliminary inspection of Owner's premises. **The Specifications do not cover additional labor or materials as may be required to perform this Agreement after previously concealed portions of the premises have been opened to inspection by the demolition operation. Such additional labor and material shall be included in a change order excuted by the parties prior to commencement of the extra work involved.**

We recognize the laws are constantly changing. It is important that you check the laws in your state.

Contractor's License # _____ Bond # _____ Expiration Date _____	This **CONTRACTOR'S ITEMIZED BID SHEETS** packet is protected under copyright and trademark laws. Reproduction of these sheets, in part and/or whole is prohibited and the reproduction of these sheets for business use is not permitted. The **CONTRACTOR'S HELPING HANDS™ PACKET** can be ordered through CRS, Inc. P.O. Box 4567, Spokane, WA 99202.

Creative Remodeling Services, Inc. © 1986 Leon A. Frechette

4-9 *General conditions.* C.R.S., Inc.

5

The beginning

For the most part, a home can be divided into three major categories. How you approach these areas depends solely on the needs of the individual—the customer. Because we don't all come from the same mold, our personalities are different as are our wants and needs. To better understand and find out exactly what your customer wants and needs, observe that person in action. This helps you to create the best environment for the customer. So what are the top three areas of concern?

- An accessible entry as well as clear passage throughout the home
- Bathrooms
- Kitchens

The order of importance, of course, is dictated by the customer. To understand the customer's requirements and abilities, listen very carefully and ask a lot of questions. Involvement in your customers' routines helps to provide the factual information you need to better serve them in one or more of these areas. Because people learn routines to accommodate their unique needs, they might be delighted to learn of other options that you can provide for their ease and safety. This chapter focuses on the entire home. Bathrooms and kitchens are covered in the following chapters.

Physical abilities

Physical limitations, no matter what they are, can affect all of us in one way or another. As mentioned throughout this book, this includes everyone—not just a person who uses a wheelchair or walker. An individual might have been involved in an accident or have physical traits (height, strength, vision, and hearing) that affect how that individual is able to live and function within and around the home environment. If you are aware of these individual physical abilities and comprehend them, it not only helps your approach in communicating but also in understanding a potential customer. Let's start with four of the five human senses: vision, hearing, smell, and touch.

Vision

Vision is an important human element that helps us to stay safe both in and out of our normal environments. Unfortunately, many with vision impairments have had to try to adapt to the living situations they were dealt, although much can be done to alleviate problems. Low vision or even blindness should not affect how people live in their own homes. We can help by providing adequate lighting throughout the home and by providing environments designed to promote easy maneuverability and avert accidents. As we get older, the following conditions often characterize our eyesight:

- We begin to lose the ability to focus.
- We have a harder time adjusting to different levels of lighting during the day as well as at night.
- Our performance might slow down because of our eyes' responses to glare from high-sheen countertops, painted walls, tiled floors, etc.

Medical procedures or devices might not always be the answer, but I remember what my grandmother said the day the patch came off her eye after cataract surgery. As we were leaving the doctor's office, she stopped to look around outdoors when she suddenly said, "Wow! Everything is so green. Look how green everything is. Everything is so beautiful!" I don't know how you would have responded, but I had chills up and down my spine.

When selecting and installing lighting, consider the following:

- Areas of lighting should be nonreflective (low-sheen laminates, paints, or tiles).
- Lighting should be nonglare as well.
- Consider using natural light before incandescent/tungsten, halogen, or fluorescent lighting. Natural light is an equal mixture of all colors of light, so if you add or subtract one color, you affect all the other colors to varying degrees. As we get older, our eyes yellow. This yellowing distorts how we perceive objects (i.e., the object's colors and/or its visual relationship to other objects). To understand this better, imagine your eyes as a camera lens. If you put a yellow filter over the lens, the lens will reproduce colors differently because it allows more yellow light through than any other color. Different sources of light emit different colors and

these colors either pass through or are blocked by the filter. If your eyes are yellowing, it is best to use lighting that has more yellow and red because those are the colors that yellowing eyes see. The following types of lights are recommended for use in some circumstances and are ranked in the order of importance:

~*Incandescent/tungsten*—a harsher light that creates an edge to objects, allowing them to be more easily seen. The yellow and red characteristics of this light give better definition to objects.

~*Halogen*—similar to tungsten, except the color characteristics are more constant over a tungsten bulb. It is also a brighter light and can add dimension when other lights are being used. It is a good light to highlight ceilings and walls, for example. In this type of situation, conceal the light source so you do not have to diffuse the light in order to reduce glare.

~*Fluorescent*—a softer light that tends to blend objects into the background, making them harder to see. It gives off blue and green colors, which are harder on the eye. The yellowing eye might not see the blue portion of the light and might see only parts of the green—but picks up the yellow light that constitutes part of the green (yellow + cyan = green). Full-spectrum fluorescent lights are available that allow the eyes to see items in more of a natural state, but the light is still a soft light.

- In hallways, elevators, and so on, lights should be recessed, and wall-mounted lights should be indirect.
- Lighting should be ample for visual communications.
- Install dimmer switches so lighting is adjustable.
- Uniform lighting should be maintained in a room no matter how a person is positioned—sitting or standing.

Some of the areas that need attention, for example, are edges and outside corners of countertops. If you fabricate the edge in a different color, then it is easier to distinguish where the countertop ends and where it starts. Figure 5-1 shows Wilsonart Gibraltar, a stone-like solid surfacing material. With over 30 colors and patterns available, you shouldn't have any trouble designing a countertop that will work for your customer. The low sheen of the product makes it easier on the eyes as well.

As you consider lighting options and window selection and/or placement for your customers, don't overlook the importance of nat-

5-1 *To prevent injuries, round corners and use contrasting/designed counter edges to alert people with limited vision.* Wilsonart International Inc.

ural light or forget that windows have benefits that go beyond bringing light into a home. The following information on daylighting and windows was provided by the American Lung Association of Michigan.

Daylighting is the technique of using natural light from both the sun and the sky and incorporating it into the home via windows, doors, and skylights. When used properly, daylighting has many benefits. It can provide the occupants of the home with greater energy efficiency and lower energy bills. Daylighting has also been shown to have positive effects on both the mental and physical well-being of people who are exposed to and receive an adequate dose of natural light each day.

To use daylighting wisely, it is important to realize that different solar directions provide different types of daylighting. Seasons of the year affect daylighting as well. In the summer, the sun's rays are more intense than in the winter when the sun is lower on the horizon and creates less warmth. Light from the north has cool, bluish hues resulting from mostly indirect light reflected from the sky. The light from the north never shines directly into north-facing windows but provides an even, consistent light in the room.

Light from the south provides more light and heat than from any other direction. Because this light is the brightest and most direct, it can cause glare and profuse heat in a room. Precautions should be taken to ensure that the light from the south is used properly to avoid fading and excessive glare. Such precautions include putting shades on the southern exposed windows and building a roof overhang that can block the sun's most intense rays.

Light that enters the house from its east-facing side is generated by the sun's early morning rays. It lacks the heat of the midday to late afternoon western sun. For those who like the early morning sun, it is best to locate the kitchen, living rooms, or bedrooms on the east side of the house.

West light provides direct light to those rooms located on the west side of the house. It can be quite intense in both brightness and heat. When using the light from the west, it is recommended that shades or curtains be installed to help control the amount of light entering the house in order to avoid excessive solar heat in the summer. Landscaping can also provide additional protection from the sun's warm western light. Planting trees in a south/southwestern location can provide a buffer from the sun while helping to filter the hot summer sunlight.

If you are constructing new and have the opportunity to orient the home in relation to the sun, consider siting the home so the backside faces south/southeast for maximum solar gain and daylighting. This side should have several windows, thus allowing for the rooms to be warmed naturally by the sun and lit by natural light. The front side, facing north, would have fewer and smaller windows to minimize air leakage problems from northwestern winds and to provide greater energy efficiency.

Windows enhance the beauty of a home while providing light, air, and a view of the outdoors. When selected and placed properly, windows can help with a home's energy efficiency. With the new and improved window technology, homeowners are now able to select from a variety of window glass options designed for specific purposes. The most common consumer needs for windows are energy efficiency (including insulation from cold temperatures and winds); protection from solar heat; control of outside noises; and protection from ultraviolet rays that can cause fading in home furnishings.

Window placement and the different sizes and directions windows face play a role in the admittance of light into a room. Horizontal windows placed high on the wall reflect light off the ceiling and cast it into the room. Because the light is high, the room might appear darker near the floor. Wide windows in the middle of a wall provide even more light in the room, while light from tall, long windows casts an equal amount of light on the wall across from the window but do not illuminate the whole room. Bay windows light the area of the bay but not the whole room. Large windows that extend from floor to ceiling provide the most uniform light but can create glare and profuse heat if not covered by blinds or shades during the times when the room receives the sun's most intense rays. Another option when using large windows is to choose windows that have a solar control incorporated in the window. Also, to maximize the benefit of cool summer breezes, windows should be placed in a way that provides cross ventilation and can serve as a means of natural air exchange.

Skylights are an attractive option to help bring light and ventilation into a home. Because people with disabilities are often unable to enjoy being outdoors as much as others, having a home filled with natural light and fresh air breezes is important to help create a friendly, comfortable, and cheerful home. Roof windows and skylights can help to provide an enjoyable outdoor connection. Because skylights provide natural light, they can be especially helpful to individuals with visual impairments. Velux-America Inc. offers units that can be opened and closed (and sunscreening accessories operated) at the touch of a button on a remote unit. Systems can be programmed to operate one unit, all the units within a room, or even "whole-house" control from one keypad. A rain sensor is even included to ensure that units close in case of an unexpected storm.

Because you are in the construction business, you know that every home has a few areas that appear to be continuously dark and gloomy, no matter what you do to enhance them. For prospective homeowners with limited vision, these dark areas are potentially hazardous, uncomfortable, and depressing. One way to give these areas the uplifting feeling of being outdoors is to illuminate them with natural lighting. A company that can help is SOLATUBE North America Ltd. With their 10" (25 cm) tubular skylight system and its unique roof-mounted reflector and mirrored tubing, you can capture daylight (possibly even moonlight) and transfer it into the home. You don't have to worry about making structural changes to install this unit since the tubing fits nicely between rafters.

SOLATUBE's highly reflective anodized aluminum tubing pulls natural light down from the reflector into dark spots by way of a ceiling-mounted diffuser that disperses the light (Fig. 5-2). A single unit can illuminate an area of 100 sq. ft. (9.3 m²) which makes it ideal for bathrooms, hallways, walk-in-closets, garages, and for those long narrow kitchens, as shown in Fig. 5-3. Wherever there is a need for improved lighting, consider a product such as this to bring indoors the feeling of outdoors. It's a natural cost- and energy-efficient source of lighting.

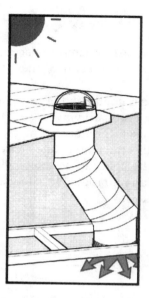

5-2
The unit's high performance is enhanced by facing the reflector south. SOLATUBE North America Limited

5-3
The diffuser dress rings (available in silver, gold, or white finish) coordinate with today's decor. SOLATUBE North America Limited

How many times have you gone to the movies or taken a trip by plane and noticed the lights running down the aisles? This same type of installation can be used in a home setting for steps, hallways, and ramps. Tempo Industries, Inc., with their Solution System has products to accomplish just that. Their products feature:

- Individually removable light lens
- Individual replacement lamps
- Convenient socket extension for ease of lamp replacement
- Parallel wiring, so one bulb does not affect the others
- Available in 12 or 24 volts

The series 1900—Carpet/Step Nose is comprised of two parts (see Fig. 5-4): a durable flexible vinyl cover and hard vinyl base. The base has a flange on the tread side that is used for attachment, by means of screws, to the tread. A system like this puts the light exactly where it is needed: at the nose of the step. The lights are visible walking up as well as down the stairs. It provides an unmistakable safety element in addition to offering an attractive accent.

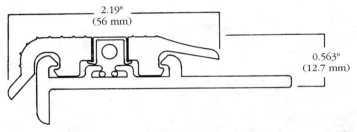

5-4 *Shipped fully assembled in straight lengths up to 12' long. Flanges are designed to accept carpet.* Tempo Industries, Inc.

Hearing

For me, hearing is an important element of life. After working around construction tools for many years, I have had to accept the fact that I do not hear as well as I used to. Even with a bell wired into the phone system, if another electronic device is on and the frequency is about the same or there is background noise, I will not hear the phone. My wife has a similar hearing problem (especially when she removes her glasses)—I find myself talking with myself a couple of times before she hears me—of course, she calls it "selective hearing." All kidding aside, over 24 million Americans have hearing disabilities. Unfortunately, there are many who are not aware they even have a hearing problem and if they do, they will not admit to it. Others might hide their hearing losses by not wearing their hearing aids.

Hearing is a round-the-clock monitoring system—even when we are asleep, our sense of hearing works overtime just waiting for the alarm to go off so we can start another day. Some people, depending on the level of their hearing impairment, might have to rely on other means or devices to wake them up (especially in an emergency situation or one relating to security), to hear the phone, or just to know who is outside their door.

One such device is the ALERTMASTER AM-6000 Wireless Notification System by Ameriphone, Inc. This product and its accessories can easily cover all the activities of a home such as:

- A telephone ringing
- A doorbell ringing
- A sound that requires monitoring, such as a crying baby
- The activation of other in-home audio alarm devices
- A motion sensor for entryway monitoring
- A visual signaler (i.e., a lamp flashing with distinct patterns for different alerts)
- An alarm clock/timer that can activate a bed shaker
- A personal signaler (a lightweight receiver) clipped to a belt that can deliver different vibrating motions up to 80 feet away by any activity in the home

The system is totally wireless. All you need to do is plug in the monitoring unit, and in the event of a power outage, the battery backup will kick in (batteries not included). Protection and security couldn't be made any easier (Fig. 5-5).

Changes are definitely in order and as professionals, we can help to make them possible—to help potential customers gain both independence and physical comfort to carry out daily activities within

5-5 *The bed shaker awakens an individual with a powerful shaking motion.* AMERIPHONE, Inc.

their own environment. The following are some of the changes we can make:

- Install acoustical sound-absorbing materials (i.e., carpet, acoustical wall panels, and acoustical ceilings. Products such as these can often correct a poor acoustical environment.

- Install sound-deadening materials in walls (especially those shared by neighbors) that allow the hearing impaired the freedom to hear higher sound volumes without disturbing anyone. This works great in apartment complexes or multifamily housing.

- Install exterior doors with side lights on the hinge side of door or far enough away from the latch to prevent burglaries.

- Equip existing exterior solid doors with 180° peepholes. For wheelchair users, the peephole should be located in an appropriate position.

- Install a video entry security intercom system (Fig. 5-6). This communication system by AIPHONE Corporation has a PanTilt control button remote that controls the door camera to go up and down and side to side. With its infrared CCD door camera, the room station can see the entry area even in total darkness. Other features include an electronic door chime with volume control, a picture brightness control, backlight control to adjust for bright sunlight, and a control button for an optional electric door release.

- Use three-way light switches to signal a person's entry into a room. For private rooms (such as bedroom or bathrooms) add an extra light switch on the outside wall that individuals can "knock" by flicking the switch. Consider using a different color for this switch—perhaps red.

- Install one single duplex electrical receptacle next to all telephone jacks. Also install a receptacle in areas where special equipment might be installed in the future, for instance, install a receptacle up high and close to the trim of each window to simplify the later installation of an automatic drapery opener system. One system that might surprise you is by Makita (Fig. 5-7). This completely programmable system, which can be preset to open and close draperies up to four times a day, can be retrofitted into an existing home automation system or used as a stand-alone feature in any home. It is also operable with a wall switch or with the standard remote control unit from as far away as 33' (10 m) (Fig. 5-8). One advantage of an automated home system is that it appears as if the house is occupied at all times. Not

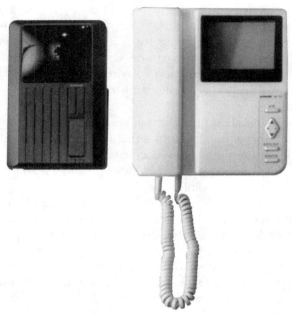

5-6 *A monitor button allows a person to observe the outside undetected.* Aiphone Corporation

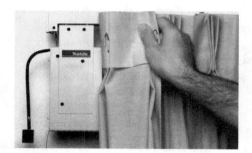

5-7
In the event of a power outage, draperies can be opened or closed manually. Makita U.S.A., Inc.

5-8
Automatic drapery opener with remote control. Makita U.S.A., Inc.

only does this add to the lived-in effect by having the drapes automatically open and close, but the system also allows sunlight to enter the house for plant sunning. It can also help with energy control and can be set to close during the heat of the day for additional energy savings and to protect furniture, carpeting, and other home furnishings from the harsh effects of sunlight.

- Consider head and hand-reach clearance when installing ceiling fans. A minimum of 8 feet from the floor to the bottom of the fan should safeguard from accidents.
- Install motion sensors for exterior lights to signal visitors. Lights should be visible from inside the home.
- Isolate sounds from the heating, ventilation, and air-conditioning (HVAC) systems. Insulate (or install insulated ductwork) for at least 10' (305 cm) of the return air duct to reduce stray sounds.
- Provide visual access to the outdoors with windows and skylights. This helps to bring the experience of nature inside.
- Eliminate concrete walkways and slabs. Areas such as these deaden vibrations.
- Consider installing low-partition walls or no walls at all between rooms. When planning an open space design, be sure to work with your customer closely—such a design helps the hearing impaired to read lips from a distance.
- Use balusters instead of walls in stairways and lofts—again, this creates an open area design.

Tips you can apply to assist the hearing impaired in bathrooms and kitchens will be discussed in later sections.

Smell

What would it be like not to be able to smell fragrant flowers—or not to be able to smell smoke or toxic fumes from a fire? As with vision and hearing, our abilities to detect and identify odors decline dramatically as we get older, so special precautions must be taken to prevent our customers from ending up in unnecessary tragedy:

- Avoid, if it is at all possible, locating living quarters above a garage. Carbon monoxide from a running car can be fatal. Carbon monoxide is an invisible and odorless gas, which results from incomplete combustion of fossil fuels that occurs in gas heaters, stoves, fireplaces, and automotive engines. At low levels, this gas mimics flu-like symptoms and causes nausea, headaches, shortness of breath, dizziness, anxiety and irritability, premature birth, miscarriage, low birth weight, and learning and memory defects in the developing fetus.

At higher levels, carbon monoxide can cause heart or brain damage, and eventually will suffocate its victims, putting them to sleep permanently. It can take as little as three minutes, depending on the level of concentration. Over 2,500 people in the United States die each year of carbon monoxide poisoning, and over 10,000 will be hospitalized (National Center for Health Statistics). Air-Zone II (Enzone Incorporated), one of the first electronic carbon monoxide detectors, can be mounted near ceiling level where carbon monoxide gas migrates. The unit plugs into an electrical receptacle but can be backed up by batteries if there is an electrical failure (Fig. 5-9).

5-9
Detector should be installed at eye level or above, but not closer than 6" to the ceiling. Enzone, the largest manufacturer of home safety test and monitoring products

For added safety, the relay output feature can be interfaced with a consumer's home alarm system. Enzone also offers two accessories, the "strobe light" attachment and the "garage door opener" attachment to enhance the unit. The strobe light attachment emits a strobe light impulse to alert the hearing impaired about carbon monoxide gas. For those with attached garages, the remote garage door opener will automatically open the garage door if potentially dangerous levels of carbon monoxide are released when a car is started.
• Install smoke detectors that can detect smoke, gas, and fire and which will indeed alarm any individual who is unable to identify these odors.

- In conjunction with any alarm system, provide an immediate escape route for each bedroom. Consider using windows with openings larger than required of egress windows in your area, and install them below the required sill height—preferably below waist height, but check with your customer. There should be a wide sill that must be able to support a person's weight. A sill 17" to 19" (43 to 48 cm) wide makes it easier for a wheelchair user to pull up onto it, balance, and then pull legs through the window opening. A wide surface for proper balance is essential. A window installed at 33" (84 cm) from finish floor to top of sill permits viewing for a seated person and for children. Avoid narrow vertical windows and tint windows at the high point of the sun's exposure through the window. If windows such as Pella were installed, then the unit could be fitted with Slimshade—blinds that fit between the panes (Fig. 5-10). Another option would to use pleated shades, which can be pulled during the sun's most intense part of the day. Be sure to consult with your local building department before giving a customer a bid on this type of installation.

5-10
Blinds fitted between panes are free from dust and safe from damage. Pella Windows and Doors

Touch

This is one of those senses that professionals tend to forget during the design stages. It is not so much that it's forgotten—it's just not thought of, but it should be! Touch is one of those senses that if disturbed, interrupts the balance of life. Individuals with limited touch sensitivity are subject to falls, prone to accidents because they are unable to distinguish between hot and cold, and can easily bruise themselves when they bump a table corner. It is important to keep pathways clear, and furnishings should have soft-eased and round corners. In bathrooms and kitchens, special measures must be taken; these are discussed in later sections.

Personal requirements

To have a better understanding of customers' personal requirements is to know the basic fundamentals involved in their range of motion, any other physical limitations, and overall measurements for equipment such as wheelchairs, crutches, canes, and walkers. Pets also need consideration. The equipment mentioned previously can certainly help individuals who have obvious difficulty with walking. Some customers have limitations that might not be so apparent. For example, damage to muscles, joints, or nerves, which can affect the ability to fully extend, bend, or even lift arms, legs or hands, can result in limited reaching, bending, or gripping.

Range of motion

Range of motion is one of the most important elements to know when designing for any individual. Simply put, the range of motion refers to the degree to which a joint can move and the person can bend and reach. This includes:

- Forward reach
- Upward reach
- Downward reach
- Side-to-side reach

The range of motion determines just how we as individuals are able to use the space around us safely, efficiently, effectively, and comfortably—this reachable space is always the most used space. For people in wheelchairs, this usually translates to the space that we know as the backsplash space, the space between the top of the countertop and the bottom of the upper cabinets. In this space, use undercounter rollout storage, and fill in this area with appliances, open shelves, or cup hooks. These simple modifications allow for this space to be usable without reducing the appearance of the project. However, reaching is only a small part of it. If a person is unable to bend, kneel, or even squat, then the range of motion is affected. For any individual, young or old, the following conditions can interfere and restrict physical abilities to function comfortably:

- High-blood pressure
- Balance problems
- Stiff joints that can affect elbows, hips, knees, shoulders, back, neck
- Shortness
- Tallness
- Thinness
- Largeness or extra weight
- Pregnancy

Such physical traits can affect how someone is able to perform any of the following tasks:

- Prepare meals.
- Pick up a piece of paper off the floor.
- Get a dish from an overhead cabinet.
- Get a pan from a lower cabinet.
- Open cabinet doors.
- Load or empty a dishwasher.
- Set a table.
- Open an oven door.
- Sweep the kitchen floor. For those who are unable to bend over, Rubbermaid Incorporated has a product called the All Pro Dirt Catcher Broom. This product is unique because the dustpan is held in place with one foot while both hands are on the broom's nonslip handle, all without leaning over except to pick up the dustpan and store it back on the handle (Fig. 5-11).

To learn what your customers are capable of doing, form alliances with their physical and occupational therapists to learn their home assessments and building recommendations. This coalition not only gives your offerings credibility, but creates a competitive edge and provides a built-in marketing opportunity for the creation of new projects, thanks to referrals which PTs and OTs can provide. If a therapist is not involved, ask your customers to describe their limitations and their capabilities to help you design an area that best meets their specific needs. I think it is important when working with a customer not to put yourself in a situation where you act the role of a therapist. Ask questions only if you need to see the customer do simple tasks like reaching for a glass from an upper cabinet. I suggest that a therapist or some other qualified person be present.

As a professional, you are in a position to inform the customer about the wide range of appliances, fixtures, and easy-access cabinetry now available, as well as to create design features that allow for wheelchair access. Understanding the characteristics of your cus-

5-11
*This would make a
thoughtful thank-you gift
for your customers.* Rubbermaid
Incorporated

tomers and their range of motion will enable you to design environments to fit their needs.

Manual dexterity

It is not enough to just know the range of motion. You also need to know if customers have good mobility in their hands. You might say this goes "hand in hand." What I am referring to is if hands and fingers can move freely in order to turn, twist, grab, grasp, pinch, rotate household items.

For example, good manual dexterity can determine whether a person is able to perform the following tasks:

- Open a door either by pushing or pulling.
- Maneuver a door handle and open the door at the same time.
- Turn a house key in a door lock.
- Maneuver a thumb latch.
- Unhook a hook from the eye on a gate.
- Pull a dining room chair out from the table.
- Close the bag on a loaf of bread.
- Load a dishwasher.
- Take clothes out of a dryer or load up a washing machine.
- Fold or iron clothes.
- Open a cabinet door.
- Grasp onto a cabinet drawer knob or handle.
- Hold onto a broom.

- Unlock a window or open a skylight.
- Turn on or off a faucet.
- Open or close a sink drain.
- Rotate an appliance knob.
- Take ice cubes out of a tray.
- Plug in or unplug an electrical cord.
- Slide a volume control bar on a stereo system.
- Use an index finger to turn on a toggle light switch.
- Rotate a dimmer switch.
- Operate a remote control.
- Type on a computer.

While this list represents only a small fraction of normal daily activities, it does encompass what it takes for us to maintain and survive within and around our own home environments. For a person unable to accomplish any of these functions, carrying out daily activities comfortably becomes a challenge as well as a struggle. That is why it is important for you to understand all this. Additionally, just knowing what your customer is capable of doing can help you determine all changes necessary for the customer. Sometimes just lowering a light switch or getting an after-market device to allow a person to open a door can make all the difference in the world. A prime example of this is Leveron by Lindustries, Inc., which converts existing doorknobs into lever handles in less than two minutes. A product like this not only solves the problem immediately but can cost less than replacing the existing knob with a new handle (see Fig. 5-12). Installing products that don't require the full use of fingers will instill confidence in a person who is having difficulty using his or her hands. All

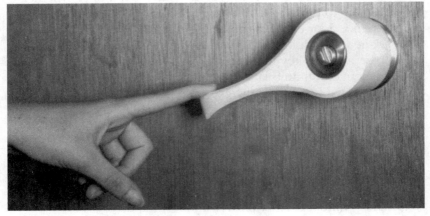

5-12 *Opening a door couldn't be easier.* Lindustries, Inc.

these individuals want is the comfort and assurance that it can be done all on their own.

Freedom

The freedom to move about is another key element to consider. My grandmother does not venture too far from the house—her only form of exercise is walking from the kitchen to the living room to the bathroom to the bedroom and occasionally a walk or two around the garden. What is important to her is be able to get outside once in a while and to be able to move around the house freely. A house can pose all kinds of barriers for individuals as they age and for those who use support devices, including any of the following:

- Another human being
- An animal
- A wheelchair
- A scooter
- A walker
- A cane
- Crutches
- Braces

A frequent obstacle is that there is not enough room for both the person and the special equipment required for mobility. This is especially true in older homes with the following characteristics:

- Doorways are too narrow.
- Hallways are not wide enough.
- The layout of the room doesn't allow efficient room to maneuver once furniture is placed.
- Bedrooms are too small to include both the bed and the equipment.
- Rooms are too small in general.
- All floor levels are not easily accessible.
- There is not enough room on the side and in front of an entry door to maneuver.

Some of these characteristics exist in new homes as well. Those who are building a new home can incorporate appropriate changes during the framing stage. But for those living in older homes who do not plan (or want) to move, your careful planning can help create a home in which residents can continue to carry out normal daily activities. While some of these areas can be corrected by simple modifications and/or products, others require major renovations. It is important in situations like this to go through the design steps carefully in order to keep project costs down. It is also possible, depending on the person, the structure, and the design of the home, that the work can be done in phases. This is certainly something worth checking out—as always, work with your customer.

Throughout the rest of this book, I suggest areas where improvements can be made and where special products could be used to rectify the situation. Concentrate on those areas that are vitally important, and by all means don't sell customers something they don't need. As described in chapter 1, customers might have had bad experiences with construction professionals. It is up to those who enter this business to help change customer attitudes—and the only way this will happen is if you are a savvy professional!

Specifications

As with anything else in the construction business, it is nice to have a starting point—real measurements from which to work. The purpose of this section is to help you establish some basic measurements and guidelines that you can use in designing. The measurements given are just basic information to alert you to the fact that you do indeed need to think about certain areas when it comes to equipment and individuals. It is your responsibility to check measurements carefully. An inch in either direction can make a world of difference to the person who has to use, work, and live with the finished product. Your customers' needs are important, so consider them at all times. Be sure to consult with them during all phases of the job. Even if you don't think it's important, check with the customer. Mistakes are costly—you have a reputation to protect and as a professional it is your sole responsibility to make sure your customer is content, secure, and happy in the environment you create.

Support devices

Accessibility standards came into effect mainly because individuals using assistive devices and adaptive equipment didn't have adequate access to public and commercial facilities. The fact was that individuals with disabilities were restricted from going place to place freely because accommodations for them were never designed into structures, curbs, ramps, entryways, sidewalks, hallways, and so on. The constant push for independence has led to a very slow victory; changes are being made. Now this accessibility concept is carrying over into the residential market. To understand the changes required for assistive devices and adaptive equipment, you must understand the equipment being used. I strongly recommend checking the yellow pages under the following headings:

- Home Health Care Equipment Supplies
- Hospital Equipment & Supplies
- Medical Equipment & Supplies

Take the time to visit a home health care center and check out the different types and dimensions of assistance equipment. It wouldn't hurt to add to your library specifications on such equipment. You never know when the information will come in handy. In this section, I outline a few basics to get you started. Think about all the different types of wheelchairs on the market today; each year manufacturers make them lighter and smaller. Stay abreast of these changes (Figs. 5-13 through 5-16).

Dimensions

The dimensions shown in some of the diagrams listed throughout the rest of this book are averages in some cases and minimums in others. If extra room is available, then exceed those minimums as much as possible. This allows users of special equipment the extra room needed to maneuver without injury. Figure 5-17 gives an overall view of the dimensions of an adult-sized wheelchair including the user. Knowing these dimensions helps you as you create a universal, barrier-free, and adaptable/adjustable design for the entire home.

Standard arm wheelchair

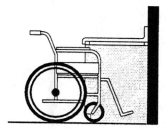

Desk arm wheelchair

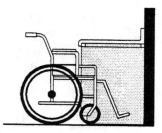

Sport model wheelchair

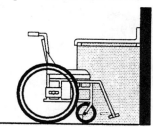

5-13 *Examples of wheelchair styles.* National Kitchen & Bath Association

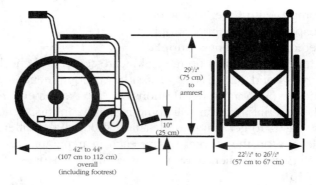

5-14 *Standard arm wheelchair.* Whirlpool Home Appliances

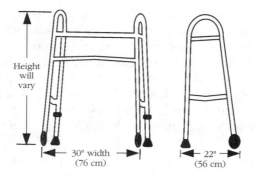

5-15 *Most walkers require a turning radius of 4 to 5 feet, depending on the build of the person.* Whirlpool Home Appliances

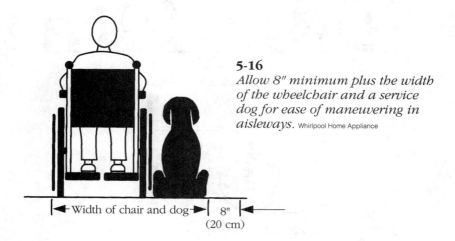

5-16
Allow 8" minimum plus the width of the wheelchair and a service dog for ease of maneuvering in aisleways. Whirlpool Home Appliance

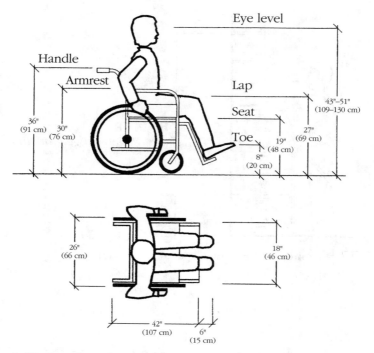

5-17 *Based on the average size of a wheelchair.* National Kitchen & Bath Association

Heights and reach ranges

The following information will help you to better understand the users' capabilities and the minimum space required:

- Persons who use crutches, a walker, or their arms or hands to maintain balance have a different reach range than wheelchair users (Fig. 5-18).

- To a cane user who is visually impaired, potentially hazardous objects are noticed only if they fall within the detection range of their cane (Fig. 5-19). The person walking toward the object can detect an overhang if its lowest surface is not higher than 27" (69 cm). When the person walks alongside protruding objects, overhangs cannot be detected. Since proper cane and service animal techniques keep individuals away from edges of paths or from walls, a slight overhang of no more than 4" (10 cm) is not hazardous when the leading edge is between 27" (69 cm) and 80" (203 cm) above the finish floor. If the item is below 27" (69 cm), then the item can protrude any amount.

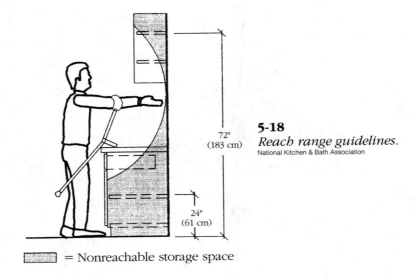

5-18
Reach range guidelines.
National Kitchen & Bath Association

▨ = Nonreachable storage space

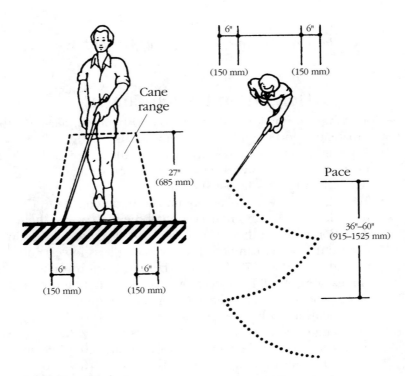

5-19 *Cane technique.* ADAAG, 7/26/91, as published in the Federal Register

- Where a wheelchair user does a parallel approach to cabinets, shelves, closets, lockers, and drawers, the maximum high-reach to knobs, controls, and pulls is 54" (137 cm) and it is 9" (23 cm) for a low-side reach (Fig. 5-20).
- For an unobstructed forward approach, the maximum high reach is 48" (122 cm) and a minimum of 15" (38 cm) for low reach.
- Clothes rods should not be more than 54" (137 cm) above the finished floor or more than 21" (53 cm) from the chair.
- A side reach over an obstruction such as a counter is limited to 46" (117 cm) high when the countertop is 24" (61 cm) in depth and not over 34" (86 cm) in height.
- A forward reach over an obstruction, again, such as a counter, is limited to 44" (112 cm) high when the countertop and clear knee space extend out between 20" (51 cm) and 25" (64 cm) (Fig. 5-21). When the countertop and the clear knee space extend between 0" and 20" (51 cm), then the maximum height is 48" (122 cm).

Clear floor space

Clear floor space means just that—an open area where no obstruction will interfere with the user maneuvering any assistive equipment. Consider the following:

- For a perpendicular (forward—Fig. 5-22) or parallel (side— Fig. 5-23) approach to a drinking fountain, for example, 30" ×

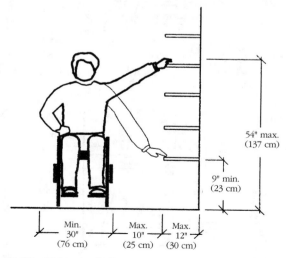

5-20 *Side reach limits.* National Kitchen & Bath Association

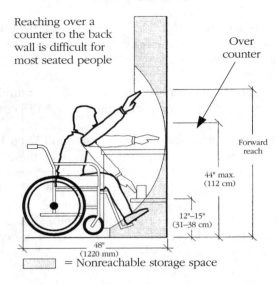

Reaching over a
counter to the back
wall is difficult for
most seated people

Over
counter

Forward
reach

44" max.
(112 cm)

12"–15"
(31–38 cm)

48"
(1220 mm)

▨ = Nonreachable storage space

5-21 *Reaching over a counter to the back wall is difficult for most seated people.* National Kitchen & Bath Association

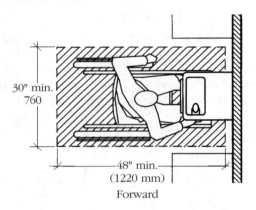

30" min.
760

48" min.
(1220 mm)

Forward

36" max.
(91 cm)

5-22 *With the required knee space below a unit, drinking fountains are easier to use.* Eastern Paralyzed Veterans Association

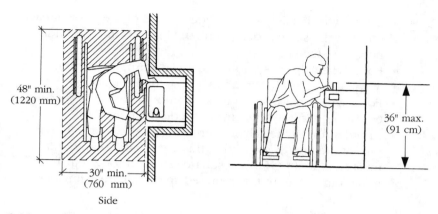

48" min.
(1220 mm)

36" max.
(91 cm)

30" min.
(760 mm)

Side

5-23 *Built-in models that require a side approach are also acceptable.*
Eastern Paralyzed Veterans Association

48" (76 × 122 cm) of clear floor space is needed for a wheelchair user. If you are going to install a drinking fountain, the minimum the unit needs to extend from the wall is 17" (43 cm) and the unit should not be more than 36" (91 cm) above the floor to the top of the spout.

- A 32" (81 cm) minimum clear width at doorways is required if the passage point is not over 24" (61 cm) in depth. If the area is more than 24", then the minimum clear width is 36" (91 cm). This includes wheelchair users and persons using assistive equipment such as canes and walkers.
- If a wheelchair user and a nondisabled person are side by side in the same space, then the required clear width of the space is 48" (122 cm) (Fig. 5-24).

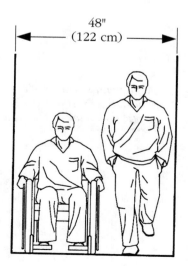

48"
(122 cm)

5-24 *The minimum requirement is 48".* Eastern Paralyzed Veterans Association

- If two wheelchair users are side by side or are passing each other in the same space, then 60" (152 cm) in clear width is necessary (see Fig. 5-25).
- For a wheelchair user to make a 360° turn, a clear floor area 5' square (25 sq. ft., or 2.3 m²) is needed (Fig. 5-26).
- For a wheelchair user to make a smooth U-turn, a space of 60" by 78" (152 by 198 cm) is needed (Fig. 5-27).
- In order for a wheelchair user to make a left- or right-hand turn at the end of a corridor, this area in the shape of a "T" must fit in a 60" (152 cm) square (25 sq. ft. or 2.3 m²) minimum space. In this required space, all areas must be a

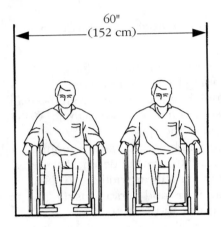

60"
(152 cm)

5-25 *The minimum requirement is 60".* Eastern Paralyzed Veterans Association

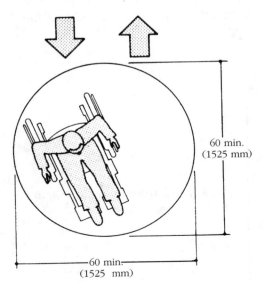

60 min.
(1525 mm)

60 min.
(1525 mm)

5-26
A clear illustration of a wheelchair maneuvering in a 60" diameter space. Council of American Building Officials (CABO)

minimum of 36" (91 cm) wide with the leg of the T-shape being at least 60" (152 cm) long as shown in Fig. 5-28.

- An accessible route around an obstruction more than 48" (122 cm) wide must have a clear space as shown in Fig. 5-29.
- An accessible route around an obstruction less than 48" (122 cm) wide must have a clear space as shown in Fig. 5-30.

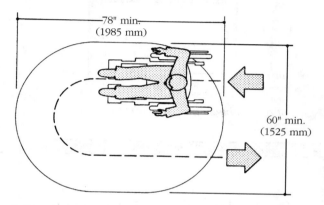

5-27 *A smooth U-turn in a wheelchair.* ADAAG, 7/26/91, as published in the Federal Register, CABO

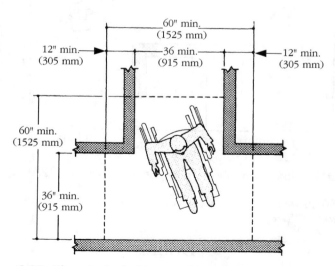

5-28 *The dashed lines indicate the minimum length of clear space needed on each arm of the T-shaped space in order to complete the turn.* CABO

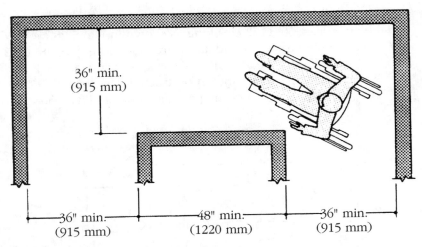

5-29 *Width of accessible route for a 90° turn.* CABO

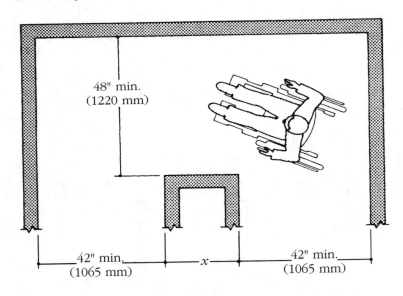

NOTE: Dimensions shown apply when *x* < 48 in (1220 mm).

5-30 *Maneuvering a wheelchair around an obstruction less than 48".* CABO

Doors

It is very important not to overlook the width of doorways and approaches to the front and latch/hinge sides of doors. Enough room must be provided so the person with disabilities can use the door with comfort. You also have to consider the type of hardware that will best fit the individual who uses the door. This is not a requirement, but installing a metal kickplate at the bottom of the door helps protect the door from possible damage from assistive equipment. The following information will help you to remember these important areas:

- Entry doors should have a net (clear) opening of 32" minimum measured from the doorstop to the door face when the door is in a 90° open position (Fig. 5-31).

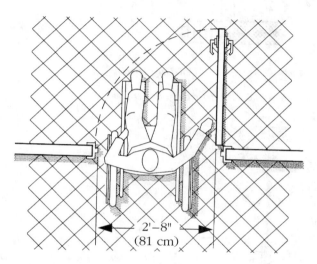

5-31 *Wheelchairs and other assistive equipment require a net (clear) opening that is at least 32".*
Eastern Paralyzed Veterans Association

- Whether a door is hinged, sliding, or folding, the clear doorway width is still 32" (81 cm) (Fig. 5-32). If you just need a little extra space in the doorway of a hinged door, consider using "Swing Clear" hinges by Stanley. These hinges can be installed on existing doors that are 1⅜" (35 mm) or 1¾" (44 mm) thick. When the door is in the 95° swing position, it will be completely free of the opening (Fig. 5-33). Before pulling out any existing door frames, think about these types of hinges; they could save you both time in labor and materials.
- The maximum force for pushing or pulling open interior doors, including sliding/folding doors, should not exceed 5.0 pounds. For fire and exterior doors, contact your local building department for requirements.

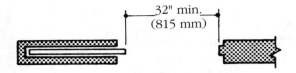

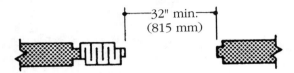

Sliding door

Folding door

5-32 *Clear doorway width.* CABO

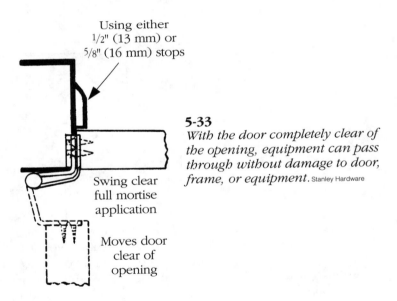

Using either
1/2" (13 mm) or
5/8" (16 mm) stops

5-33
With the door completely clear of the opening, equipment can pass through without damage to door, frame, or equipment. Stanley Hardware

Swing clear
full mortise
application

Moves door
clear of
opening

- If you install a door closer, adjust the sweep period of the closer so that from an open position of 70°, the door will take at least 3 seconds to move to a point of 3" (8 cm) from the latch, measured to the leading edge of the door.

Power Access produces an automatic door operator (Model 4300) that converts most interior and some exterior hinged doors to power operation. This product has important built-in safety features—both mechanical and electrical. The operator arm is not attached to the door. Instead, a wheel at the end of the operator arm rolls against the face of the door, pushing the door open (Fig. 5-34).

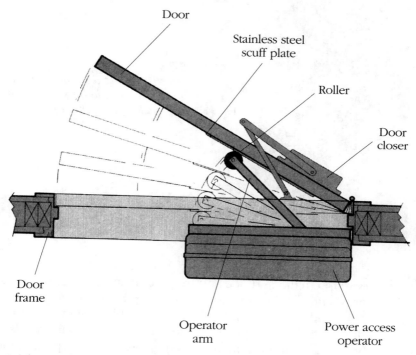

5-34 *Top view—typical installation.* Power Access Corporation

The importance of this unique feature is that the door can always be opened manually from either side without involving the operator. Traffic flow through the doorway is not hindered by the operator. The Power Access opener is always used in conjunction with a conventional door closer, either surface-mounted or concealed. If the door meets an obstruction during the opening cycle, a built-in load-sensing circuit automatically stops the operator and the arm returns to the at-rest (or closed) position. The driver motor is thermally protected and door hold-open time can be set for as long as 30 seconds. The door has the option of staying open longer if necessary (Fig. 5-35).

- Handles, pulls, latches, locks, and other operating devices on accessible doors should have a shape that is easy to grasp

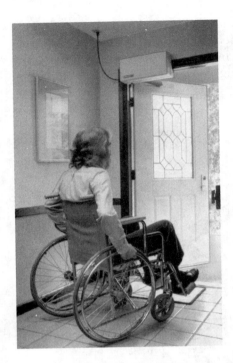

5-35
An automatic door opener can make life a little bit simpler for a wheelchair user. Power Access Corporation

with one hand and does not require tight grasping, pinching, or twisting of the wrist to operate (Fig. 5-36). Lever, push-type, and U-shaped handles are acceptable designs. When sliding doors are fully open, the operating hardware needs to be exposed and usable from both sides. Consider putting the handle between 36" (91 cm) and a maximum of 48" (122 cm) high.

Weiser Lock has designed a keyed leverset (Dane Style) to meet the requirements of the ADA, providing easy access for those with disabilities, elders, and children. It includes an extra-large turn button for easy locking action. This unit also features a unique disengaging exterior lever. Unlike most levers, when the keyed lever is locked, the outer trim turns freely without retracting the dead-locking latch. This prevents forced entries or damage to locking mechanisms. The leverset is also "panic-proof"—when the door is locked, the inside lever will always retract the latch for emergency exits (Fig. 5-37).

For those customers who find it difficult to use a key, consider installing a keyless system. Essex Electronics Incorporated has been developing such systems for over 20 years. The Keyless Entry Access Control System (Model KE-

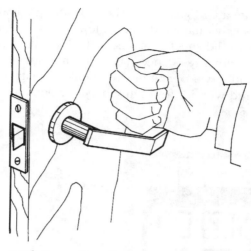

5-36 *Lever handles can be used with ease even if the hand is doubled up in a fist.* Paralyzed Veterans Association

5-37 *Dane Style, keyed leverset provides ease of access, a stylish appearance, and enhanced security.* Weiser Lock—A Masco Co.

300) provides access privileges for up to 100 individuals and the ability to restrict access during certain hours. The system knows when to allow the door to open, how long to leave it open, and when an unauthorized person is attempting entry. When the unit is programmed in the alarm mode or is integrated with a subscriber alarm network, it will generate an alarm when the door is forced or held open. For higher security environments, the system can be programmed to

activate a CCTV camera. The most unique feature of the KE-300 is its virtually indestructible keypad. It is manufactured from a solid sheet of stainless steel, providing both vandal- and weather-resistance. There are no moving parts to wear out and it will operate in 100 percent relative humidity, when covered with ice, or in any harsh or demanding environment (Fig. 5-38).

5-38
You don't have to worry about losing a key. Keyless Entry is a registered trademark of Essex Electronics, Inc.

- Kickplates, if installed, need to cover the width of the door and be at least 12" (30 cm) high.
- Thresholds, if provided, should not exceed ½" (13 mm) high at any door with the exception of an exterior residential sliding door. There the maximum height for a threshold is ¾" (19 mm). Andersen Windows has designed accessory items that will allow ease of access through their patio door from either direction. The Ramped Sill Insert is available for both the interior and exterior. The interior sill is made of solid oak and the exterior is made of extruded aluminum (Fig. 5-39).

Door approaches/landings

On an exterior door (door swings to the interior) and/or slider, the landing immediately outside should be level and clear of any obsta-

5-39
Using accessory items such as the Ramped Sill Insert offers homeowners added convenience. Photo courtesy of Andersen Windows, Inc.

cles. If desired, this landing could have a ¼":1' (6 mm:25 mm) grade for drainage and still be considered "level." Depending on how a wheelchair approaches the door, the landing requires a maneuvering clearance in front and/or to the side of the entrance. The entrance itself requires a minimum net (clear) opening (width) of 32" (81 cm) for the wheelchair to pass through. As mentioned before, this 32" (81 cm) net (clear) measurement starts from the doorstop to the door face when the door is in a 90° open position or, in the case of a slider, when the door is fully opened. A wheelchair can approach a door or slider straight on, from the hinge and/or slider side, or from the latch side. Each approach requires a minimum landing size as follows:

- Straight-on approaches: Both door and slider require a minimum 32" (81 cm) width net (clear) opening by a minimum 42" (107 cm) in depth measuring out from the exterior wall (Fig. 5-40).
- Hinge and/or slide side approach: Both doors require a 54" (137 cm) minimum width (with the measurement starting from the latch side and measuring back toward the hinge/slide side) by a minimum depth of 42" (107 cm) (Fig. 5-41).
- Latch side approach: Both doors require a minimum 32" (81 cm) width net opening plus 24" (61 cm) (with the measurement starting from the hinge/slide side and measuring back toward the latch side) by a minimum depth of 42" (107 cm) (Fig. 5-42).
- Two doors in series: The minimum space between two hinged or pivoted doors in series should be 48" (122 cm) plus the width of any door swinging into the space. Doors in series should swing either in the same direction or away from the space between the doors (Fig. 5-43).

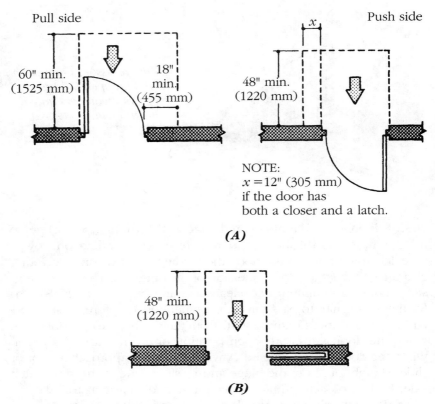

5-40 *(A) Front approaches—swing doors. (B) Front approaches—sliding doors and folding doors.* CABO

Handrails

Most of us, I would guess, have installed handrails for adults. But what about children who cannot reach the handrail or even get their small hands around the handgrip? It is important to remember the needs of children as we design:

- For children under five years of age, you might want to consider using a handrail that is between 1" (25 cm) and 1³⁄₁₆" (30 mm) in diameter.
- For children between 5 and 8 years of age, consider a handrail that does not exceed 1¼" (32 mm) in diameter.
- For children between 8 and 12 years of age, consider a handrail that does not exceed 1¾" (39 mm) in diameter.

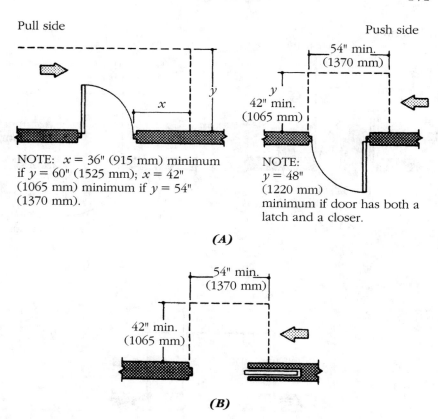

Pull side

Push side

NOTE: $x = 36"$ (915 mm) minimum if $y = 60"$ (1525 mm); $x = 42"$ (1065 mm) minimum if $y = 54"$ (1370 mm).

54" min. (1370 mm)

y

42" min. (1065 mm)

NOTE: $y = 48"$ (1220 mm) minimum if door has both a latch and a closer.

(A)

54" min. (1370 mm)

42" min. (1065 mm)

(B)

5-41 *(A) Hinge side approaches—swinging doors. (B) Slide side approaches—sliding doors and folding doors.* CABO

- Mount the handrail at a height between 24" (61 cm) and 38" (97 cm).

For adults, handrails should follow these specifications:

- The diameter or width of the gripping surfaces of a handrail should be between 1¼" and 2" (32 and 51 mm) (the ADA shows it as a maximum of 1½" ([38 mm]) in diameter) or the shape should provide an equivalent gripping surface. If handrails are mounted adjacent to a wall, the space between the wall and the rail should be 1½" (38 mm) (Fig. 5-44).
- Handrails may be located in a recessed area providing the recess is a maximum of 3" (76 mm) deep and extends at least 18" (46 cm) above the top of the rail (Fig. 5-45).

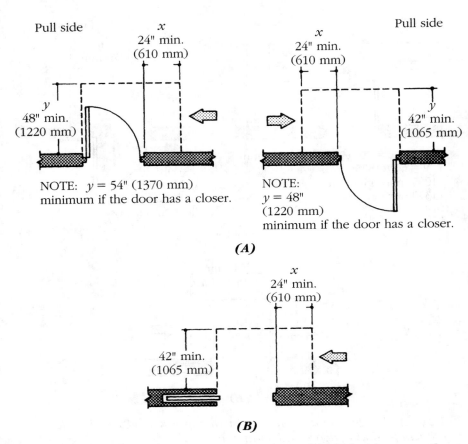

Pull side   *x*
24" min.
(610 mm)

y
48" min.
(1220 mm)

NOTE: *y* = 54" (1370 mm)
minimum if the door has a closer.

x
24" min.
(610 mm)   Pull side

y
42" min.
(1065 mm)

NOTE:
y = 48"
(1220 mm)
minimum if the door has a closer.

(A)

x
24" min.
(610 mm)

42" min.
(1065 mm)

(B)

5-42 (A) Latch side approaches—swinging doors. (B) Latch side approaches—sliding doors and folding doors. CABO

- Consider placing handrails between 34" and 38" (86 and 97 cm) from the landing to the top of the gripping surface (Fig. 5-46).
- For stairs, if the handrail is not continuous, it should extend a minimum of 12" (30 cm) and be parallel with the top landing. The bottom handrail should continue to the slope for a distance of the width of the tread from the bottom riser to a post. The handrail should then extend from that point 12" (30 cm) and be parallel to the ground or landing. The handrail extensions (metal) of 12" (30 cm) at both the top and the bottom of the stairs must be looped back and tied into the posts in order to support themselves.

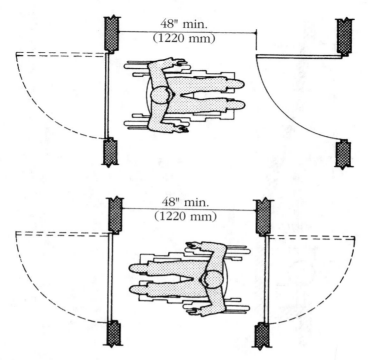

5-43 *Two hinged doors in series.* CABO

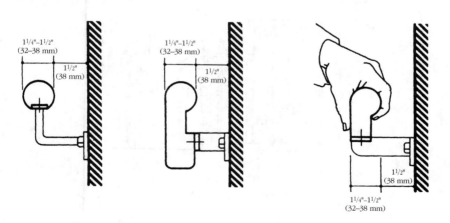

5-44 *Size and spacing of handrails.* ADAAG, 7/26/91, as published in the Federal Register

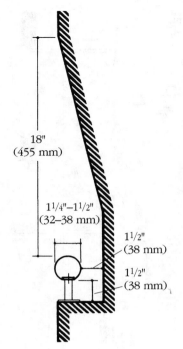

5-45
Cross section of a recessed handrail. ADAAG, 7/26/91, as published in the Federal Register

18"
(455 mm)

1¼"–1½"
(32–38 mm)

1½"
(38 mm)

1½"
(38 mm)

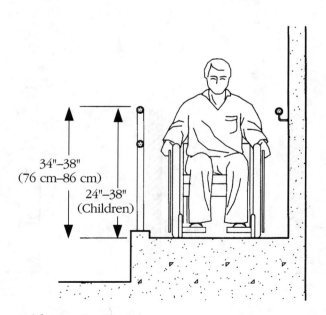

34"–38"
(76 cm–86 cm)

24"–38"
(Children)

5-46 *Handrail height.* Eastern Paralyzed Veterans Association

Ramps

Ramps are a related concern. Whether the ramp is for a wheelchair user or someone who has difficulty using stairs, it is an important issue that needs to be settled so you know how to bid the job properly. You might also want to suggest that the customer have the area around the ramp landscaped to better integrate its design with the house and surrounding yard. The good news is that, unless you are building a concrete ramp, the general construction requirements are the same as for decks, including:

- Span distance
- Setting of posts
- Live and snow loads

I recommend you work closely with your local building department for your state's accessibility regulations. In general, consider the following points:

- Single-family residences have no dimensional requirements regarding ramp width, but I recommend a minimum 36" (91 cm) and suggest you consider 44" to 48" (112 to 122 cm) if you are going to install the handrails to the inside. Commercial work requires 36" (91 cm) interior and 44" (112 cm) exterior clear.
- Level landings are needed at both the top and the bottom of the ramp. In addition, a 60" (152 cm) landing the same width as the ramp or greater is needed after every 30" (76 cm) elevation change. If the ramp changes direction at a landing, the minimum landing size is 60" × 60" (152 × 152 cm).
- Guardrails need to be mounted along both sides of the ramp, and handrails should mounted to the inside.
- The top of a handrail (gripping surface) must be between 34" and 38" (86 and 97 cm) from the ramp surface. Consider installing a second handrail about 24" (61 cm) from the ramp surface.
- The handrail at the top and bottom should extend at least 12" (30 cm) and be parallel with the landing and/or ground.
- A clear space of 1½" (38 mm) should be between the handrail and the surface to which it is mounted.
- Use 2" × 6" decking boards and install them the short way (width of ramp) to provide better traction for wheelchair tires. The installation of a nonslip surface is also required.
- The maximum slope of a ramp in new construction is 1:12, but a slope of 1:16 might be easier for a wheelchair user to navigate (Fig. 5-47). Find out what slope (within code limits) your customer prefers.

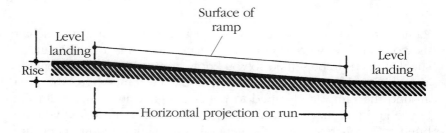

Maximum rise			Maximum horizontal projection	
Slope	in	mm	ft	m
1:12 to < 1:16	30	760	30	9
1:16 to < 1:20	30	760	40	12

5-47 *Components of a single ramp run and sample ramp dimensions.* ADAAG, 7/26/91, as published in the Federal Register

- The transition at the point where a concrete walk or drive meets the ramp should be smooth and level with the landing. The landing should be at least as wide as the ramp, and the length should be a minimum of 60" (152 cm); 72" (183 cm) according to the Uniform Building Code (UBC).
- To protect the surface from the weather, consider incorporating a roof into the structure (Fig. 5-48).

To add a ramp to an existing porch that has a couple of steps, you need to ask yourself the following questions:

- Are the porch and steps made from wood or concrete?
- Do the steps land on a concrete pad or sidewalk?
- How wide are the steps?
- Are there guardrails on the steps?
- Will the ramp be permanent or temporary?

To give you a brief overview of what this project might involve, I assume the porch, steps, guardrails and handrails are made of wood and that the steps are 36" (91 cm) or less in width. First remove the steps and sections of the guardrails on either side of the steps (up on the porch) so that when you complete the ramp and install the handrails, there is 36" (91 cm) clearance.

Depending on how the main post was installed, you might have to remove some of the porch decking to be able to remove the posts and reinstall them in the porch framework. If you have a crawl space, you can work from the underside.

When designing your ramp, keep in mind everything that has been mentioned previously (in the ramp section) and up to this point

5-48 *An incomplete ramp showing a roof added to the design.* C.R.S., Inc.

(Fig. 5-49). Build the ramp framework and seal it, including the underside of the ramp joists that contact the concrete; then install 2" × 6" decking.

For those professionals who seek a modular ramp, Rampit, Inc., has quite a selection, offering wood aluminum, all aluminum, portable (large or small), and aluminum channel ramps.

Their large wood aluminum ramp system (shown in Fig. 5-50) has the following features:

- Aluminum side stringers
- 2" × 10" treated lumber deck treads
- 2" × 4" treated lumber handrails
- Adjustable aluminum support assemblies
- Custom sizes available

Curb ramps

Wherever an accessible route crosses a curb, a curb ramp should be provided. If the curb ramp is located where pedestrians must walk across the ramp or where it is not protected by handrails or guardrails, it should have "flared sides." Curb ramps with "returned curbs" can be used where pedestrians would not normally walk across the ramp. In this area, plantings or some other nonpedestrian surface should be used to discourage pedestrians from walking across the ramp. "Built-up" curb ramps should be located so they do not project into traffic

Wheelchair ramp

NOTE: Length of ramp is not to scale.

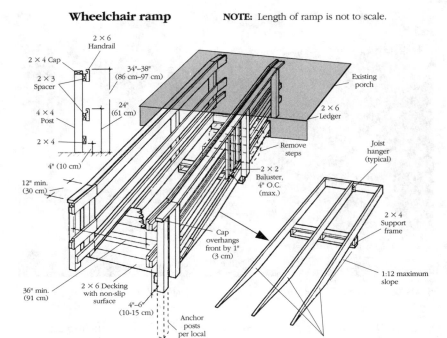

- 2 × 6 Handrail
- 2 × 4 Cap
- 2 × 3 Spacer
- 4 × 4 Post
- 2 × 4
- 4" (10 cm)
- 12" min. (30 cm)
- 36" min. (91 cm)
- 2 × 6 Decking with non-slip surface
- 4"–6" (10-15 cm)
- Anchor posts per local code
- Cap overhangs front by 1" (3 cm)
- 34"–38" (86 cm–97 cm)
- 24" (61 cm)
- Existing porch
- 2 × 6 Ledger
- Remove steps
- 2 × 2 Baluster, 4" O.C. (max.)
- Joist hanger (typical)
- 2 × 4 Support frame
- 1:12 maximum slope
- 2 × 6 Joists

5-49 *Wheelchair ramps should have at least 36" clearance between handrails and a slope no steeper than 1:12.* Technical drawing courtesy of Workbench Magazine

5-50 *Reusable, modular, and good looking.* Rampit, Inc.

vehicle lanes, or they should be located within accessible parking spaces or their access aisles (Fig. 5-51).

- A curb ramp should have flared sides with a slope of 1:10 maximum. This is to prevent pedestrians from tripping if they were to walk across the ramp. The ramp itself must be at least 3' (91 cm) wide with a slope no steeper that 1:12 and the surface must be nonslip.
- If the beginning of the curb ramp is less than 48" (122 cm) from a building or wall, for example, then the slope of the flared side should not exceed 1:12.

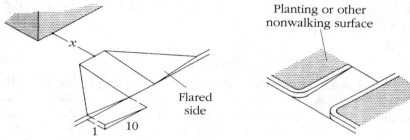

NOTE: If $x < 48"$ (1220 mm), then the slope of flared sides shall not exceed 1:12.

(A) Flared sides

(B) Returned curb

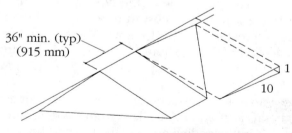

(C) Built-up curb ramp

5-51 *Three examples of curb ramps.* CABO

Parking space

There should be at least one accessible parking space that is 8' (244 cm) wide × 20' (610 cm) long (minimum) with a minimum 5' (152 cm) wide access aisle. This area accommodates a vehicle that un-loads a wheelchair from side doors. Vans with side-mounted lifts require 8' (244 cm) of space with an access aisle of 8' (244 cm), the equivalent of two 8' (244 cm) parking stalls (for a total of 16' or 488 cm). This is important to know, especially when working on resi-dences. If the home is equipped with a standard double-car garage and the family has two vehicles of which one is a van, there wouldn't be enough room in the garage for proper access to the van. In re-ality, this home should have a three-car garage—one stall empty for proper access. For all commercial areas and public facilities in-cluding multifamily dwellings (with the exception of single-family or duplex residential), a sign is needed to alert van users to the presence of the wider aisle.

Stairs

When stairs are properly constructed, they can be successfully uti-lized by persons who are visually impaired. The uniform riser height is 7" (18 cm) maximum and 4" (10 cm) minimum; tread width is 11" (28 cm) minimum. If you are allowed in your particu-lar area to go beyond the 7" (18 cm) maximum in riser height, I wouldn't recommend it. In fact, you are better off to go below 7" (18 cm) maximum height for ease of use. Open risers are not per-mitted and this is a practice that should be carried over into the res-idential market. The underside of the nosing should not be abrupt and should have a radius of curvature at the leading edge of the tread that is no greater than ½" (13 mm). Risers should be sloped or the underside of the nosing should have an angle not less than 60° from the horizontal. The nosing should project no more than 1½" (38 mm) (Fig. 5-52).

Another important consideration when constructing stairs—and ramps—is the installation of a tactile warning system (grooves paral-lel to the steps) in the landing areas at the top and bottom to alert vi-sually impaired individuals of the imminent presence of stairs (or a ramp) and the direction (up or down). Commercial and multifamily requirements call for top and bottom landings that extend out from the stairs (or ramp) a distance that is at least equal to the width of the steps or a maximum of 48" (122 cm). The tactile warning should be-gin at least 24" (61 cm) out from the first step (or the ramp) and ex-tend back toward the steps (or ramp) to within 8" to 12" (20 to 30 cm). Consult with your building department to confirm requirements in your area.

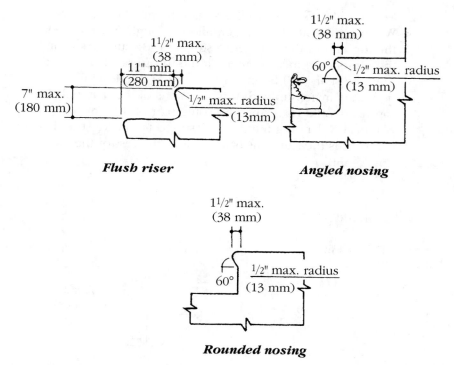

5-52 *Examples of acceptable nosings.* C.R.S., Inc.

Stair construction

Over the years I have built some beautiful stairs, but I confess that stairs are not my strong suit. Stairs can be time-consuming and they really make you think—mathematically—to correctly calculate measurements for risers (height) and treads (width).

To simplify the process for you, some tools, charts, and diagrams are included to help you design stairs. However, before getting into these items, there are some basics to review before calculating the risers and treads:

- Remember to cut off the bottom of the stringer by the thickness of the tread material. Otherwise, the first riser will increase (possibly to a height exceeding the codes) by the thickness of this material (Fig. 5-53A). At the same time, lowering the stringer by the thickness of the tread material will increase the top riser height by the same thickness. This is necessary because the tread thickness will shorten the top riser by this amount. Also, the top step is part of the finish floor—not another tread.

- There is always one tread less than the number of risers.
- When laying out the stringer, allow enough stock to tie in the top end of the stringer to supports. Be sure to maintain the same tread measurement at the top step. Also, consider how the stairs will be incorporated into the design as well as how they match up with the directions of the material. The top riser could be formed by some part of the finished platform or landing framework (supports). Make sure that this riser is the same measurement as the rest of the risers (Fig. 5-53B).

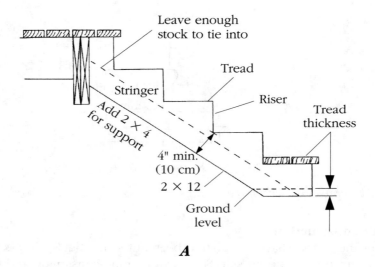

A

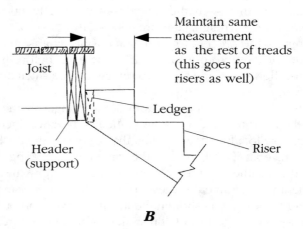

B

5-53 *Stairs-to-ground basics.* C.R.S., Inc.

Basic stairway layout
The following information should prove helpful before you lay out your stringers:

- The sum of all unit runs (tread less nosing) = total run.
- The sum of all unit risers = total rise. This is measured from the surface of the finished platform to a level point on the ground (existing slab or poured pad). To find a level point (on the ground) from which to measure, place one end of a level about where the stringers will land. Point the other end toward the place where the stringer will attach to the platform. If your level is not long enough, use a straight 2" × 4" with a level on top of it.
- As the angle of a stringer changes, so does the riser-tread ratio. There are three general rules for riser-tread ratio (excluding tread nosing; I recommend the nosing extend beyond the riser from 1" to 1⅛" (25 to 29 mm):
  ~Rise plus tread width = 17" to 18" (43 to 46 cm)
  ~Rise times tread width = 72" to 76" (183 to 193 cm)
  ~Sum of two risers plus tread width = 24" to 25" (61 to 64 cm)
- An "ideal" ratio for wooden steps is a 7" (18 cm) rise with a 10" to 11½" (25 to 29 cm) tread while the "ideal" ratio for concrete steps is a 6" to 6½" (15 to 17 cm) rise with a 12" to 13" (30 to 33 cm) tread. Be sure to consult your building codes for the requirements that apply to your area.
- In residential construction, avoid risers more than 8" (20 cm) and treads less than 9" (23 cm). Commercial stairs have a maximum 7" (18 cm) rise and a minimum 11" (28 cm) tread.
- Try to keep the angle to the ground 34° to 37°.
- Maintain the same height for risers as well as treads. A ⅜" (10 mm) difference is allowed between the largest and smallest risers and treads.
- Treads should slope forward about ⅛" (3 mm) for drainage.
- Maintain a stairway at least 36" (91 cm) wide.
- Consider using a 2" × 12" for a stringer. This would give about 11½" (29 cm) tread widths. The use of three stringers instead of two for the stairway system will stop the springy or spongy feeling on treads as they span the distance between two stringers.
- Maintain at least 4" (10 cm) of the stringer once the risers and treads have been cut out. For extra support, add a 2" × 4" on the inside of each stringer. If you have a middle stringer, attach a 2" × 4" to each side with screws. Do not hammer because you could break off the tread on the stringer (Fig. 5-53A).

- When stairs are going to end at ground level, be sure they land on a concrete pad. Finish the outside edges and broom the pad for traction. The landing should extend beyond the stairs a distance equal to the width of the stairs (36" or 91 cm). Of course when assistive equipment is going to be used be sure that the pad is a minimum of 72" (183 cm) in length. Also hold the stringer, including the kicker plate, off the concrete pad by using an aluminum post standoff or PVC spacers. This will prevent the material from soaking up water. Otherwise, make sure that the kicker plate is treated wood that can hold the stringer up and off the concrete pad.

Stairway construction tables

You will find Tables 5-1 through 5-3 handy when working on stairway layouts.

Table 5-1. Stairway layout

Approximate angle to floor line	Rise in inches	Tread run in inches
30½°	6½ (165)	11 (279)
32°	6¾ (171)	10¾ (273)
33¾°	7 (178)	10½ (267)
35¼°	7¼ (184)	10¼ (260)
37°	7½ (191)	10 (25)
38½°	7¾ (197)	9¾ (248)
40°	8 (203)	9½ (241)

Adapted from: Blue Book, Swanson Tool Co., Inc.

Table 5-2. Decimal equivalents of 8ths, 16ths, 32nds, and 64ths

Inches	Decimal Equivalent	Inches	Decimal Equivalent	Inches	Decimal Equivalent
¹⁄₆₄	0.015625	¹¹⁄₃₂	0.34375	⁴³⁄₆₄	0.671875
¹⁄₃₂	0.03125	²³⁄₆₄	0.359375	¹¹⁄₁₆	0.6875
³⁄₆₄	0.046875	⅜	0.375	⁴⁵⁄₆₄	0.703125
¹⁄₁₆	0.0625	²⁵⁄₆₄	0.390625	²³⁄₃₂	0.71875
⁵⁄₆₄	0.078125	¹³⁄₃₂	0.40625	⁴⁷⁄₆₄	0.734375
³⁄₃₂	0.09375	27/64	0.421875	¾	0.750
⁷⁄₆₄	0.109375	⁷⁄₁₆	0.4375	⁴⁹⁄₆₄	0.765625
⅛	0.125	²⁹⁄₆₄	0.453125	²⁵⁄₃₂	0.78125
⁹⁄₆₄	0.140625	¹⁵⁄₃₂	0.46875	⁵¹⁄₆₄	0.796875

Inches	Decimal Equivalent	Inches	Decimal Equivalent	Inches	Decimal Equivalent
5/32	0.15625	31/64	0.484375	13/16	0.8125
11/64	0.171875	1/2	0.500	53/64	0.828125
3/16	0.1875	33/64	0.515625	27/32	0.84375
13/64	0.203125	17/32	0.53125	55/64	0.859375
7/32	0.21875	35/64	0.546875	7/8	0.875
15/64	0.234375	9/16	0.5625	57/64	0.890625
1/4	0.250	37/64	0.578125	29/32	0.90625
17/64	0.265625	19/32	0.59375	59/64	0.921875
9/32	0.28125	39/64	0.609375	15/16	0.9375
19/64	0.296875	5/8	0.625	61/64	0.953125
5/16	0.3125	41/64	0.640625	31/32	0.96875
21/64	0.328125	21/32	0.65625	63/64	0.984375

Adapted from: Blue Book, Swanson Tool Co., Inc. (Refer to appendix C for metric equivalents)

Table 5-3. Decimal equivalents of 12ths

12th	Decimal equivalent
1"	0.083333
2"	0.166666
3"	0.25
4"	0.333333
5"	0.416666
6"	0.5
7"	0.583333
8"	0.666666
9"	0.75
10"	0.833333
11"	0.916666

Adapted from: Blue Book, Swanson Tool Co., Inc. (Refer to appendix C for metric equivalents)

Calculating risers

Just for practice, assume you are working on a platform that is 6'3" (191 cm) off the ground (Fig. 5-54).

1 The total rise of this platform is 6'3" or 75" (191 cm).
2 You want a 7" (18 cm) rise per step, staying close to the 35° angle (Table 5-1).
3 To determine the number of risers, divide 75" (191 cm) by 7, which equals 10.714 risers.
4 Since 0.714 is over one half of a riser (round 10.714 to 11), divide 75" (191 cm) by 11, which equals 6.818" (17.3 cm).

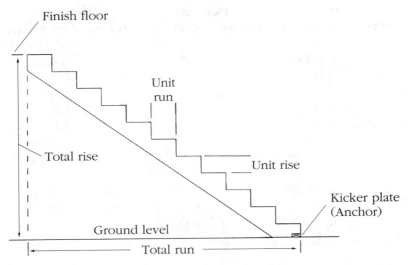

5-54 *Remember, total rise is measured to the top of the finished material's surface.* C.R.S., Inc.

5 Refer to Table 5-2. The closest you can get to 0.818 is 0.8125, which is ¹³⁄₁₆". Your figure now becomes 6.8125, which is 6¹³⁄₁₆" (17.3 cm).

6 To recheck the total rise, multiply 6.8125 by 11 which equals 74.9375.

7 Since 0.9375 = ¹⁵⁄₁₆ (23.8 mm), you will be short by ¹⁄₁₆" (1.6 mm) of your total rise of 75" (191 cm). Rather than attempting to divide 0.625 evenly between the 11 risers (adding 0.0057 to each riser), just add ¹⁄₁₆" (1.6 mm) to the bottom riser to reach the total rise. My experience is that if the bottom riser is within ⅛" (3 mm) of other riser heights, you won't notice the difference when walking the stairs and neither will your customer.

Calculating treads

Now that you have established 11 risers at 6¹³⁄₁₆" (17.3 cm), you need to calculate the 10 treads (remember, there is always one less tread than riser). Applying the three general rules, we have:

1 6¹³⁄₁₆" (17.3 cm) (Rise) + 11" (28 cm) (calculated run) = 17 ¹³⁄₁₆" (45.3 cm) (17" to 18" ([43 to 46 cm]) is ideal).

2 6.8125 (17.4 cm) (Riser height) × 11 (run) = 74.9375 (190 cm), or 74¹⁵⁄₁₆" (72" to 76" ([183 to 193 cm]) is ideal).

3 6.8125 (17.3 cm) + 6.8125 (17.3 cm) (sum of two risers) + 11"
(28 cm) (run) = 24.625 or 24⅝" (62.6 cm) (24" to 25" ([61 to 63
cm]) is ideal). Therefore, we have 10 treads × 11" (28 cm)
(run) = 110" (279 cm) (9.166, Table 5-3) for a total run of 9' 2"
(279 cm).

Calculating stringer length

Continuing with the same example:

1 Rise of 75" (191 cm): 75 × 75 = 5,625 (36,290 cm)
2 Run of 110" (279 cm): 110 × 110 = 12,100 (77,841 cm)
3 5,625 + 12,100 = 17,725 (114,131 cm)
4 The square root of 17,725 (114,131 cm) = 133.13526 ÷ 12 =
11.094 or 11' 1 (338 cm) ⅝₄". Add 12" to 24" (30 to 61 cm) to
this figure for waste. In this particular case, the question is,
"Can you cut the stringer from a 12' (366 cm) 2× or should
you go up to a 14' (426 cm) piece?" How lucky do you feel?

How would you like to solve hundreds of building problems at
the touch of a button? A new calculator, the Construction Master IV
(Calculated Industries, Inc.) shown in Fig. 5-55, can solve riser and
tread calculations in a matter of minutes. The stair key instantly finds
the number of risers and treads, riser height, tread width, and any
overage or underage.

5-55
The Construction Master IV.
Calculated Industries, Inc.

This calculator can also add, subtract, multiply, and divide in feet-inch-fractions, decimal feet (tenths, hundredths), inches and fractions, decimal inches, yards, meters, centimeters, millimeters, board feet, and even square and cubic dimensions. Besides stair solutions, it also has rafter solutions for commons, jacks, and hips and valleys—even irregular hips. It has a "paperless" tape for reviewing the last 20 entries. If you don't already have one, you should! Contact Calculated Industries, Inc., at 800-854-8075.

Another tool that can help with the layout of risers and treads on stringers is Swanson's "Big-12" Square. This compact tool incorporates a rafter/framing square, stairway layout gauge, protractor, tri- and miter-square, and layout scribes with easy-to-read numbers (Fig. 5-56).

The Swanson Speed Square comes with an illustrated *Blue Book* for roof and stairway layouts. This 62-page, pocket-sized manual gives complete instructions on basic roof construction with all rafter length tables as well as complete stairway building instructions including figuring proper tread width and rise, stairwell opening sizes, overhead clearance, stringer layout, and so forth. Some of the information contained in this chapter is from the *Blue Book*. If you don't already have one, I would strongly recommend you add it to your

5-56 *The Big-12 Square.* Swanson Tool Co., Inc.

collection and put it to good use. You might have to purchase the tool in order to get the *Blue Book*, but you will find the tool a valuable addition to your collection.

Other stair considerations

Stairs can give anyone trouble, especially stairs leading to a basement or those that are close to an outside entrance. Water or tracked-in snow can cause hazardous footing. Extra measures need to be taken in these areas. For better traction and to help the visually impaired locate the nose of the stairs, the R.C.A. Rubber Co. has a good selection of different styles of rubber stair treads. The #555VI has a 2" (5 cm) wide abrasive strip recessed right into the tread. Because it is 12½" (32 cm) deep and is available in lengths of 3' to 6' (91 cm to 183 cm), you can cover the entire tread in most cases. For extra antislip protection, consider them for your next project—commercial, multifamily, or residential (Fig. 5-57).

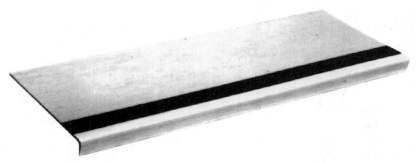

5-57 *VI Abrasive strip rubber stair treads.* The R.C.A. Rubber Company

Products

All along I have mentioned products that can make a difference in the lives of your customers. Depending on your particular project, you might find these products to be "just what the doctor ordered." Staying abreast of these products helps you and your customers achieve a well-planned project. More important, they help your customers achieve independence!

Home designs

For new construction, the following three plans illustrate carefully thought-out designs. They are part of a collection from HomeStyles

Publishing and Marketing Inc. The blueprints are designed by licensed architects or members of the American Institute of Building Design (AIBD), and each available plan is designed to meet nationally recognized building codes at the time and place they were drawn.

Although the presentation might vary depending on the size and complexity of the home and the style of the individual designer, the blueprints for most home designs include the following elements:

- Exterior elevations
- Foundation plans
- Detailed floor plans
- Cross sections
- Interior elevations
- Roof details
- Schematic electrical layouts
- General specifications

The following design plans as well as others can be ordered by calling 800-547-5570:

- Plan #I-1914-H—A lattice-railed porch wraps the facade of this comfortable ranch. Inside, living spaces are free-flowing, emphasizing ease of accessibility. An island kitchen opens to the family room, and the dining and living rooms unfold into each other. Wide windows overlook the backyard. Double doors to the yard enhance the master bedroom. Its private bath has plenty of room to maneuver and features a separate tub and shower and a roomy wardrobe. Two secondary bedrooms share a full bath. Garage access is conveniently nearby (Fig. 5-58).
- Plan #I-2290-H—Natural light floods the interior of this spacious home. Guests can leave their coats in the island closet before moving into the formal living and dining rooms, where radiant windows overlook the backyard. Just to the right of the entry is the library. An oversized work island adds to the kitchen's efficiency, and the bayed breakfast nook also overlooks the backyard. The neighboring family room boasts a fireplace and sliding glass doors to a covered patio. The private master suite has double doors opening to a cozy deck and a wardrobe with plenty of room for clothing and accessories. All manner of comfortable amenities are in the bath, including a refreshing spa tub and roomy shower. Guests will feel right at home in the good-sized secondary bedroom, which shares a convenient hall bath (Fig. 5-59).

"Great Room" Concept in Economical Design

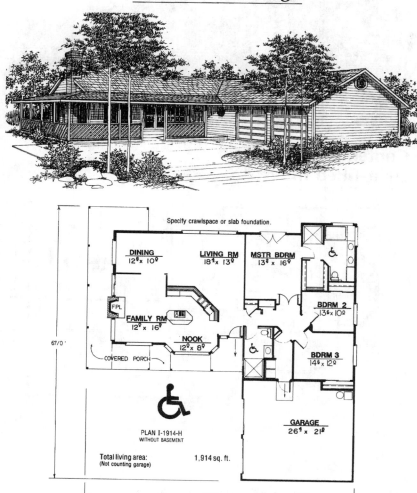

5-58 *"Great Room" concept in economical design.* HomeStyles Publishing and Marketing, Minneapolis MN, 1-800-547-5570

- Plan #I-2726-H—This spacious ranch-style home has plenty of room to move around in. The centralized living area boasts a corner fireplace that spreads warmth and ambiance to the family room, bayed breakfast nook, and island kitchen. Double

Contemporary Exterior, Light-filled Interior

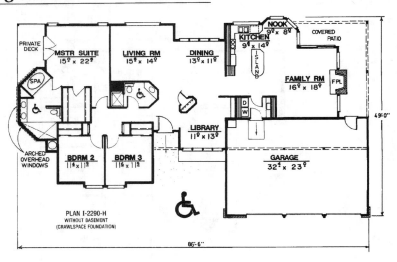

PLAN I-2290-H
WITHOUT BASEMENT
(CRAWLSPACE FOUNDATION)

Total living space: 2,290 sq. ft.
(Not counting garage)

5-59 *Contemporary exterior, light-filled interior.* HomeStyles Publishing and Marketing, Minneapolis MN, 1-800-547-5570

doors open to the backyard from the family room. Twin doors also introduce the living room to the right of the sidelighted entry. An island closet is convenient for dinner guests to hang up their coats before moving on to the formal dining room. The corner master bedroom features a large wardrobe and private bath. Guests or children will appreciate the privacy of the three secondary bedrooms, which share a hall bath (Fig. 5-60).

Space to Maneuver

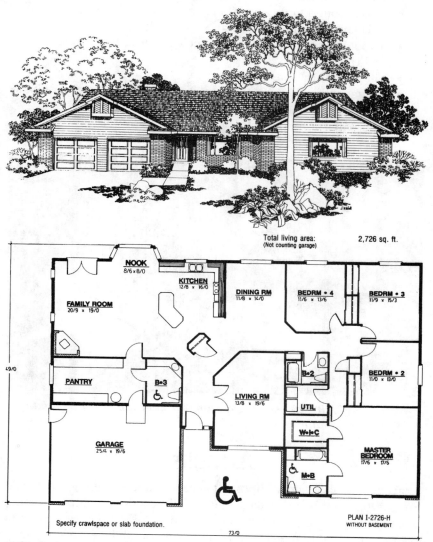

Total living area: 2,726 sq. ft.
(Not counting garage)

NOOK
8/6 × 8/0

KITCHEN
12/8 × 16/0

DINING RM
11/8 × 14/0

BEDRM • 4
11/6 × 13/6

BEDRM • 3
11/9 × 15/3

FAMILY ROOM
20/9 × 19/0

BEDRM • 2
11/0 × 13/0

PANTRY

B•3

B•2

LIVING RM
13/8 × 19/6

UTIL

W•I•C

GARAGE
25/4 × 19/6

MASTER BEDROOM
17/6 × 17/6

M•B

Specify crawlspace or slab foundation.

73/0

49/0

PLAN I-2726-H
WITHOUT BASEMENT

5-60 *Space to maneuver.* HomeStyles Publishing and Marketing, Minneapolis MN, 1-800-547-5570

Accessible workshops

Once the house has been designed for full accessibility, you might
consider creating and building a fully accessible workshop. You'll
need to be creative in your design and work closely with the cus-

tomer. Find ways to make standard tools accessible, using ideas like the following (which were provided by *Workbench* magazine):

- A roll-around table saw where the base has a fold-down off-feed table and built-in storage for saw blades
- A router table that allows a wheelchair user to operate the tool (Fig. 5-61)
- A lowered drill press or bandsaw
- A rotating workbench that can stop at different tool positions
- A Ferris wheel style tool caddy
- Arm extensions specially designed to grab tools

5-61 *By modifying an existing design, a router table can be used by a person with disabilities.* Photo courtesy of Workbench Magazine

Access

I have talked about how important access is, and sometimes just making the door or hallway wider gives full access to your home. But what about getting to the basement from the first floor, or getting to your home if the home is built into the side of a hill—or even getting off the porch to the sidewalk? The following products can assist in those areas as well as others.

Platform lift

Access Industries, Inc. has a product called Porch-Lift which is a vertical platform lift. The following are some of the many features of a platform lift:

- It requires less space to install than a ramp.
- It can be used indoors as well as out.
- It allows full access to the home—basement or second floor.
- It is more attractive than a ramp.

Figure 5-62 shows the Model PL-LD. It was designed for use in applications where a compact, low-rise lift is needed. The standard platform is 36" × 38" (91 × 97 cm) and has lifting heights of 48" (122 cm) and 72" (183 cm). It can be used in lighter commercial applications. Platform lifts can be used to solve an array of accessibility problems.

5-62
A platform lift is an easy solution to full access. Access Industries, Inc.

Chair lift

When there is not enough room for an elevator or a platform lift, then the solution could be a chair lift. Individuals who are comfortable in a home and don't want to move out of it shouldn't let stairs interfere with daily activities. A stair lift gives accessibility, independence, and freedom. Figure 5-63 shows Electra-Ride (manufactured by Bruno Independent Living Aids). The chair can swivel 45° and 90° at the top and bottom of the stairway. When the footrest is folded, the unit has a total width of 15¾" (40 cm). Standard lengths of track are available in 16' (488 cm) and 20' (610 cm) lengths and can be cut to size. No special wiring is involved because the system is powered by two 12V batteries, which are continuously charged by a battery charger that plugs into any receptacle. A product such as this can help make any home that restricts an individual's freedom into a home that can be fully enjoyed.

Elevator

For existing or new homes, there is the option of installing an elevator. A residential unit can be installed in a space little over 20 sq. ft.

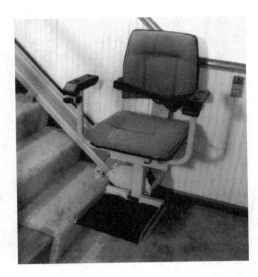

5-63
Now a customer can ride with comfort. Bruno Independent Living Aids, Inc.

(1.9 m²), or about the size of some closets. You can choose an electric winding drum or hydraulic elevator system. Make sure there is battery backup, emergency lighting, telephone, door locks, handrails, and options for accessory items. You must also decide on the size of the cab. Even if there is no wheelchair user in the home at the time of installation, should the cab be large enough to accommodate a wheelchair? Look ahead! Figure 5-64 shows the Estate by Waupaca Elevator Company. This unit is finished with recessed oak wall panels (walnut and cherry available), an unfinished floor, drop-ceiling lighting, and scissors gates. This particular elevator has two exits, which adds convenience and increased mobility to any home.

Outside elevator

When you find the perfect spot to build on a lake, it will probably be on the side of a hill. Some of the world's most appealing property is often difficult to access. Although stairways can be constructed, the sheer length and steepness of the climb would make anyone tired just thinking about it. This shouldn't discourage a customer from building—not when outside elevators are available. An elevator by Garaventa (Canada) LTD (Hillside Elevator Division) can ease the discomfort of having to climb a set of steep stairs. Besides giving a great view of the surrounding area, an elevator can add value to the property. Garaventa can custom-design a unit just right for your project. They can also provide an enclosed cab to protect passengers from Mother Nature, a handrail, and a seat (Fig. 5-65). An elevator enhances your customers' lifestyle; they can enjoy the view while going for a ride!

5-64
Be sure the width of the cab can accommodate a wheelchair. Waupaca
Elevator Company, Inc.

5-65 *What a view!* Garaventa (Canada) LTD.

Recreational lifts

We covered access to a lake place, but what about a pool or spa at home? How does someone with disabilities access those recreational pleasures? The pool or spa in many cases is a place for individuals to enjoy the water, exercise, and to heal. The difficulty of getting into and out of the facility defeats the purpose. Help is on the way—companies that manufacture such access equipment can make this process a real comfort.

Aquatic Access Lifts offers sling-type lifts for in-ground and above-ground pools and spas. Their lifts are powered by water pressure, either from a plumbed-in line or just straight from the garden hose. No electricity is required and it takes less than two gallons of water for each cycle. The up and down motion is controlled by a turn of the valve handle. Seats are available with no arms or two arms and with or without seatbelts, and the seats turn freely. The Pool Lift AG shown in Fig. 5-66 allows a person to ride up to 30" (76 cm), turn over the wall, and ride down 30" (76 cm) into a 4' (122 cm) deep pool. The handle shown allows the user to manually swing the seat over the water. It is not automatic and will require some arm muscles. Even at that, it still adds to the dignity of independence.

Spectrum Pool Products has a product called the Freedom-lift. This fully automatic (four-way control valve) adjustable spa lift enables an individual to reap the benefits of hydrotherapy. The water-powered drive system provides a smooth and dependable ride that is controlled

5-66 *One way to enjoy the afternoon.* Aquatic Access Inc.

by the user. Each lift has a comfortable pull-out leg support system. All structural components are TP 304 stainless steel (polished finish). The range of motion is 25" (64 cm) raising capacity, 120° rotation. The unit comes complete with mounting hardware, hoses, plastic seat, seat belt, stationary inner arm, and pull-out leg support. Gaining independence is what it is all about (Fig. 5-67).

5-67 *One sure way to enjoy the spa.* Spectrum Pool Products

Because the two lifts mentioned previously are powered by water pressure, they have a water discharge. It is important that the discharge hose not be placed so as to create a cross connection situation. For example, if you want to discharge the water into the pool, make certain that the end of the discharge hose is not located below the flood line (deck) of the pool. If the end of the discharge hose is actually in the pool's water and the water supply suddenly creates a siphoning effect, the pool's water could be drawn into the water system, contaminating the water supply. If you are installing one of these lifts, be sure to check with your plumbing inspector for the proper location of the discharge hose.

Heat

We all need it, we've got to have it, we can't live without it—heat. The majority of homes are heated with convection heat; unfortunately, this type of heat warms the air while drying it out. How efficient is this type of heat? What about heat that can be directed right at the source?

Radiant heat offers an alternative. Because air is transparent to radiant heat, it doesn't get nearly as warm or as dry as with convection heaters. Because there is no air movement, there are no drafts. Only those objects that get in its path get instantaneous heat, and that's good. Radiant heat does not require floor space, flues, piping, ducting, filters, or tanks. Maybe we need to go back and evaluate how we heat our own homes! Radiant ceiling panels can supplement a heat source; because they are up and out of the way, the hazard of accidental burns or fires is reduced. They can be placed in those areas where supplemental heat is needed. One company that has such a product is made by SSHC, Inc., called the Enerjoy Peopleheater.

- Panel sizes range from 2' × 2' × 1" (61 × 61 × 2.54 cm) through 4' × 8' × 1" (122 × 244 × 2.54 cm).
- The units are individually (zone) controlled and can be painted to complement any decor.
- There is no noise or odor and they are nonallergenic and maintenance free—no moving parts.
- Panels are lightweight and easily installed on ceiling, flush, or T-bar applications.
- According to the company, they offer 20 to 50 percent lower operating costs than other conventional heating systems— electric, oil, and gas.

Radiant heating can be an ideal comfortable money-saving solution to today's heating problems (Fig. 5-68).

Have you ever given much thought to the thermostat? To someone with reduced hand strength or limited vision, a daily task such as adjusting the thermostat can be very difficult. Honeywell's Easy-To-See Round thermostat and Easy-To-Use Accessory put precise temperature control into the hands of people with limited vision, coordination, or hand strength. Some of the features of the Easy-To-See Thermostat (Fig. 5-69) include:

- Enlarged cover ring with raised numbers so users can see and feel the temperature range
- Low-glare design for people with limited vision
- Raised setpoint knob and indicator arrow for easier adjustment
- Ratchet mechanism in setpoint knob that provides a click to be heard and felt at every two degrees of movement, with a stronger click at every 10 degrees
- Optional decorator ring specifies "Heat," "Cool," or "Off"

5-68
With radiant ceiling panels directly in the area, there's no excuse not to have a cozy atmosphere. SSHC, Inc.

5-69
Easy-To-See thermostat can aid the visually impaired.
Honeywell Inc.

The Easy-To-Use Accessory (Fig. 5-70) has the following features:
- Circular extension ring allows brushing or rolling the temperature setting dial into place
- Fits over 1993 and later models of the Honeywell round Easy-To-See Thermostat

Nothing is more comforting than a fireplace. It just seems to make a home the way it should be. Heat-N-Glo Fireplace Products, Inc., is one company offering a gas fireplace with a remote control. This would be ideal for my grandmother! She wouldn't even have to get off the couch. It's amazing how a simple remote can improve the life of someone who has difficulty getting up. This particular type of fire-

5-70
*Thermostat accessory makes
adjusting the thermostat dial
easy for people who have
difficulty grasping and
turning conventional dials.*
Honeywell Inc.

place is direct-vented; in other words, it vents out the back of the unit
to the outside using a 5" (14 cm) and 8" (20 cm) coaxial pipe. All air
for combustion is taken through the outer 8" (20 cm) pipe, and exhaust gases are eliminated through the inner 5" (14 cm) pipe. A fixed
panel of glass on the front of the firebox creates a sealed combustion
chamber, eliminating the loss of warm air into a chimney system, heat
that is often lost with conventional fireplaces. A unit such as this is
great for remodel projects because you don't have to worry about a
chimney (Fig. 5-71).

5-71 *The comforts of home.* Heat-N-Glo Fireplace Products, Inc.

Summary

All the information given in this chapter and in remaining chapters applies to the commercial market. Use this information as a guide and apply it to the residential market. It would be a good idea to pick up some of the publications I have recommended (and will continue to recommend) throughout *Accessible Housing*. Pick up copies of A117.1 and *Accessible Design for All—An Illustrated Handbook: Washington State Regulations (1995)*. These two alone cover anything that I haven't covered, especially where the commercial market is concerned. My intent for writing this book is to help you to better understand the residential market, where standards don't apply. Keep in mind before doing any bidding and work to consult with your local building department concerning this area of accessibility.

Summary

6

Bathrooms
and kitchens

Up to this point, valuable information has been provided to help you modify, build new, and better understand what is involved in universal, barrier-free, and adaptable/adjustable design. Now it is time to step into two rooms that probably require more understanding on your part than any of the other rooms in a home: the bathroom and the kitchen. Activities in these two rooms help us all to start each new day. For people with disabilities, however, these rooms can be their worst nightmare. As with widening hallways, doorways, or building ramps, the bathroom and kitchen need special attention to help individuals feel comfortable in them and able to utilize the facilities in these areas with full control. People with disabilities need to start their days just like nondisabled individuals.

As Gene Rothert's story in chapter 1 should remind us, one way to better understand our roles as professionals is by role reversal. Only then will we truly feel what individuals have gone through—and are still going through—every day of their lives.

There is no better way to learn more on this subject than through the National Kitchen & Bath Association (NKBA). This organization promotes professionalism, helps to establish good ethical business practices, and provides leadership and direction for the kitchen and bathroom industry. Certification by the NKBA as a kitchen and bathroom designer (CKD/CBD) will put you a step ahead of the competition, and recognition of this certification can only build confidence in your customers. In addition, you can enjoy financial rewards by increasing the fees for your professional services. There is always more to learn about this subject.

Bathrooms and kitchens are areas in which your barrier-free designs can make a vital difference in the lives of your customers, and you can receive pure satisfaction in helping to solve real problems here. At the same time, you can create a viable business. What could be better?

Bathrooms

It's wonderful, in the construction business, to meet and conquer challenges and obstacles, especially in the remodeling field. This means that we need to put our hammers down occasionally and take some time to check out new products and learn new construction methods and techniques that could benefit both our customers and ourselves. Of course, these tools can be found in trade publications, in books, at seminars and trade shows, and from organizations that you can join. It is your responsibility to keep abreast of changes within this business. You might also want to check out my book, *Bathroom Remodeling* (McGraw-Hill, ISBN #0-8306-4479-2), for a thorough discussion of remodeling this important room from the ground up. What you know could determine whether or not you get a job you bid on. Don't wait for a customer to come to you with a problem you don't know how to solve.

One issue on the minds of customers—and therefore important to you—is whether or not barrier-free designs can be incorporated into their bathrooms. The answer is yes, of course. To what degree is another matter, but many of us are not sure exactly what this process entails, and some of us are just plain frightened of the subject. Don't wait so long to understand this area that you begin to lose jobs! By now you should have grasped the concept of barrier-free design: it makes life a little easier and more convenient for the customer. Barrier-free bathrooms for individuals who are disabled, as well as for older adults who have reduced balance and mobility, pose a challenge in design.

Design specs

Whether you are planning a new design with your customer or just working on a remodeling project, put yourself in the position of the wheelchair user. Begin your barrier-free design with the overall floor area, and consider the following when bidding on barrier-free bathrooms:

1 Begin with a minimum clear floor area that is 5' (152 cm) square (25 sq. ft., or 2.3 m²) to allow wheelchair users to make a 360° turn (Fig. 6-1).

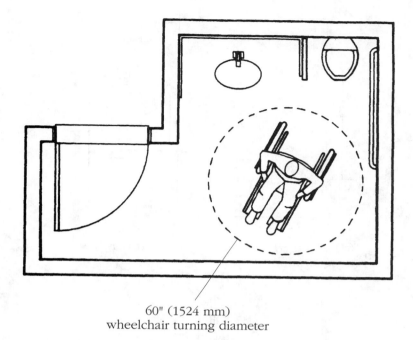

60" (1524 mm)
wheelchair turning diameter

6-1 *Required space for a wheelchair to make a 360° turn.* Eastern
Paralyzed Veterans Association

2 You should have at least 30" × 48" (76 × 122 cm) of clear
floor space in front of a wash basin to allow a forward
approach and this clear floor space can extend up to 19" (48
cm) under the wash basin (Fig. 6-2).

3 Insulate or conceal hot water pipes under a roll-under vanity
top (34" (86 cm) maximum from top of counter to floor and
29" (82 cm) minimum from underside of sink to floor) to
prevent burns (Fig. 6-3).

4 Install loop or single-lever faucet handles.

5 Faucets should be equipped with anti-scald temperature
controls.

6 Figure 6-4 is an overall view of the clear floor space required
for wheelchair access to a toilet and wash basin (not a stall).
The minimum required space in front of the toilet is 48" (122
cm). According to Fig. 6-4, the 48" (122 cm) can be obtained
but it depends on the depth of the toilet to be installed (i.e.,
its distance from the wall). Otherwise, you might require an
area (from wall to wall) somewhere between 75" and 79"
(191 and 201 cm).

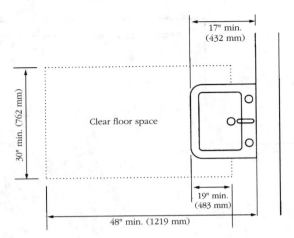

6-2 *Required floor space for a barrier-free wash basin.* American Standard Inc.

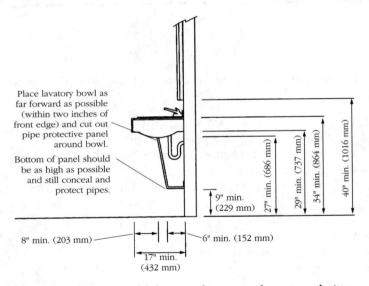

6-3 *Don't forget to add the panel to cover the exposed pipes.*
American Standard Inc.

7 Notice the height and placement of the handrails and toilet paper dispenser in the water closet (W.C.). The toilet should be mounted between 17" and 19" (43 and 48 cm) to the top of the seat (Fig. 6-5), but check with your customer. They might appreciate having the seat higher or lower. The floor dimensions given in Fig. 6-5 are allowed for a slide wheelchair transfer in a stall.

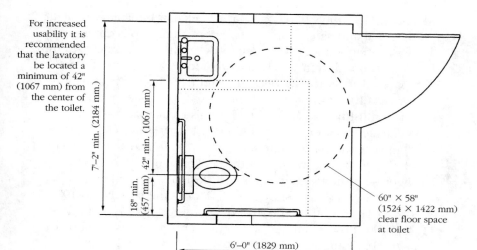

For increased usability it is recommended that the lavatory be located a minimum of 42" (1067 mm) from the center of the toilet.

7'-2" min. (2184 mm)

42" min. (1067 mm)

18" min. (457 mm)

6'-0" (1829 mm)

60" × 58" (1524 × 1422 mm) clear floor space at toilet

6-4 *Notice the 18" (462 mm) from the center of the toilet to the interior wall.*
American Standard Inc.

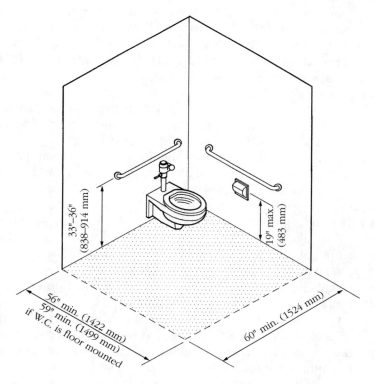

33"–36" (838–914 mm)

19" max. (483 mm)

56" min. (1422 mm)
59" min. (1499 mm) if W.C. is floor mounted

60" min. (1524 mm)

6-5 *Three-dimensional view of a wall-mounted toilet.* Eastern Paralyzed Veterans Association

8 Figure 6-6 shows two common wheelchair transfers to toilets: diagonal and side approaches. Be aware that placement of a wash basin immediately to the side of the toilet precludes the side approach transfer. To accommodate a side transfer, the space adjacent to the toilet must remain clear of obstruction for 42" (107 cm) from the centerline of the toilet and a wash basin must not be located within this clear space.

9 A transfer shower stall should be at least 36" (91 cm) square with seat and have a minimum of 36" × 48" (91 × 122 cm) of clear floor space in front of the stall (Fig. 6-7).

10 Figure 6-8 shows the proper seat design and maximum measurements for a shower stall. Mount the seat 17" to 19" (43 to 48 cm) off the floor or as requested by the customer.

11 A roll-in shower can be used in the same space as a standard bathtub, requiring a minimum of 30" × 60" (76 × 152 cm) without a seat (but install a grab bar around the stall). The minimum clear floor space is 36" × 48" (91 × 122 cm) (Fig. 6-9).

12 Another option is an easy-access bath with removable seat (standard 5' (152 cm) tub) or a permanent seat unit (5' (152 cm) plus a 15" (38 cm) allowance for the seat). There must be 30" (76 cm) of clear floor space in front of the tub when approaching from the end (head) and 48" (122 cm) if the tub is approached straight-on (side) (Fig. 6-10).

13 A motorized tub lift can lower a person into the water automatically or, for the less disabled, a removable bathtub seat is convenient. (There are also bathtubs with doors in one side; see Fig. 6-25 later in this chapter.)

14 An enlarged bathroom door should have a minimum 32" (81 cm) clear width (36" (91 cm) is preferred) from the doorstop to the face of the door when it is open in a 90° position to provide access for a wheelchair.

15 The bathroom door should open outward. If a person should fall up against the door, the door can still be opened. (This would require 5' (152 cm) clear for the door in the hallway—a pocket door might be a better choice.)

16 Install easy-to-grasp (lever) door handles on all doors.

17 Hallways leading to the bathroom should be widened up to 60" (152 cm); and install low-pile carpeting, direct glue down (carpeting), wooden floors, or nonslip floor materials to ease the use of walkers and wheelchairs. Individuals who do not need the assistance of a wheelchair might find handrails

18—30   18
455—760   455

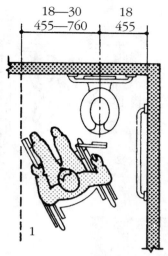

1

Takes transfer position,
swings footrest out of
the way, sets brakes.

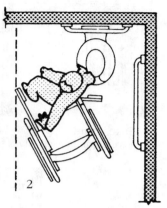

2

Removes armrest,
transfers.

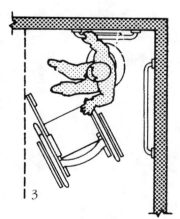

3

Moves wheelchair out
of the way, changes
position (some people
fold chair or pivot it 90°
to the toilet).

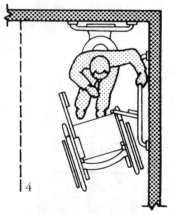

4

Positions on toilet,
releases brake.

(A) Diagonal approach

6-6 *Two wheelchair transfers.* CABO

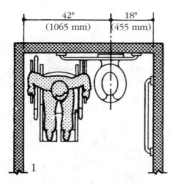

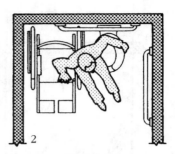

Takes transfer position,
removes armrest, sets brakes.

Transfers

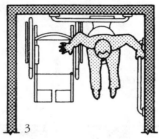

Positions on toilet

(B) Side approach

6-6 *Continued.*

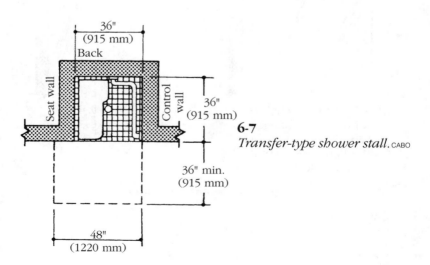

6-7
Transfer-type shower stall. CABO

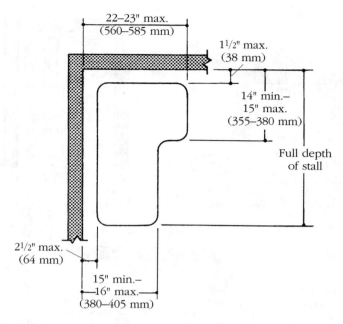

6-8 *Shower seat design.* CABO

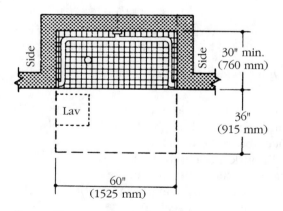

6-9 *Roll-in type shower stall.* CABO

installed in the hallway convenient. If you install handrails here, consider a railing system that blends in with the decor of the home so the rails don't look institutional. The handrails should be securely installed so that they can hold up to 250 pounds applied at any point.

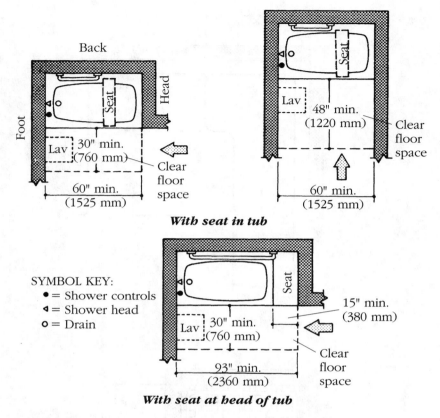

SYMBOL KEY:
- ● = Shower controls
- ◀ = Shower head
- ○ = Drain

With seat in tub

With seat at head of tub

6-10 *Clear floor space at bathtubs.* CABO

18 Consider lowering the mirror below the 38" (97 cm) maximum required height (bottom edge of the reflecting surface above the floor).

19 Install nonskid floors in the bathroom.

20 Provide adjustable-height storage.

21 Install a toilet specifically designed for wheelchair users or simply an extended seat.

22 Don't forget wall-mounted grab bars in tub/shower areas and around the toilet (diameters should be 1¼" to 1½" ([32 to 38 mm])). The space between the grab bar and wall should be 1½" (38 mm) and the unit should be secure enough to hold 250 pounds applied at any point on the grab bar. If you are remodeling the bathroom, or building new, reinforce walls behind the tub/shower and toilet with ¾" (2 cm) plywood to ensure adequate support for grab bars (or the future placement of grab bars). Using a zigzag grab bar keeps wet hands from slipping. Figure 6-11A shows grab bars installed in a bathtub area without a permanent seat while Fig. 6-11B shows them installed with a permanent seat at the head of the tub. Figure 6-12 features grab bars installed in 36" × 36" (91 × 91 cm) and 30" × 60" (91 × 152 cm) shower stalls.

23 Provide an all-direction shower head.

24 Cabinet hardware should include "D" pulls.

25 Light switches located on the wall outside the entry to bathrooms eliminate the need to enter a dark room. Better yet, install movement sensors that turn the lights on when a person enters the room and turn them off again when the person leaves the room. A similar approach is to use a delayed-action switch that leaves the light on for a few moments after the switch is turned off.

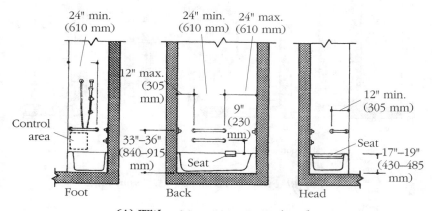

(A) **Without permanent seat in tub**

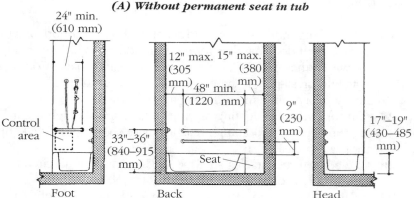

(B) **With permanent seat at head of tub**

6-11 *Grab bars in bathtub area.*CABO

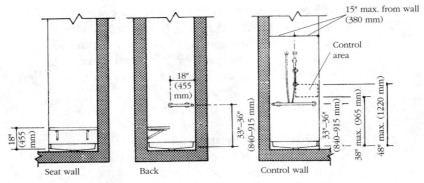

(A) 36" by 36" (915 mm by 915 mm) stall

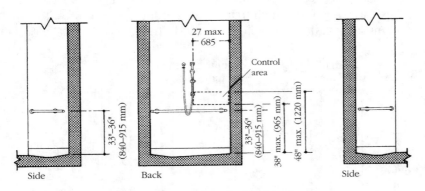

NOTE: Shower head and control area may be on back wall (as shown) or on either side wall.

(B) 30" by 60" (760 mm by 1525 mm) stall

6-12 *Grab bars in shower stalls.* CABO

26 Consider mounting switches adjacent to doors and horizontally aligned with door handles for ease in locating. Make sure they are within the reach of everyone who uses the space. Consider installing press-pad switches, which are easier to use for almost everyone than traditional toggle switches.

27 Plan for overhead lighting as well as task-specific lighting in the shower and grooming areas to make shaving and makeup application easier.

28 All electrical receptacles shall be GFCI (ground fault circuit interruptor) protected as required by the NEC.

29 For individuals who are hearing impaired, the bath light and fan should have a single switch that turns them on and off simultaneously.

30 For visually impaired persons, natural lighting, nonglare lighting, and adjustable lighting are useful.

31 Self-closing plumbing fixtures prevent accidentally leaving the water running.

32 Install a phone in the bathroom that uses an overhead light to indicate an incoming call.

The diagrams in Fig. 6-13 show two possible configurations of a bathroom with a roll-in shower. This particular shower fits exactly within the dimensions of a standard bathtub. Because the shower does not have a lip, the floor space can be considered part of the required wheelchair maneuvering space. These bathroom designs, therefore, provide enough floor space to be considered barrier-free and could be used to provide accessibility in an area where space is limited. The alternate roll-in shower (Fig. 6-13B) also provides sufficient room for the "T-turn."

This is not the final word on the subject, by any means. These are simply guidelines to be used as starting points. It is important that you be sensitive to your customer's needs to make sure that what you design and build does indeed work comfortably—and you need to know this before you start the project!

Customer specifics

One of the most frequently asked questions from a customer is "Can I make my bathroom bigger?" As you probably know from experience, enlargement is usually not an option, but still it is worth considering. Many factors come into play when determining whether enlargement is possible, and you need to ask yourself the following questions when looking at a job:

- Is the bathroom in question on the main floor?
- What kinds of rooms surround the bathroom?
- Is there living space above or below the bathroom?
- How many people live in the home?
- How many bedrooms are there?
- If you were to use space from a nearby room to enlarge the bathroom, would it detract from the resale value of the home? Will it make the other room smaller than 70 sq. ft. (6.5 m²), with a minimum 7' (213 cm) in any dimension, thus making the room nonhabitable?
- Would it cost too much to enlarge the existing bathroom?
- Is the customer planning to build an addition in the future?
- Can you plan a bathroom in the new addition?
- How large is the laundry room?

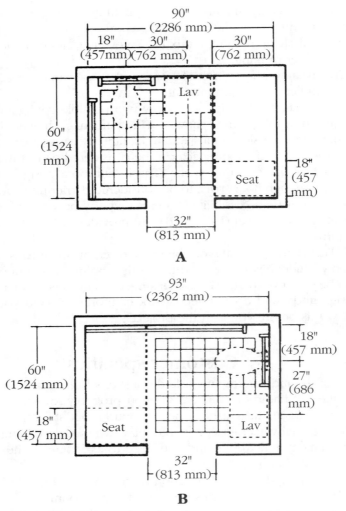

6-13 *Two barrier-free designs.* ADAAG, 7/26/91, as published in the Federal Register

- Would it be possible to add bathroom facilities to the laundry room?
- If there is more than one bathroom, would it be easier to remodel or enlarge one of them?
- Does the master bedroom have a bathroom?
- Is there room in the master bedroom for a new bathroom?

Kids' bathrooms

With commonsense planning and today's exciting new safety features, we can protect our most precious national resource—our children. In planning space needs for children, it might help to sort their activities of daily living into three categories: activities that can be done independently without difficulty or assistance, activities that are done with difficulty and/or minimal assistance, and activities that can be accomplished only with great difficulty or complete assistance. Use this analysis to pinpoint specific needs.

The clever kids' bath by Kitchen & Bath Design (shown in Fig. 6-14) features good universal design that is invisible (it blends right into the aesthetics) and emphasizes safety.

6-14 *This shipshape room is a secure home port for kids.* Gary White, CID, CKD, CBD, Kitchen & Bath Design, Newport Beach, CA

Some of the things we can do as professionals to secure kids' environments include the following:

- Install an adjustable hand-held shower head (Fig. 6-15). Nessie by Friedrich Grohe is a brightly colored hand-held shower that offers a bubbly, splash-free water flow engineered specifically for children. With their own special hand shower, children might look forward to bathtime.
- Place a temporary platform at the side of the tub for safe entry and exit.

6-15 *Nessie—named after the Loch Ness Monster.* Grohe America, Inc.

6-16 *The 24" bevel mirror cabinet is used in a recessed application.* Robern, Inc.

- Create a space for platform or step stool storage. Figure 6-16 shows a good example of pull-out step stools for children to reach the faucet or see themselves in the mirror.
- Lower mirrors and cabinets.
- Install a medicine storage lock box. Protect children from accidental poisonings or other dangers from prescription medications, razors, cosmetics, and personal care items all normally stored in a bathroom. Figure 6-17 shows a Safety Lock Box by Robern, Inc., in both the open and secured positions.
- Install grab bars, especially at the entry to the shower and tub.
- Install slip-resistant flooring.
- Use single-control lever-style scald-resistant faucets. Figure 6-18 shows a SCALDSafe Tub Spout Hot Water Sensor (Resources Conservation) that automatically shuts off the water flow when the water temperature reaches 114°, well below 120° (where scald injuries begin to occur).
- All electrical receptacles should be GFCI-protected as required by the NED. You might want to childproof the receptacles (i.e., secure them behind plastic covers when not in use). Shatterproof light fixtures are also recommended.

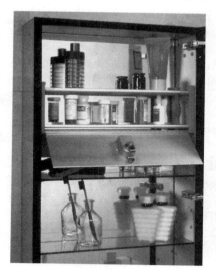

A   *B*

6-17 *Open (A) or closed (B) for secure storage. This storage compartment can be located anywhere a shelf can be placed in the cabinet.*
Robern, Inc.

6-18 *SCALDSafe—Hot Water Sensors by Resources Conservation, Inc.*

Accessible products

Product awareness plays a very important role in your design. These are the products that have to conform to your customer's needs. Stay on top of barrier-free products—be sure that your personal library is up to date. It wouldn't hurt to visit supply houses to investigate the newest and latest products. If you have not already done so, establish relationships with your local rehabilitation center, occupational therapists, physical therapists, and so on; they have access to products through channels that might not be available to the general public. The following products are worth checking out:

Plumbing

American-Standard and Pressalit together have created a Multi System Bathroom. The Pressalit products are capable of moving up and down and sideways on the Multi Track system, providing flexibility for individuals with physical limitations by allowing bathroom fixtures and other accessories to be moved to more comfortable levels and to gain additional space. This special feature allows individuals to remain independent as long as possible. Independence is very important to your customers!

The Multi System Shower Chair can easily be adjusted: the seat and support arms can be repositioned both vertically and horizontally and components can be added or removed. The Ceratherm (American-Standard) valve and hand-held Sport provide the ultimate in convenience and safety with two built-in anti-scald protections and an anti-chill feature.

The Multi System and Tilche wash basin combination can be adjusted for everyone from the tallest adult (or an adult with back pain) to the smallest toddler. Furthermore, this height-adjustable wash basin can be set for comfortable use from any wheelchair, even from those with trays or electronic controls mounted on the armrests. The smooth, light-pressure Wrist Blade lever handles on the Lift faucet (with ceramic disk valve) complete the versatility and comfort of this Multi System Lavatory (Fig. 6-19)!

6-19 *You may choose a simple shower seat or select the larger contoured shower chair with backrest (shown).* American Standard Inc.

Be aware that this system incorporates a flexible drain assembly, which might violate plumbing codes because of the depth of the trap seal. When the wash basin is adjusted to its lowest position, the flexible drain results in a trap seal depth of 8" to 9" (20 to 23 cm), which exceeds the code maximum of 4" (10 cm). Because there are so many benefits to this product, contact your local building/plumbing department for information on obtaining "alternate approvals."

Kohler's Interlude Lavatory permits full wheelchair accessibility and convenient countertop installation for residential and commercial use. The wash basin slopes to the rear, positioning the drain out of the way of a wheelchair user's legs. The attractive half-round shape and straight front permit forward positioning of the wash basin in the countertop for easy reach. The wash basin measures 19¾₆" × 24⅛"

× 6⁷⁄₁₆" deep (23 × 61 × 16 cm) and conforms to the latest accessibility requirements for toe, leg, and knee clearances. Figure 6-20 shows Kohler's Touchless faucet.

6-20 *Design of Interlude Lavatory.* Photo courtesy of Kohler Co.

Showers/tubs

Universal-Rundle produces a 64" × 64" × 80" (163 × 163 × 203 cm) gel-coated fiberglass one-piece unit especially designed for wheelchair users called the Liberte. The unit comes with grab bars (1½" ([38 mm]) O.D.), a slip-resistant floor mat, a fold-down seat (either left or right), and an entry ramp (Fig. 6-21).

Aqua Glass creates a Special Care unit with a unique style. The model SC6183 presents both aesthetics and utility in one handsome 5' (152 cm) acrylic tub/shower unit designed for the bather's maximum comfort, convenience, and confidence. Access to the bathing area is made easier by a removable teakwood transfer seat and five strategically positioned stainless steel grab bars. The unit features a hand-held shower with a bar mount that allows varying height adjustments, and a soap dish and corner shampoo shelf molded into each unit. An optional dome light is also available (Fig. 6-22).

Maxx Inc. offers an acrylic shower stall that is 55" × 48" × 84¾" (140 × 122 × 215 cm). The model 54HS has two molded soap trays, 54" and 30" (137 and 76 cm) above the shower floor and on the same side as the valves are installed. Two wall brackets are installed 42"

6-21
A good bird's eye view of the shower stall from the top down. Universal-Rundle Corp.

6-22 *This unit fits nicely into the wall.* Aqua Glass Corporation

and 66" (107 and 168 cm) above the floor for use with a hand-held shower. One stainless steel seamless 1" (25 mm) diameter, 18-gauge curtain rod is installed 76" (193 cm) above the shower floor. The unit can be ordered with a seat which has two 30" (76 cm) grab bars or without a seat, in which case there will be three grab bars, all installed 36" (91 cm) above the floor horizontally (Fig. 6-23).

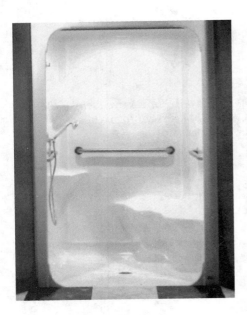

6-23
Notice the shower floor is even with the floor. Maax Inc.

Jacuzzi Whirlpool Bath refines the shower with its J-Dream shower and steam system. This state-of-the-art shower unit contains easy-glide, tempered glass doors as well as a newly designed electronic control system featuring a user-friendly control pad with color diagrams and digital readouts. The J-Dream offers a customized, hand-held showerhead and 16 vertical, programmable jets. The unit incorporates a soothing steam system with overhead cascade and sculpted seat. An optional stereo system that includes an AM/FM radio, CD player and four speakers can be added. The unit measures 60" long × 36" wide × 85" high (152 × 91 × 216 cm) (Fig. 6-24).

Florestone Products Company has an assortment of quality shower and bath products. Call them at 800-446-8827 for a copy of their *Barrier-Free Wheelchair Accessible Institutional,* which covers baths, showers, shower receptors, and bath/shower combinations. They also carry utility sinks for use in laundry rooms.

Silcraft Corporation offers the model Access 3700, which is a side-entry personal-size spa, tub, and whirlpool bath. With its comfortable seat and contoured interior, this unit was designed for maximum comfort, relaxation, and accessibility, while requiring minimum space. The swing-away door allows easy entry and exit. No longer is it necessary to climb over the edge of the tub: a customer can simply slide in and enjoy luxury and convenience. The system is designed to be used with or without a transfer device. A removable access panel allows a lift and transfer device to roll under the tub (Fig. 6-25).

6-24
J-Dream by Jacuzzi Whirlpool Bath.

6-25 *Designed to be installed into a standard 5' tub recess area.* Silcraft Corporation

International Cushioned Products has a unique bathtub that comfortably conforms to the body once hot water is added. This bathtub is also available as a whirlpool bath. The nonslip surface of this tub minimizes the risk of a fall and greatly reduces the chance of injury should a fall occur (Fig. 6-26).

6-26
*A product that is soft and durable
and saves energy.*
International Cushioned Products

E. L. Mustee & Sons, Inc., have designed a product called DURABASE which is a fiberglass shower floor that can replace a standard 5' (152 cm) bathtub. The shower floor system features a molded fiberglass 30" × 60" (76 × 152 cm) floor and 12" × 60" (30 × 152 cm) entry ramp. The two-piece unit can be used in new construction and is ideal for commercial installations in hotels/motels, hospitals/nursing homes, and other related locations. Replumbing is not required (Fig. 6-27).

6-27 *Entry ramp provides easy ADA-approved wheelchair access on a slip-resistant surface.* E.L. Mustee & Sons, Inc.

Faucets

Gemini Bath & Kitchen Products' ARWA-Clinic faucets are fitted with handles requiring low operating force. The Clinic handle is a "no-grasp" variation and requires only an elbow, arm, or back of the hand (closed fist) to operate. It is molded from unbreakable, easy-to-clean thermo-engineered polymer material. The main advantages of this unit include:

- The basic position of the handle can be quickly adjusted for greater flexibility of flow control.
- It is resilient and manufactured with high-viscosity chemically resistant material, which offers safety against accidents.
- The standard grips can be custom formed to special user needs.

This faucet covers a full range of applications in residential, nursing homes, clinics, hospitals, and the medical/dental market (Fig. 6-28).

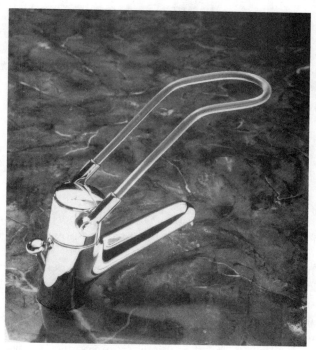

6-28 *A well-designed faucet.* Gemini Bath & Kitchen Products

Alsons has three sleek European-styled hand showers, one for every lifestyle. The zesty Massage Action Model 425 provides a full invigorating massage spray, or it can switch over to a fine tingling full-body spray. The practical Clog-Free Full Spray Model 426 produces a strong comforting full-body spray through unique rubber orifices. Mineral deposits in these orifices can be dislodged by gently rubbing the orifice with your fingers, keeping the hand shower clog-free. The Classic Full Spray Model 427 brings new styling to the traditional multiholed spray plate to produce the classic gentle rain of a sprinkling can (Fig. 6-29).

6-29
Hand-held shower makes life a little simpler. Alsons

Interbath introduces InTouch ORGANIZATION with an array of practical accessories to decorate the bath or shower wall including the following items:

- The Basket stores shampoo bottles of any description, right side up or upside down, as well as the occasional rubber duck and almost anything else.
- The Soap Dish has small elastomer buttons to keep soap high and dry; its slots permit quick drainage.
- The V-Shelf holds other things, from sponges to toothpaste. Hang brushes or other items from two integral hooks on the backside.
- The Racquet Shelf is a flat, specially woven nylon net that captures toothbrushes, razors, and other slender items.
- The Hook is a convenient accessory on which to hang yet more items.
- The Ring holds the wash cloth or drying hosiery.

Figure 6-30 shows The Handshower Caddie, which includes a 24" (61 cm) Hi-Lo Slide Bar, The Basket, The Soap Dish, The Hook, and The Classic II Massage Shower on an integral three-position mount. The bar has self-adhesive backing and is easily installed. Screws and anchors are included for optional installation. Accessories slide easily onto the Bar and can be instantly adjusted for the most convenient reach.

6-30
*An easy way to improve
any bathing area.* Interbath, Inc.

Shower doors

Tub-Master Corporation has a barrier-free shower door that offers individuals with special needs safe and easy access to their showers. The door folds completely out of the way for almost full access to the shower area. The panels of the door are translucent Polystyrene that won't crack or shatter and allow light into the bathing area (according to the manufacturer). The specially designed bottom track creates a small dam but still allows easy roll-over for a wheelchair user (Fig. 6-31).

Sterling Plumbing Group features a revolutionary design and unique concept: the door slides back, swings out, and swings inward to disappear. The FreeStyle unit is designed without top and bottom tracks, which eliminates the possibility of bumping your head on the upper track, and it allows no collection of water, mildew, and bacteria. Overall, this provides clean and easy access to the tub/shower that your customers and their children will enjoy using (Fig. 6-32).

Lighting/ventilation

Natural lighting adds real value to any home. It also helps give small areas a feeling of the outdoors. Whenever possible, try to include nat-

6-31 *Makes it easy for wheelchair maneuvering.* Tub-Master Corporation

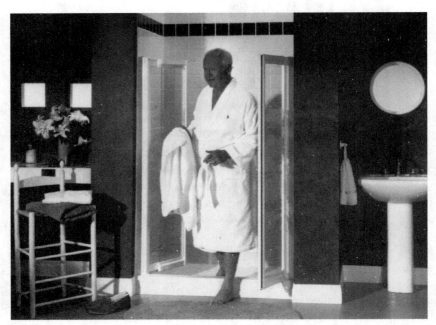

6-32 *Safe and convenient access for people of all ages.* Sterling Plumbing Group, Inc., A Kohler Company

ural lighting. Figure 6-33 is a good example; it shows a bathroom featuring a curtain of glass blocks that fill the room with natural light. The two different patterns and sizes of glass blocks give this curved exterior wall a distinctive look (12" × 12" ([30 × 30 cm]) Decora and 6" × 6" ([15 × 15 cm]) Argus from Pittsburgh Corning Corporation). The glass blocks let in light but protect the bather's privacy by distorting

6-33 *It's almost like bathing outside.* Pittsburgh Corning Corporation

the view from either side. The mirror on the adjacent wall complements the openness of the bathroom.

Broan produces SensAire bath fans designed to automatically turn on in response to motion, increasing humidity, or both—removing damage-causing moisture from bathrooms and other commonly used areas. In situations when it is difficult to turn on and off a switch, this product offers "hands-free" operation. The unit is designed to use a switch if desired and is controlled by a single two-wire receptacle (normally modern units require three wires), which makes it great for retrofit. It is also available as a fan/light/night-light combination.

Unique products

Hinge-It Corporation has an exciting product that can be used in spaces that are ordinarily overlooked (i.e., behind a bathroom door). This is a great place for a Eurorack. The model 3000 three-loop design offers users six 18" (46 cm) wide areas for towels or for hanging hand washables. Because it hangs off existing door hinges, it is easy to install without measuring, holes, or marks: Just pop the pin and drop it in the adjustable brackets. A heated version—great for warming up towels—is also available (Fig. 6-34).

White Home Products Inc. provides a solution to the universal problem of storage. The automatic Closet Carousel makes closet space (minimum 6' × 4'6" ([183 × 137 cm]) deep) more efficient and helps to make newly created storage space both practical and luxurious. This has always been my wife's dream—to step from the bathroom into a walk-in closet featuring a carousel that operates at the push of a button.

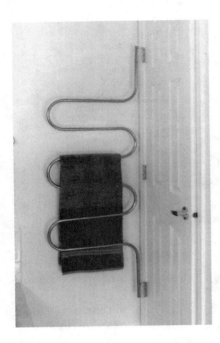

6-34
*So convenient your customers will
use it every day.* Hinge-It Corporation

PPP Manufacturing Company has a unique tub stopper called Flip-It. Made of chrome-plated ABS plastic and delrin, it replaces linkages, stoppers, buckets, and spring tub stoppers with one unit that fits directly into the drain. No tools or hardware are needed for installation. The product was designed to eliminate troublesome trip lever parts and stoppers and the bending or stooping required to close a drain. Now with a simple flip of the toe, a drain can be closed or opened (Fig. 6-35).

Assistive equipment/products

To millions of Americans, a simple, common, and personal daily activity can be awkward, difficult, or painful: using the toilet and effectively handling toilet paper. This difficulty affects the aging, those suffering illness, or anyone who is physically disabled.

Now with the introduction of a remarkable product called Lu-bidet, people with special needs (and everyone else) can experience a new dimension in personal hygiene. It is a dignified solution for those who need assistance using the toilet. The product can be mounted for right- or left-handed operation on most toilets to deliver a warm-water wash and air dry, simply and easily, every time you use the toilet. This is a good product to consider when there is no room for another plumbing fixture (Fig. 6-36).

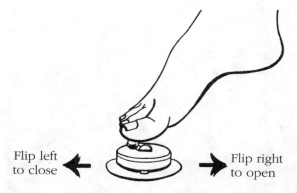

Flip left
to close

Flip right
to open

6-35 *No bending or stooping—just open or close with a simple flip of the toe.*
PPP Manufacturing Company

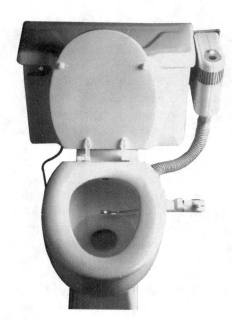

6-36
A product such as this can make a difference in our lives every day. Lubidet USA Inc.

Frohock-Stewart Inc. features bath safety products designed for independent living. For 40 years they have specialized in the design, manufacturing, and marketing of safety products for bathrooms. Figure 6-37 features the following products:

- Wall grab bars
- Transfer bench with back
- 5" (13 cm) elevated toilet seat
- Toilet guardrails

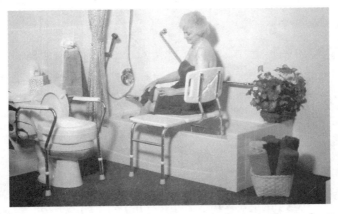

6-37 *After-market products can assist in independent living.* Frohock-Stewart Inc.

HEWI, Inc., manufactures an L-shaped shower seat that is designed to meet the requirements of ADA and ANSI. The seat is made of high-quality nylon with corrosion-resistant steel inserts in the frame and mounting bracket. The solid nylon slats offer the additional advantage of a nonporous surface which is sanitary and easy to clean. Nylon is always comfortable to the touch because it retains a moderate temperature and does not transmit static electricity. The 28½" (72 cm) wide seat is available in 13 colors to complement any interior design (Fig. 6-38).

T.F. Herceg, Inc./Handi-Move International offers a variety of permanent and portable SUREHANDS Lift & Care Systems for homes and workplaces. The automatic adjusting body support ensures a gentle, easy, and secure transfer without the use of a sling. This unit provides the freedom to raise and lower a person while the support automatically adjusts and embraces the thorax as it is raised. Users with active arm and upper body movement can, in many cases, transfer independently.

SUREHANDS systems are available in a variety of models and offer assistance in transferring, bathing, hygiene care, positioning, standing, walking and exercising (Fig. 6-39). When installing a product such as the track-mount system shown in Fig. 6-39, make sure that there is adequate framing for support.

Guardian Products Inc. has quite a collection of home comfort and safety products. One that I found interesting was the tub grab bar shown in Fig. 6-40. This bilevel grab bar allows for a proper grasp when entering or exiting a tub. It has a texture-coated finish for a sure, nonslip grip. Large rubber lined pads fit securely yet won't mar the existing tub surface and can be installed without the use of tools. And, since it is portable, your customer can take it when traveling or visiting.

6-38 *The L-shaped seat requires wood blocking in the wall for adequate support.* Hewi, Inc.

6-39
Finally, a lift and care system as versatile as a pair of hands.
T.F. Herceg, Inc.

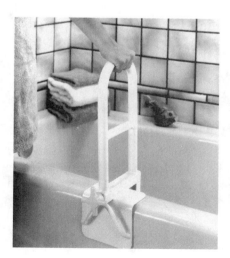

6-40
Height above tub wall is 15".
Guardian Products Inc.

Finally, Sears' Home HealthCare catalog is also full of home care products—give them a call at 800-948-8800 to receive your copy.

All of the products shown or described in this section represent only a small fraction of the home care products available. When requesting information or asking for a catalog, be sure to request a full-line catalog. The full-line catalog will show all the products available from each company. Some companies will customize their products to fit your particular job. If you are unable to find what you are looking for, be sure to ask the companies listed throughout *Accessible Housing*. The important thing is to stay on top of what's available.

Kitchens

As *Accessible Housing* has already pointed out, "barrier-free design" is one way to make life easier, more convenient, and more pleasant for everyone. Whether it's a child in a wheelchair because of multiple sclerosis or an older adult with arthritic joints, people who are disabled have a variety of special needs that can be met with barrier-free design and construction. The same considerations applied to bathrooms also apply to kitchens.

Gary White, CID, CKD, CBD, of Kitchen & Bath Design comments:

Over a quarter of a million people are seriously injured in the kitchen and bath of their own homes each year. In fact, the kitchen and bath are the two most dangerous things you own next to your automobile. All of us are aware of the value of seatbelts, antilock brakes, and air bags for our vehicles, but what do you know about pressure-balanced valves or ground fault devices in your home? And the good news is proper safety design is also good looking and easier to clean.

The latest trends in materials, styles, appliances, and related products for the kitchen are discussed in following section.

Accessible kitchens

Some of the information contained in this section is from the *Kitchen Industry Technical Manuals* published by the NKBA (mentioned earlier in this chapter). In general, kitchens require three special considerations in barrier-free design:

- Wheelchair mobility
- Work space comfort
- Accessibility to cabinets and storage spaces

When planning a kitchen for a wheelchair user, be sure to know the wheelchair's measurements, and don't forget that the user might change to a different-sized wheelchair in the future. Of special importance is the front-to-back measurement—including foot rests—because this measurement determines the turning radius, which is normally 60" (152 cm) (25 sq. ft. or 2.3 m²) for a full 360° turn. The clear floor space for cabinet-to-wall and cabinet-to-cabinet is 60" (152 cm) minimum.

- The usual height at the top of a wheelchair armrest is approximately 29" (74 cm). This is important for easy movement under countertops.
- Space for knees requires a height that is at least 24" (61 cm) from the floor and approximately 30" (76 cm) in width (36" ([91 cm]) is preferred).
- The recommended countertop height is a minimum of 27" (69 cm) from the finished floor to the underside of the countertop and should be no greater than 34" (86 cm) to the finished top. The maximum thickness of the countertop is 2" (5 cm).
- For a 24" (61 cm) standard countertop depth, the first 19" (48 cm) is considered to be easy access for the user—the remainder is ideal for storage.
- The toe kick of the cabinet should be 6" (15 cm) maximum in depth and 9" (23 cm) minimum in height.
- Breadboards, chopping blocks, or pull-out work surfaces are most functional when installed 27" (69 cm) off the floor and are a minimum 30" (76 cm) wide and 24" (61 cm) deep. Depending on the manufacturer of prebuilt cabinets, you might find the maximum width for a bread board will be 24" (61 cm). Be sure to ascertain your customer's preferences (Fig. 6-41).
- Insulate hot water pipes and drains in the open area under the sink to prevent burns.
- Remember, entry doors should have a net (clear) opening of 32" (81 cm) measured from the doorstop to the door's face when the door is in a 90° open position. Use a lever-style door handle. Again, the force required to push or pull interior doors open cannot exceed five pounds.

Cleanup area

Meal preparation under sanitary conditions and cleanup go hand in hand. Be sure to discuss with your customers their specific needs in this area. The following are general specifications and suggestions:

- The sink should be shallow, only 5" to 6½" (13 to 17 cm) deep.
- The faucet should be a loop or single lever (Fig. 6-42) for easy operation.

6-41 *Chopping block kit that includes a 2¼" high drawer box and 1¼" solid maple box.* Kraftmaid Cabinetry, Inc.

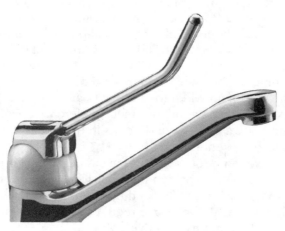

6-42 *Accessibility Handle #512 by Franke.* Franke Inc.

- Consider an infrared sensor faucet that automatically activates the water flow at preset temperatures.
- The drain should be located at the rear, especially if a garbage disposal is installed. The whole idea is to keep the knee space below the sink clear.

- Hot water dispensers prevent individuals from having to lug pots of water to and from a range.
- Install a second basin with a side-mounted faucet located in a lower counter.
- Install a mechanical basin that lowers and raises with the touch of a button (Fig. 6-43).

6-43 *With a touch of a button, the unit can adapt to a wheelchair user or someone tall.* Real Life Design—GE Appliances

Manufacturers are designing products every day to meet ADA regulations as well as the needs of consumers. Kohler Co. offers AS-SURE, a complete work station with the addition of an optional polyethylene cutting board, colander, and drainboard. This enameled cast iron wheelchair-accessible sink features a front apron that curves gently inward to bring the basins closer to a wheelchair user. The overall measurement is 36" × 24" (91 × 61 cm) (Fig. 6-44).

The ASSURE sink is equipped with two basins—a large 20⅝" × 15⅞" × 6¼" (52 × 40 × 16 cm) basin and a smaller one, measuring 6½" × 18⅛" × 4¼" (17 × 46 × 11 cm). The faucet deck has been brought forward for easy reach. The faucet shown in the picture is "Coralais," also by Kohler. Notice the integral pull-out spray head. The single-handle model comes with a standard 9½" (24 cm) spout and a push button control on the head for easy one-touch switching from stream to spray.

Pedal Valves, Inc., introduces the PEDALWORKS Faucet Controller. This product can address several needs associated with faucet knobs, for example:

- How to turn on the faucets when hands are messy.
- How to turn on the water when hands are full.
- How to avoid wasting hot and cold water while rinsing dishes. .

6-44 ASSURE—*A complete work station by Kohler Co.*
Photo cortesy of Kohler Co.

PEDALWORKS is installed into the sink cabinet with the pedal heads in the toe kick area. The user presets the temperature and pressure (the water is kept on at all times) with the faucet knobs; the pedal is used to turn the water off or on. A latch to hold the pedal down is incorporated into this design and is activated when the user pushes in a toe button located on the pedal shaft. Engaging the latch also allows the user to switch to regular hand control—turning the faucet off and on by hand. These features provide complete operational flexibility (Fig. 6-45).

Ultraflo Corporation produces a push button electronic plumbing system. The system is installed using only one supply line instead of the conventional two lines (hot and cold). Water usage in kitchens and bathrooms (including showers) can be activated by a solid state switch pad at each receptacle, allowing the user to select the correct temperature at the touch of a button. The switch can be mounted in the face of a cabinet for easy access for wheelchair users. Individual temperature and flow rates are preselected to assure consistency and are adjustable to suit any user's preferences (Fig. 6-46). This product could be used both in the residential and commercial markets.

Other considerations

When designing an accessible kitchen, don't forget the following:
- Use glare-free lighting and lower or install switches, thermostats, and rheostats no higher than 48" (122 cm) off the floor. Electrical receptacles should be no lower than 15" (38 cm) off the floor. Also consider that the electrical service panel should be reachable and accessible. Be sure to consult

6-45
It's a great convenience.
PEDALWORKS™ is a trademark of Pedal Valves Inc., Luling, LA

6-46 *Stretching across a basin to turn on faucets is no longer necessary.* Ultraflo Corporation

with your customer, because "reachable and accessible" for you might not apply to the customer. Consider installing the panel in the kitchen area.

- Install glare-free cabinets with low-gloss laminate.
- Install or lower wall cabinets closer to the countertop and install roll-out shelves (Fig. 6-47) and drawers with full extension glides. If you are not able to lower upper cabinets, then consider the Liftshelf Storage Retrieval System by Accessible Work Systems Inc. This unique system operates on 115 volts and comes complete with harness and switches and in widths of 18" and 21" (46 and 53 cm). A rocker switch powers a set of shelves to pivot out and down from an overhead storage cabinet to the countertop below. In the

6-47
*A pull-out base mini-pantry
cabinet that is accessible
from both sides.* KraftMaid Cabinetry, Inc.

down position, the shelves are accessible even from a
wheelchair.

- Install pull-out trash cans, swing-out spice racks, or roll-out
  half-blind shelves (lazy Susans), and a pull-out ironing board.
- Vary countertop heights; for example, install a dishwasher in
  a countertop height of 45" (114 cm), counters at the standard
  36" (91 cm) height, and a center work island at a lower 28"
  (71 cm) height.
- Use solid surface material for countertops before considering
  tile (harder to clean), but tile is OK for backsplashes.
- Round corners around all countertops.
- Use soft-ease edges on countertops.
- Install some type of built-in hot plate/cutting board. Vance
  Industries, Inc., has a product called the Surface Saver—a
  tempered glass food preparation product. The nonporous
  surface will not burn, mark, stain, or scorch and is impact-
  resistant. Their portable unit can be installed into the counter
  by using a mounting frame, available in stainless steel, white,
  or almond (Fig. 6-48).
- Install drawer organizers. Figure 6-49 shows a silverware
  organizer by Vance Industries, Inc., that easily trims for a
  custom fit and increases drawer capacity without requiring
  drawer modification.
- Install slide-out baskets under the basin (Fig. 6-50).

6-48 *The nonporous surface provides a sanitary surface for preparing food.* Vance Industries, Inc.

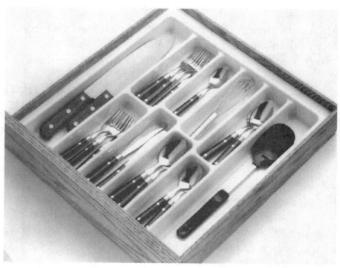

6-49 *Neatly organizes any drawer.* Vance Industries, Inc.

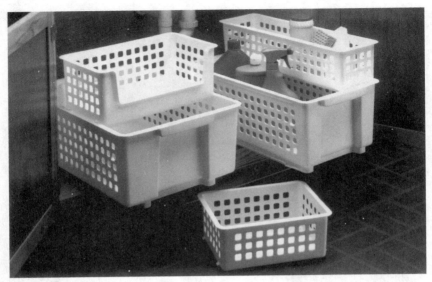

6-50 *Household supplies slide into easy reach with this storage system.*
Slide'n Stack Sliding Basket, Rubbermaid Incorporated

- Install an automated shelving system for kitchens or pantries. White Home Products has a system that provides over 30 sq. ft. (2.8 m²) of storage in one central location. Shelves rotate vertically, utilizing full cubic footage (Fig. 6-51).
- Use loop- or D- and C-shaped pulls for cabinet and closet hardware.
- Make sure that a fire extinguisher is located within easy reach of the oven and range.
- Don't forget the details—provide an adjustable height towel holder.
- A mirror suspended above the cooking area allows extra vision for a seated person.

Hearing impaired

People who are deaf or hard of hearing have special needs in the kitchen. Consider the following suggestions:

- Eating areas should be sized to encourage the use of round tables that give individuals a clear view of each other.
- The range hood light and fan should have a single switch that turns them on and off simultaneously.
- The garbage disposal switch should include a light to signal when the unit is on.

6-51
This unit comes complete with battery pack operation in the event of a power failure. White Home Products Inc.

- The kitchen should be open to the family room and/or dining area for a clear sight line. The sink should face both the activity areas and the entry, if possible; don't block visibility by hanging cabinets over peninsulas.

Vision impaired

If your customer is vision impaired, consider the following:
- Edges of counters should be a different color and corners should be rounded.
- The range or cooktop should have a "hot surface" indicator light so the user can tell whether the burner is on or off.
- Dryers should feature audible lint signals that sound when it is time to clean the lint screen—this would be especially helpful to individuals who have difficulty seeing light-colored lint.

Appliances

The correct placement of appliances can help your customers work safely and effectively in their kitchens.
- Lower or install the wall oven and microwave between 24" (61 cm) and 48" (122 cm) from the bottom of the appliance to the finish floor. Install a pull-out or rolling table beneath the appliance (Fig. 6-52).

6-52
This rolling table can easily be moved around the kitchen to assist in food preparation, serving, or cleanup. Real Life Design—GE Appliances

- Raise the dishwasher 6" to 8" (15 to 20 cm) off the floor and locate the unit so it is accessible from either side (Fig. 6-53). Asko features a compact dishwasher that measures 19½" high × 21⅞" wide × 22⅞₆" deep (50 × 56 × 57 cm), which means this unit can fit on or above standard countertops, similar to the installation of a microwave (Fig. 6-54).
- Change the gas range to an electric unit with staggered burners and mount easy-to-hold and easy-to-turn controls on the top and to the front or below the unit to eliminate reaching across hot burners. Figure 6-55 features a self-cleaning smooth top range (model #6898V4V) by Magic Chef. The slanted control panel features recessed control knobs that are easy to hold and to turn. In addition, the front positioning of the knobs and signal lights on the control panel make this range easier and safer for wheelchair users.

6-53
The same rolling table can be used when unloading the dishwasher. Real Life Design—GE Appliances

6-54
This unit can be installed where full-sized dishwashers won't fit! Asko, Inc.

6-55 *Even a drawer for storing pots and pans.* Courtesy of Jenn-Air

- Built-in cooktops also need staggered burners and mounted easy-to-hold and easy-to-turn controls on the top and toward the front (Fig. 6-56).
- Install a retractable downdraft hood that is raised at the touch of a button.
- Consider installing a side-by-side refrigerator. The width of the doors makes them lightweight to open and puts foods within reach.

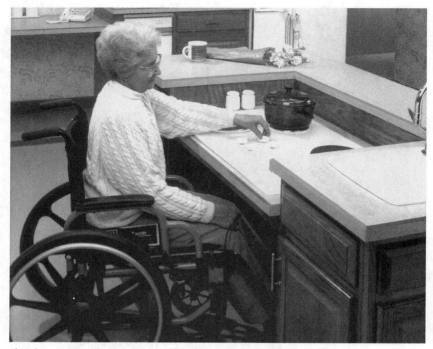

6-56 *Good example of an installed built-in cooktop.* Whirlpool Home Appliances

- Place a compact refrigerator next to a bed, family room chair, or bathroom counter to save trips to the kitchen.
- Consider installing a compact range-sink-refrigerator unit (mini-kitchen) with an undercounter refrigerator.

Dwyer Products Corporation offers a mini-kitchen unit as well as kitchen design options for easy accessibility by the physically disabled in Series HC (accessible kitchens) and Series AH (adjustable accessible kitchen). Numerous modifications and options are available, allowing builders and remodelers the flexibility to design a kitchen to meet individual needs. Dwyer's units can be integrated into any decor, including commercial and institutional applications. For free design assistance, contact Dwyer at 800-348-8508 (Fig. 6-57).

King Refrigerator Corporation has been manufacturing mini-kitchens for over 60 years, and they have a variety of combination units that might fit your project. The stainless steel top helps keep maintenance needs down. One advantage of this type of compact unit is that it can help convert a room without a major renovation (Fig. 6-58).

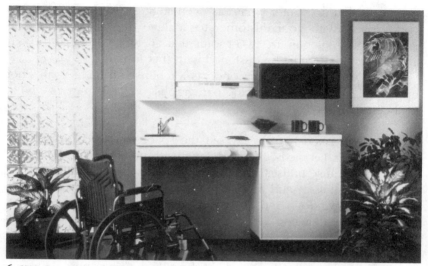

6-57 *Great product to incorporate into a bedroom.* Dwyer Products Corp.

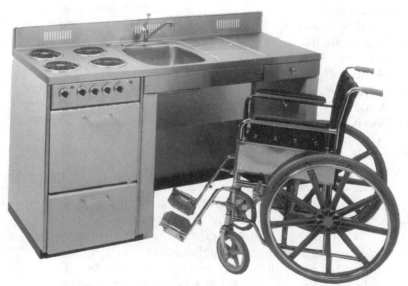

6-58 *Model KF60E-HAN specially designed for wheelchair users.*
King Refrigerator Corp., Glendale, NY 11385

Layout

The information up to this point should help to get your design in motion. The following section should help you to complete the design. As I have stressed repeatedly, the most important thing to remember is that no matter what has been suggested, you still need to work closely with your customer to achieve the best design. The bathroom and kitchen are two rooms that are very personal to your customer, so they must be designed with that in mind.

Linda Nitteberg, CKD, of Concepts Kitchens and Baths shares her input on design in the following paragraphs, which summarize what has been discussed so far:

I'm often asked how to lay out the space for a person in a wheelchair. Let me begin by saying there's no one right answer to this because houses are all different. They come in different shapes and sizes and they have doors in different places and too many windows and all those kinds of things. But in general, an L-shaped kitchen allows the best access in and out of the space. It's unobstructed. A wide, short U is often a good choice. It has to be wide enough that a person in a wheelchair can encounter other individuals and also be able to turn around. Most kitchens that I design, most bathrooms for that matter, are occupied by a nondisabled person as well as a wheelchair user. For this reason, multilevel counter surfaces are a real good choice. Another reason multilevel is real necessary is that we just have a terrible time in this industry with certain appliances, dishwashers just don't get down low enough to fit under the counter height that is necessary for most people in wheelchairs. While I'm harping about appliances, ovens are another pet peeve. Some manufacturers make ovens with doors that swing open from the side. Side-hinged doors are really great for a person in a wheelchair. I'm very disappointed that one of the brands that I used on a real regular basis has decided to go with a drop-down door instead of a side-hinged door. It's really frustrating to be in the position of designing and not have the products available that you'd really like to spec out.

When doing a multilevel design, I like to put in two sinks, one at the standard height of about 36" (91 cm) and of course that one will be over by the tall dishwasher. The second sink oftentimes can go in a low island. Speaking on the subject of heights, a small woman often needs a finished counter height of 30" (76 cm). A man, because he is generally taller, can often use a finished counter height of 33" to 34" (84 to 86 cm), that's compared with our standard norm of 36" (91 cm). There are ways to do this that are creative, attractive, and very usable. I like to incorporate desks, eating bars, tables.

Another solution that's real helpful for wheelchair users is to go with a 10" (25 cm) toekick to help deal with the footrest problem. In general, I avoid long runs of cabinets. I prefer to have small usable work stations where a person can park and do specific tasks with the tools at hand.

You might be wondering what kind of storage is best. It must be reachable. It must be accessible. Review the measurements you've taken. Look particularly at upward reach and lower reach. Most of us can access storage in that range, access that is between shoulder and hip. That's not very big. For some of us, it's even less big than others. I refer to these as the inches of maximum reach. Consider lowering the wall cabinets. I often set wall cabinets right on the countertop. Sometimes I use that backsplash space and fill it with appliance gadgets, open shelves, cup hooks. These modifications allow for this space to be usable without reducing the appearance of the project. Full-height pantry, oven, and linen cabinets provide good storage solutions. They provide drawers at the perfect height for your client. It is easier to manage a drawer than to manage a roll-out shelf behind a door, although a roll-out shelf is much better than nothing!

What can we professionals do to improve the home environment of our customers in wheelchairs? Most of the design elements I speak about and I use are included in cabinet catalogs that we have easy access to. Sitting squarely and closely to the counter is a problem for a wheelchair user because of the footrest. Like I said, the footrest sticks out a foot beyond the front of the chair. This often results in twisting a person's back and can result in further injury, or at the very least, discomfort. One of the tricks that I've come up with by accident is angling the counter so that instead of having 90° angles or 180° straight runs, I like to use angles that are about 130° to 160°. This brings the countertop closer to your left and right hands as you sit in your wheelchair.

I incorporate as many things as I can that pull out and over the customer. Features such as wastebaskets, vegetable bins, spice racks, roll-out shelves, sink tilt-outs, ironing boards, pull-out tables are all very nice. It's my opinion that every kitchen should have good sturdy full-extension chopping blocks. I like to incorporate one next to the cooktop and one in the sink area.

Base cabinet doors are a perpetual problem . . . because of the footrest. Try designing with narrow doors, bi-fold doors, tambours, sliding doors, and no doors. I've designed a cabinet that's been very good for some of my customers that allows the user to roll under the sink or the cooktop. The door basically . . . has a piano hinge where the two doors come together and real super strong hinges on one side and it opens and folds back. There's no floor in the cabinet, no toe kick, no bottom rail, and the flooring surface extends all the way under the cabinet. Fairly easy to do, not terribly expensive, and works real well. The counter is still too high for a person in a wheelchair but it's a wonderful solution for a person in a cart.

Some customers find it helpful to have a pull-out cart on wheels. This can be very useful in transporting food or dishes or whatever from the cooking area to the serving area. Customers with upper body weakness might find it difficult to lift a pot of boiling water. You can design so that they can slide a pan from the cooktop to the sink and back and forth without having to lift it. A sink with a slanted bottom might be desirable if a person has a really bad grip or bad weakness in that it would allow them to get things in and out of the sink.

We professionals must plan for and incorporate support systems. It costs so little to put in bracing while the wall is open. A 2" × 6" placed between 30" and 35½" (76 and 90 cm) makes life easier for the user of the facility even if it's years down the road. Be sure when you do that you leave little notes, or documentation, as to where you've done it. Life would be so much more convenient for people in wheelchairs and carts if all door openings were 36" (91 cm) or all aisles and hallways were 48" (122 cm), and I feel that eventually, if we're militant enough about it, these will become the architectural norms.

The turning radius for a person in a wheelchair is usually 60" (152 cm). Turning radius is defined as the area it takes for a person in a wheelchair to turn 360°. Avoid three-point turns. Situations and designs where you force a person to do three-point turns should really be scrutinized. Sometimes you don't have any choice, but look for options. Three-point turns, first of all are tiring, secondly they're frustrating, and many times they're unsafe. Don't trap a person in a wheelchair and force him to back out. Keep in mind the triangle theory—draw it down on paper—a triangle with a 3', a 4', and a 5' side. Hopefully that'll be a real good visual reminder for you that it stands for the following: 3' (91 cm) doorways, 4' (122 cm) halls and aisles, 5' (152 cm) turning radius.

Convenient work centers

If an existing work station is not suitable for use by a family member, the description below (with the help of *The Less Challenging Home* by Whirlpool Corporation) suggests ways you can modify the design to make it more convenient. However, unless the limitation is only temporary (such as a broken leg), the best solution might be to re-design the kitchen to use a more suitable work center.

Efficient kitchens generally are designed around a work triangle formed by the location of the refrigerator, sink, and range. The arrangement of the "work center" around this triangle depends on the space available. Four of the more common work centers are described below:

U-shaped work center

Figure 6-59 shows a typical U-shaped work center. This design features some specific advantages:

- It provides room to maneuver a wheelchair.
- It provides room for two people to work.
- It reduces kitchen traffic flow problems.
- It reduces risk of bumping into appliances.

This design might be inappropriate for people with low vision or who have difficulty maneuvering across wide open areas (e.g., people who use walkers or crutches). To adapt a U-shaped work center for their use, place appliances closer together to shorten the work triangle.

L-shaped work center

Figure 6-60 shows an L-shaped work center. Again, there are advantages to this layout:

- It provides room for kitchen traffic to flow through the room without interfering with the work triangle.
- It provides ample room for storage next to each work station.
- There is sufficient room for two people or a wheelchair.

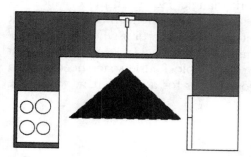

6-59
U-shaped work center. Whirlpool Home Appliances

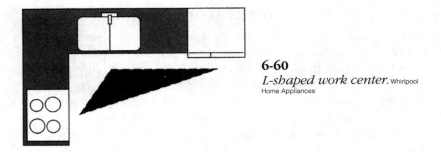

6-60
L-shaped work center. Whirlpool
Home Appliances

This layout (like the U-shaped work center) is probably also inappropriate for people who have low vision or difficulty maneuvering (because of the use of walkers or crutches) across wide open areas. To adapt an L-shaped work center for their use, place the cooking work station closer to the corner of the L.

Island and peninsular work centers

Figure 6-61 shows island and peninsular work centers. They too have their merits. One main advantage is that they shorten the work triangle for easy use by people with low vision or who use walkers or crutches. This style might be inappropriate for some disabled persons because open appliance doors might partially block aisle space needed for a wheelchair. To adapt this work center for use with a wheelchair, move the island or peninsula farther away from the main wall to increase aisle space.

Corridor and Pullman work centers

As shown in Fig. 6-62, corridor work centers put appliances across an aisleway from each other. Pullman work centers place all appliances along the same wall. These configurations might be approprate for people with low vision or who use walkers or crutches because they shorten the work triangle. However, the distance between the sink and appliances can make maneuvering in these work centers tiring when using crutches, a walker, or a wheelchair. Shortening the distance helps eliminate inefficiencies. Keep in mind that open appliance doors might partially block aisle space needed for a wheelchair. To adapt this work center for a wheelchair, widen the aisle space.

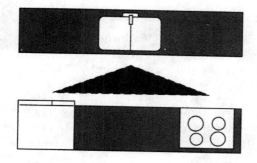

6-61
Island and peninsular work centers. Whirlpool Home Appliances

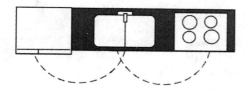

6-62
Corridor and pullman work centers. Whirlpool Home Appliances

Table 6-1 shows the recommended work triangle dimensions that are helpful in understanding the triangles shown in Figs. 6-59 through 6-62. Table 6-2 shows comfort zone dimensions that help you to better understand a person who stands/walks unassisted, walks with assistance, or just sits.

Table 6-1. Recommended work triangle dimensions

Appliance/fixture	Standard Feet (cm)	Wheelchair Feet (cm)	Walker/ crutches Feet (cm)
Total distance connecting refrigerator, range, and sink	12 to 22 (366 to 671)	14 to 24 (427 to 732)	10 to 20 (305 to 610)
Refrigerator to sink	4 to 7 (122 to 213)	6 to 9 (183 to 274)	2 to 5 (61 to 152)
Sink to range	4 to 6 (122 to 183)	6 to 8 (183 to 244)	2 to 4 (61 to 122)
Range to refrigerator	4 to 9 (122 to 274)	6 to 11 (183 to 335)	2 to 7 (61 to 213)

Source: Whirlpool Home Appliances

Table 6-2. Comfort zones in inches/feet (cm)

Comfort zones	Standing/ walking unassisted	Walking with assistance*	Sitting
Maximum upper cabinet reach:			
Over a counter	68" (173)	63" (160)	60" (153)
Without a counter	77" (196)	68" (173)	48" (122)
Maximum vision for items on high shelf	61" (155)	61" (155)	48" (122)
Maximum height of storage for daily use	74" (188)	65" (165)	45" (114)
Minimum aisle space	3' (91)	4' (122)	4.5' (137)
Minimum space between work stations:			
One cook	4' (122)	5' (152)	5.5' (168)
Two or more cooks	4.5' (137)	5.5' (168)	6' (183)
Maximum aisle space between counters	6' (183)	6' (183)	6.5' (198)

*Leaning on another person; or using a cane, crutches, or walker.

Source: Whirlpool Home Appliances

Figure 6-63 is a good example of a combination L-shape and island. Notice that the sink has been placed in the corner of the L-shape and the cooktop has been placed in the 45° corner of the island both for easy access and workability. The cabinets are by Yorktowne Cabinets, who produce a broad range of stock, semicustom, and barrier-free cabinetry.

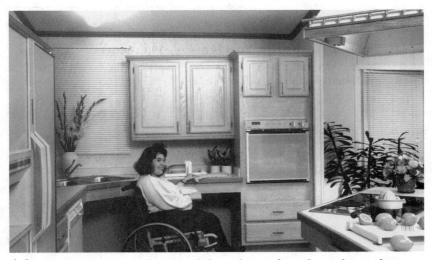

6-63 *Notice the pin rail around the exhaust fan above the cooktop.* Courtesy of Yorktowne Cabinets (Yorktowne, Inc., Red Lion, PA)

Laundry room

Another area to consider is the laundry room. The laundry room can be incorporated into the bathroom or kitchen or it can have its own separate room. Whatever the case, the same considerations apply to this room and its appliances as to the kitchen. Specifically,

- Installing the washer and dryer at different heights makes loading easier for individuals who are under 5' (152 cm) tall or who are wheelchair users.
- If there is a crawl space or an area of unusable space below the area where the washer will be installed, then lower the unit, especially if it is a top loader. An innovative design such as this can adapt standard appliances for use by wheelchair users or a short individual. This same concept can be incorporated into a closet. A recessed closet floor allows long clothing to hang properly after the closet rod has been lowered for easy access. When using a recessed area, it is important to install a "curb" around the front in order to stop a wheelchair. Recessed areas such as these will require cutting into the floor joists, which entails structural work. Be sure they are framed properly, braced, and have been inspected.
- Be sure appliances have side swing doors for easy maneuvering (Fig. 6-64).
- Controls should be located up front.
- Appliances such as washers should feature an automatic dispenser for adding bleach and fabric softener.
- Install a built-in ironing center.
- Install a table for folding clothes and be sure that it is wheelchair accessible.
- Consider installing closets and/or easy-to-reach shelving for clothes. Figure 6-65 shows a barrier-free system by Lee/Rowan. With the Track 'N Shelf system, all shelves can easily be adjusted up or down.
- Be sure there is plenty of light.

Remember the water damage repairs you have made because of leaking or flooding washing machines? Failed gaskets, worn seals, and broken hoses can release gallons of washing machine water into a home or apartment in a matter of seconds. As you know, in some cases carpeting must be replaced, and the damage to surfaces and/or the structure can require costly repairs. One way to prevent this is by installing the FloodSaver, a Washing Machine Surround. The unit has an area for the hose bibs and the waste drain, the floor pan includes a drain, and there is even a spot for the receptacle. Check into using single-lever shutoff valves. A unit such as this surround is an attractive, long-lasting solution (Fig. 6-66).

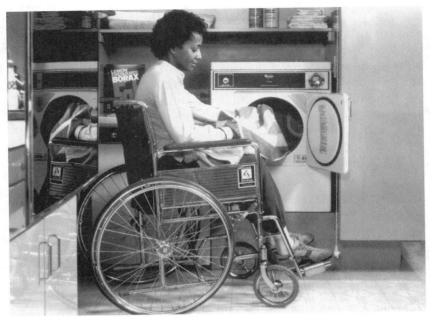

6-64 *Side swing dryer doors provide plenty of room for reaching inside the dryer while seated.* Whirlpool Home Appliances

6-65 *A system such as this makes access easy.* Lee/Rowan Building Products Division

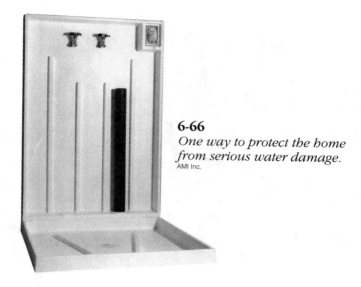

6-66
One way to protect the home from serious water damage.
AMI Inc.

Summary

Now it's time to organize that kitchen and/or laundry room. But before you do that, mentally put yourself in the place of the person who has to use these rooms. Think about overhangs or cabinets that might be in the way of someone with low vision. Does the work area provide easy access to a fire exit in the event of an emergency? Are light switches, receptacles, and appliance controls within easy reach? Is there convenient access to gas and water shutoff valves and to the homeowner's power supply box? These are only a small part of what you need to consider as a professional. While reading *Accessible Housing*, make yourself a list of the important items that will help you as you design. Consider how to combine the correct appliances, materials, and important factors that have been pointed out throughout this book and install them in ways that make the design more efficient.

Figure 6-67 shows a preliminary drawing of what to expect in a good design and the overall view of the area (outlined) that you need to consider when designing. Figure 6-68 shows a finished kitchen that has been modified from the drawing in Fig. 6-67 to accommodate a wheelchair user.

A special project

The challenge was to remodel a 1950s ranch-style house to allow the owner, Barbara Allan, a wheelchair user, to cook and entertain gra-

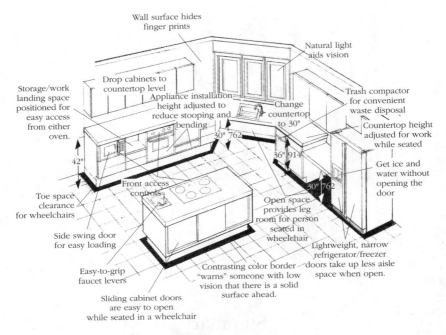

6-67 *Preliminary drawing.* Whirlpool Home Appliances

6-68 *Notice the laundry room off to the left in the photo.* Whirlpool Home Appliances

ciously and fully enjoy her backyard (discussed in the next chapter). A sunroom was added, and the dining area and kitchen were combined to provide open space and a transition to the yard. Varying counter heights and specialized cabinetry, including pull-out countertops, made the kitchen accessible, and yard improvements opened new ways for Barbara to experience her environment.

Barbara is the Director of the Access/Abilities Program for the Easter Seal Society of Washington; her story about the project was told in chapter 1. This particular project was designed by Carolyn D. Geise, FAIA, of Geise Architects in Seattle, WA. Barbara's project won

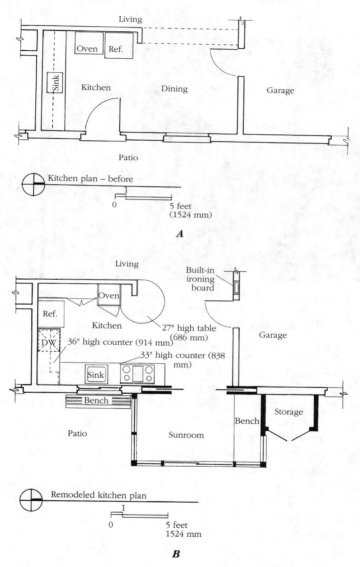

6-69 *(A) Before and (B) after. Notice the new design incorporated a U-shape design. Even though the sunroom addition was added, the overall design did not require the sunroom nor did it require any renovation to interior walls. It was all done within the existing square footage.* Geise Architects

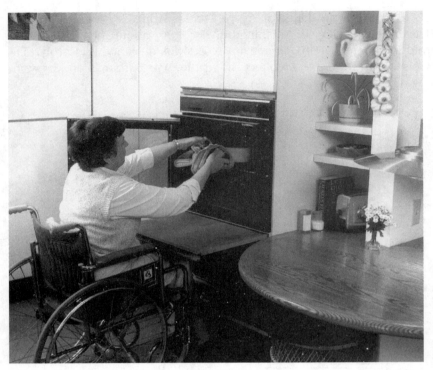

6-70 *The pull-out table just under the oven makes it easy to transfer hot items to the table. Notice the finger grip mounted on the front of the pull-out table. The microwave is located under the oven.* Geise Architects, photo by Don Normark

Geise national recognition and an award for accessibility design in 1993. Figures 6-69–6-73 show the result of this project. The captions for each figure contain important information that you might be able to use on your next project.

As a construction professional, you need to focus on the individual capabilities of your customer, both now and in the future (as the person ages). Familiarizing yourself with the materials and products now on the market that can be used to create barrier-free living is vital, but even more important is the ability to guide a customer unfamiliar with all the design and component selection possibilities so the end product works! I believe you can never have too much information on the subject.

Regardless of what you read, what you've been told, or what you've seen, be sure to contact your local building department. The kitchens, bathrooms, and laundry rooms you design have to be comfortable for your customers, so include your customers every step of the way. Remember, happy customers are good referral and reference customers. Remember also that the information contained in this

6-71 *This gives an overall view of the kitchen. The appliances have been properly laid out to allow Barbara to work with ease in her wheelchair. Incorporating a round table into the wall (center support) at the proper height to accommodate a wheelchair eliminates the need for table legs. The table is at the right height to accommodate a wheelchair. The light has been brought close to the table for a more concentrated light but the overall lighting is handled by fluorescent lights that almost cover the entire ceiling.* Geise Architects

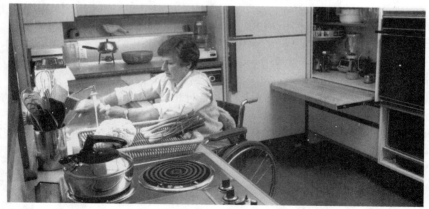

6-72 *The counter for the sink has been set at 33" (84cm) and there is room for wheelchair access underneath. This makes it comfortable for Barbara to carry out her daily activities. She can even reach the dishwasher from this position. To see the difference in the height of the countertops (33" vs. 36" [84-91cm]), look at the wall containing the refrigerator and dishwasher. A standard height dishwasher was installed because no lower units were available at that time. However, Barbara likes the extra counter space provided by a standard unit and is able to work comfortably at the 36" (91 cm) height.* Geise Architects, photo by Don Normark

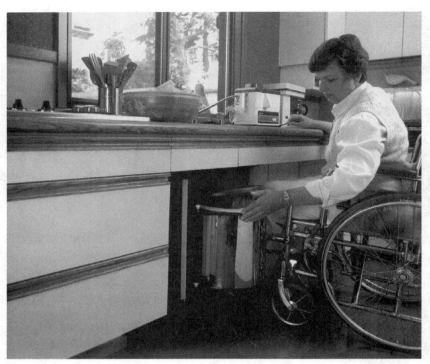

6-73 *This gives a clearer picture of the front of the sink. Notice the window has been dropped to give her a full view to the backyard. Every space has been utilized, including space at the back of the kneehole under the sink—a pivot-out garbage can has been installed here.* Geise Architects, photo by Don Normark

chapter (and the entire book) is generally intended for use in residential construction. However, as you well know, the laws that govern barrier-free issues generally apply to the commercial market (i.e., public facilities and multifamily housing), where the real emphasis on accessibility has been placed. Use those laws and standards to guide your thought process as you design.

7

Final details: Landscaping to hardware

Up to this point, you have been given all the necessary tools to enter this timely business with the self-assurance to help your customer with personal needs. If you run into an area in which you are unsure, or you feel uncomfortable about getting involved, then walk away or find help, but don't try bluffing your way through it. If you should decide to go through with such a project, it is possible that you customer will suffer the unfortunate consequences of your action. If you don't know—then ask! There is nothing to be ashamed about—be a safe and knowledgeable professional when entering this market.

This chapter covers a broad range of topics including landscaping/gardening, disposal and tear-out, products that can be used to keep the home safe while work is in progress, and hardware that can help with the installation of products mentioned throughout *Accessible Housing*.

Landscaping and gardening

It is not enough to just make the home barrier-free—what about the environment that surrounds the home? Some of us enjoy planting a garden, others like to smell the flowers, while others just enjoy feeding the birds and squirrels. Everyone, including those who are wheelchair users, should be given the chance to enjoy the outdoors. It is important for people to get outdoors and enjoy the beneficial effects of sunlight and nature.

Diane Miller, in her ongoing work with the "Welcome, H.O.M.E." project, stresses the importance of the outdoors. In chapter 1 she described the 2,000-foot wheelchair-accessible Pioneer Trail built in a scenic woodland where individuals with disabilities can enjoy nature firsthand. The specially designed picnic tables allow people with various disabilities to enjoy an outdoor picnic. One of Welcome H.O.M.E.'s future goals is to include features that will allow the visually impaired to enjoy the outdoors. What's unique is that the trail is open to the public—no calls, fees, or reservations necessary—just come and enjoy the outdoors.

There are several ways to carry your work directly to the outdoors. Let's revisit the project described in chapter 6, which was designed by Carolyn D. Geise, FAIA (Geise Architects) for Barbara Allan.

The new sunroom addition gives Barbara the opportunity to enjoy the outdoors indoors. The concrete 3' (91 cm) wide path that starts from the addition winds around the yard past the raised planting beds to the evergreen tree with its large hanging branch. The path widens to accommodate a bench, where she (in her wheelchair) can visit with friends. From her bedroom she can overlook the entire landscape, enjoy the patio just outside the bedroom door, or head down the path.

Yard improvements, such as those mentioned previously and shown in Fig. 7-1, open a new way for wheelchair users to enjoy their own environment. As you can see in the diagram, the pathway integrates the entire site. Figures 7-2–7-4 give an overall view of this project.

It is important to communicate with the customer to find out what the customer wants in a landscaping project. It would be a good idea for you to work with a landscaper who understands this market as well as the geographic area and knows what products (trees, plants, lawns) to suggest to the customer. Low-maintenance plants might be better suited for nonaccessible areas in the yard. However, don't underestimate the customer. It's possible the customer has a full-time landscaping service to care for the yard.

Access to the home—the entrance—should be carefully considered. It is important to include the entrance into the design of the landscaping, especially the front of the home. Together with the customer, decide which entrance will be the primary entrance, design that entrance for easy approach and operation—in other words, barrier-free. Design aspects to consider include the following:

- The entrance should be totally illuminated, including the surrounding area, pathway, and door.
- There should be easy access—level ground, gentle slope, and no steps.
- Pathways or sidewalks leading up to the door should be 5' (152 cm) wide.

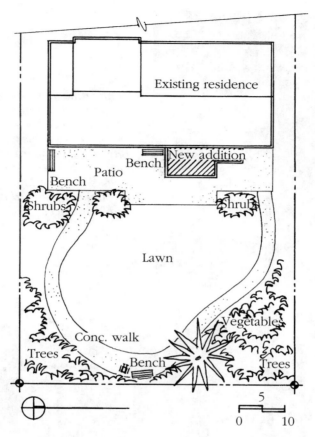

7-1 *Site plan.* Geise Architects

- The door itself should be wider than the 32" (81 cm) net opening (36"—91 cm—is better), and it should have lever handles.
- A level surface should extend at least 18" (46 cm) beyond the latch side of the door.
- On the latch side, build an exterior shelf from 32" to 44" (81 to 112 cm) off the ground to allow a person to set packages down while unlocking the door.
- Weather protection: The front entrance should be covered to protect at least three or four persons from the elements.
- A built-in bench or seat for at least two would give people a chance to catch their breath before entering the home.
- Plants should be trimmed low so as not to hide or cover the pathway or sidewalk, house, and door.

7-2
At one time there was only a window where this patio door has since been installed. Now this gives Barbara the opportunity to view landscaping and, if she prefers, she can move throughout the yard with full independence.

7-3 *Notice the built-in benches near the bedroom and a patio the full length of the home and wide enough for Barbara and her friends. The 3' path with a slight grade (less than 2 percent) gives her a wide enough area and proper slope to maneuver through the landscape.* Geise Architects, photo by Don Normark

7-4 *Here's the meeting place—the midpoint of the path. The bench allows individuals who are not disabled to sit and the extra wide space next to the bench allows the wheelchair user some comfort while visiting.* Geise Architects

Barrier-free gardening

I find the concept of barrier-free gardening exciting, as I hope you do. I love to garden, but the thought of using my carpentry skills to create a barrier-free garden is very stimulating. The fact that there is a whole new market out there waiting for the right green thumb makes good business sense, too.

For many, gardening is taken for granted; but for those with disabilities, raising a garden can be a real challenge. If you are a wheelchair user, the soil will make it difficult to maneuver around the garden. Reaching the plants is another consideration. If your customer has reduced motor skills resulting from an accident or a disease such as arthritis, bending or grasping a garden tool can be quite a struggle. The whole idea of a barrier-free garden is to raise the garden up to a comfortable level in order for the individual to work in it without discomfort. People shouldn't have to sell their property because they are unable to attend to garden maintenance. Simple changes such as creating an accessible pathway or moving higher-maintenance plants to the front of the garden can make a world of difference to people with a variety of disabilities. The whole idea refreshes the spirit. I know next year I'll be at my grandmother's getting her barrier-free garden in.

No one knows this subject better than Gene Rothert, whom we met in chapter 1. Gene is a Registered Horticultural Therapist and author of *The Enabling Garden—Creating Barrier-Free Gardens.* Manager of Urban Horticulture at the Chicago Botanic Garden, Gene oversees their Enabling Garden for People with Disabilities. His book is packed full of information to help individuals with disabilities and elders regain their independence and the spirit of working out-doors—or possibly begin a therapeutic hobby.

One chapter in his book that I found especially interesting was chapter 7, "The Design: Putting It All Together," especially the section on "The Five Essential Steps of Garden Design." Because you are in the construction business, you know that the best projects are those that have a carefully thought-out plan. Well, the same is true for a gar-den design. There is not enough space in this chapter to thoroughly discuss all of Gene's ideas, so I will highlight and paraphrase some areas from the book (©1994 by Gene Rothert, reprinted with permis-sion from Taylor Publishing Company, Dallas, TX) to introduce you to the subject matter. As I mentioned before, I suggest you work with a licensed professional landscaper. I'm not suggesting that you be-come a landscaper, but it is possible that you will build the pathways, install the raised gardens, and utilize a landscaper as a subcontractor in order to get the job completed. Sell the job as though you were selling a new home or a remodeling package.

Five essential steps

Professional garden designers and landscape architects adhere to the following five steps when designing a garden. Address these steps in the order they are listed. Actually, they are very similar to those you follow when constructing an addition or remodeling a bathroom.

1: Base information

The base plan supplies the very basic information from which the plan will emerge. Hopefully, a plot plan will be available that contains all the information you need. If such a plan is not available, then you need to establish through other means the location of the following:

- The property lines (which need to be identified by a licensed or registered surveyor)
- Utilities (water, telephone, gas, electric, and cable)—Do you know where any easements are? Are they underground or overhead?
- A septic tank—If one exists, where is it and where is its accompanying drain field?
- Any existing sprinkler lines

Concerns such as these can affect safety, expenses, and (of course) the design. The base plan, in essence, needs to include everything about the property (Fig. 7-5). If you are planning to include an addition or a deck, for example, then you need to know:

- The required minimum front yard setback
- The required minimum rear yard setback
- The required side yard setback

It's a good idea to ask the customer if the property has been surveyed; perhaps the markers are still there. Depending on the size of the addition you plan to build, the survey report can help you determine the setback requirements. If the customers are not sure, have them check with the office of the county auditor/recorder.

The survey might also show any restrictions or easements associated with the property. Entrance points and paths of underground services might have to be determined by the individual utility companies involved. Check in your local phone book under "utility companies." Sometimes they have special service numbers for locating underground utilities.

If you are working in a development, there could be covenant restrictions. Check with the association for any guidelines. Also, a subdivision should have been surveyed as part of the subdivision process. Depending upon the date of subdivision, the corner monuments (markers) might still be at the corners.

2: Site analysis

This is an evaluation of the property and includes the pluses and minuses of the site, structures, and the surrounding area. This is the starting point where you decide in what direction the project should go. You need to look realistically at the possibilities and the limitations at hand—in other words, what you have to work with (Fig. 7-6). Be sure to check things out carefully; whatever you discover could have an impact on the design and the budget. Some areas to examine and which might be of concern are as follows:

- Will the anticipated project blend in with the character of the rest of the neighborhood? This includes the landscape as well any new structures.
- Is the neighbor's home/yard/deck in full view? Do you need to build a fence?
- Consider climate and weather. What is the summer shade as compared to winter shade? What is the prevailing wind direction?
- How are drainage, soil conditions, and the grade of the property?
- Do existing structures have wall space available for vertical gardening?

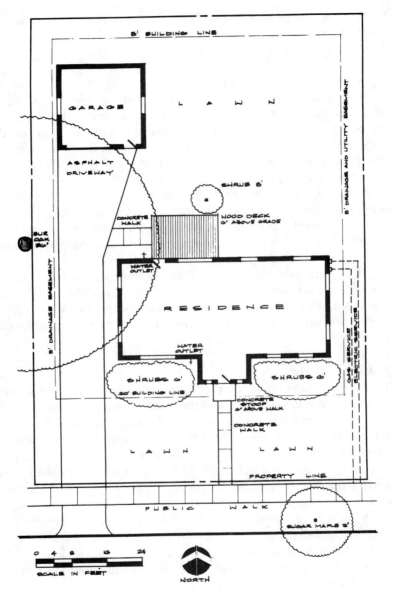

7-5 *Base plan.* From *The Enabling Garden,* (c) 1994 by Gene Rothert. Reprinted with permission from Taylor Publishing Company, Dallas, TX

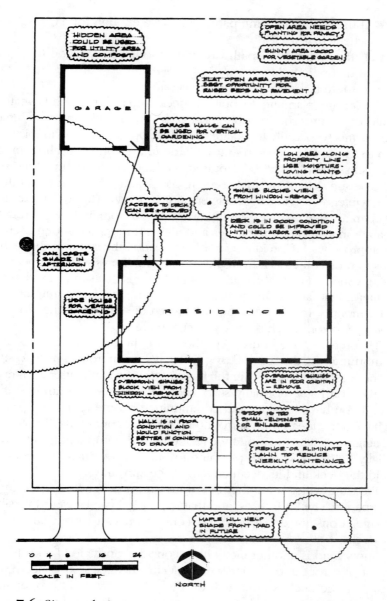

7-6 *Site analysis.* From *The Enabling Garden*, (c) 1994 by Gene Rothert. Reprinted with permission from Taylor Publishing Company, Dallas, TX

- If there is an existing patio, is it large enough for a wheelchair user?
- Is the walkway or pathway wide enough and in good structural condition?
- If there is a deck, is it fully accessible?

If you are planning to build a deck, then climate and weather should be a concern. Probably most of us build decks in the summer when plants (especially trees) are fully developed. It is easy in this situation to forget what the sun's rays will do in the winter and how much of the sun's warmth will be captured on the deck during that time period. The sun's changing angle is more concentrated in the summer than in the winter, which is why it delivers more energy. (The sun crosses the sky in an arc that changes slightly every day, becoming lower throughout autumn as winter approaches and higher throughout spring as summer approaches.) If deciduous trees are nearby, the summer shade that helps to protect the deck from the sun's harmful rays will disappear, allowing winter sunlight through. Another factor is that sunny areas in the summer might fall within the shadow of the house during autumn and winter months. In time, the sun will bleach the surface of the wood to a soft gray color, which some customers prefer.

Theoretically, if a house faces the south, the east side receives only the morning sun, the south-facing side stays warm from sunrise to sunset, the west side absorbs the full force of the sun's mid afternoon rays, and the north side normally stays cool because the sun rarely shines on it. If you have lived in your community for some years, you probably have a fair idea of the surrounding weather conditions. If not, then ask neighbors who are long-time residents. This information can be especially helpful if you are planning to build an overhead structure to shield the deck and its occupants from the sun's rays.

Freezing water is another of nature's most destructive forces; water expands when it freezes, and that expansion can cause irreversible damage. Constant expansion and contraction can cause damage to any deck.

Snow load is another element to consider. Snow load adds to the weight of a roof and an uncovered deck. This is a real concern, especially if the deck is built high off the ground. Without proper support and bracing, snow load could cause a deck to collapse. If you live in an area with high average snowfall, consult an engineer to ensure adequate and solid construction.

There are plenty of ways to make attractive shade structures, but the only way to protect the deck from the sun's harmful rays or to bring in sun to those portions that your customer wants to enjoy during the summer months (and possibly during the winter) is to plan for it:

- Find out if the customer prefers to sit in the sun or the shade.
- In what season(s) and at what time(s) of day do the customers expect to use their deck the most?
- Does the customer anticipate night use? If so, you might want to suggest outdoor lighting and a few GFCI (ground-fault circuit interrupter) protected electrical receptacles.
- What is the direction of the prevailing wind? You might want to suggest some type of buffer such as hedges, trees, and so on.
- Are there barriers to the view, such as hedges or trees that will bother the customer? Design the deck with a desirable view. If your customer is a wheelchair user, make sure that the view is unobstructed from a seated position.
- Is privacy an issue? Suggest louvers, latticework, screens, and so forth.

It might be a good idea to take the information contained within this chapter and prepare a checklist for potential customers who are undecided about issues like these. This way, they can review their needs and check the boxes on your list. It would be better to return for their answers than to sign them on the spot and start the job— only to have unsatisfied customers once the project is completed. You might also wish to consult my book, *Builder's Guide to Decks* (Mc-Graw-Hill, ISBN #0-07-015749-9) for a thorough discussion of factors involving deck placement and the ins and outs of deck construction and maintenance.

3: Checklist of needs and wish list

You have evaluated everything up to this point so you know what can and can't be done. Now it's time to find out what your customers want. Take the time to consult with your customers. Learn their priorities, their wants and needs, their wish lists. You are not looking for fine detail information but rather the basics that will help you determine how much of what they want is possible and whether it will fall within their budget. This is the time to really communicate and get to know your customers. If the customers are not sure, then the following list of items might provide some assistance and makes a good worksheet. Of course, you will want to customize this list:

- Deck
- Patio
- Walkways
- Pool
- Storage shed
- Utility shed
- Fence

- Privacy
- Arbor
- Gazebo
- Hot tub
- Assistive equipment (recreational lift)
- Irrigation system
- Lawn
- Vegetable garden
- Flowers
- Compost area
- Lights

4: The concept plans

By now you should have gathered enough information from your evaluation and from your customer to assemble some preliminary drawings. These are working plans that enable customers to visualize what they've been thinking about. It really presents an opportunity to see things in black and white before the project begins. The working plans give you and your customers a chance to work out any details and/or changes. It's a lot easier to make changes on paper than to get halfway into the project and then have to make changes.

Once customers see the concept, be prepared to come up with an alternative plan. You might want to consider offering three different plans from which to choose. Tracing paper is inexpensive, and besides, the concept drawing can be saved. You never know when you will run into a similar project.

5: The final design

Once you have worked out all the details, then you are ready for the final drawings and approval from the customer. The final plans make it easier for you, as well as any subcontractor(s) that might be involved, to bid the job. If there are subcontractors, then the final plans help them to prepare for their involvement.

Figure 7-7 is an example of a garden plan for a wheelchair user. It was designed to accommodate people with fairly restricted mobility and activity levels. It gives some ideas of what could be done. Go back and review Fig. 7-5 and notice how much and what was done with this particular property. As for plants, flowers, and vegetables, be sure to use those that are suitable for your area. Also be aware of the climate and weather since they will have an impact on the plant products you choose. It would be best, though, to leave this area in the hands of a professional who knows—a professional landscaper. Lights should be used both in gardens and around the

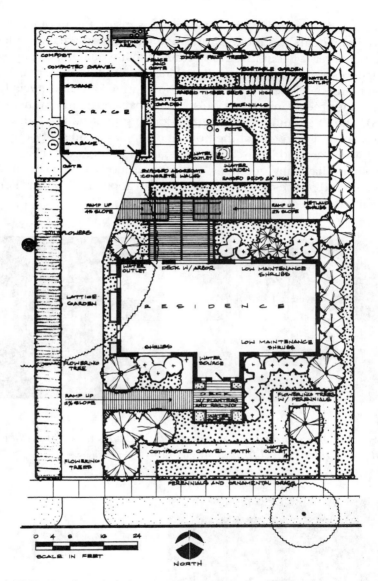

7-7 *Garden plan for a wheelchair user.* From *The Enabling Garden* (c) 1994
by Gene Rothert. Reprinted with permission from Taylor Publishing Company, Dallas, TX

site, and if there is a pool, consider lights inside the pool itself. This way individuals can move around the landscaped area and identify the pool area without massive overheads that would impose upon the neighbors. One company worth looking into is Fiberstars. For the pool, you could use Fiber-Glo, a fiber optic lighting system especially designed for the swimming pool, spa, and backyard environment (Fig. 7-8). The FS3 Illuminator is a great-looking light fixture that can be used around the pool, at the bottom of steps, on sides of ramps and pathways, around landscaped areas, and in the garden (Fig. 7-9).

If you have any questions, contact Chicago Botanic Garden. Their address and phone number can be found in appendix A under "Firms—Architects/Designers/Contractors."

A   **B**

7-8 *(A) Before and (B) after. Fiber optic provides an even and beautiful pool lighting effect from a single light.* Courtesy of Fiberstars, Inc.

7-9
The FS3 will light an area up to approximately 5' from each side of the housing.
Courtesy of Fiberstars, Inc.

Things you can do

The first aspect to consider is who will be using the barrier-free garden. If the garden is intended for a wheelchair user, this will make a difference in the size and width of rows you construct and whether the pathway should be a solid surface. Even though your customer is not now a wheelchair user, it might be possible (if there is enough space) to make your design accessible now. You will be providing for the possible future needs of the homeowner and family. Look at this as an opportunity to employ good universal design practices.

If the project is for a wheelchair user, consider the following:

- Raise the bed up 17" to 24" (43 to 61 cm) with the width not more than 48" (122 cm) and a length that is comfortable for the customer.
- The width between the raised beds must be at least 36" (91 cm).
- Provide at least 36" (91 cm) of space for maneuvering around a 48" (122 cm) raised bed. If the beds are about 24" (61 cm) wide, then the width of rows should be at least 42" (107 cm) and the end space should be 48" (122 cm). If the client needs to turn around at an intersection of the raised beds, then the intersection should be 5' (152 cm) square (25 sq. ft. or 2.3 m²) to allow for a 360° turn.
- The surface of the row needs to be of solid material so a wheelchair can maneuver.
- For raised beds, you can install treated 4× material horizontally and 6× for vertical installation.
- Raised beds can be made from cedar or redwood 2× material and the surface can have veneer bricks.
- The side of the garage or house can be used to attach a vertical wall garden. The vertical wall is a framework of cubicles made out of 2× material not to exceed 12" (30 cm). The cubicles are sized to the customer's preference. Boxes are made with one open end to fit the cubicle loosely. The plants are planted in these boxes. The boxes are filled with soil covered with 4- to 6-mil black plastic, then the plastic is covered with 1" (25 mm) square plastic-coated wire mesh with the perimeter covered with a finish moulding.
- Install hanging baskets that are tied off with a rope so the wheelchair user can raise or lower the baskets to work on them.
- Rain gutter with capped ends attached to a vertical wall could make a good planter for shaded areas.

- Old oak wine barrels also are excellent planters.
- Sewer pipe with the flared end up and chimney flues painted with bright colors make attractive planters.

If the project is for an elder, the construction methods and planters are all the same with the following exceptions:

- The raised beds should be built at least 17" (43 cm) high (Fig. 7-10).
- The sill of the bed should be capped with a 2" × 4" or 2" × 6". This makes it wide enough so someone can sit on it.
- The rows should be between 18" and 24" (46 and 61 cm) in width.
- At the ends of rows, consider a space between 36" and 48" (91 and 122 cm).
- The surface of the path should be compact for easy walking; do not use gravel.
- As plants mature, they reach the height where a person can work on them comfortably. Again, the raised beds need to be at the 17" (43 cm) height.
- For plants that don't grow upward, a simple tomato cage can be used.
- Install ¾" (19 mm) PVC as shown in Fig. 7-11.
- Consider building raised beds that are 4' × 4' (122 × 122 cm) as shown in Fig. 7-12.

7-10 *The 17" height makes it comfortable for an individual to sit on the raised bed.* C.R.S., Inc.

7-11 *Plastic can be draped over the PVC pipe for early growth.* C.R.S., Inc.

7-12 *The used brick gives a rustic look and helps bring the entire design together. In this case, the area is used for flowering plants.* C.R.S., Inc.

Disposal considerations

Every day new products enter the market, joining a wide selection of existing products, and many of them contain chemicals. It is important to verify the correct disposal of waste from these products. Protection of the environment is a major issue and disposal laws are being both added to the books and enforced. These regulations might impact your material selections because proper disposal affects costs and therefore your bid to the customer. In this case, it is far better to know before bidding the job than after the fact. This is definitely something to consider. You must be both a people-oriented professional and a professional with values, and those values should include the environment and the customer. It is our responsibility as professionals to set a good example and cooperate with governing agencies to help protect our environment. In addition, certain chemicals might affect certain customers, so be sure to ask your customers if they are concerned about any chemicals and/or products.

Tear-out

Before starting any project, evaluate the tear-out situation. This necessary step could help to prevent mistakes which, of course, tap into profits. You definitely cannot afford mistakes. Some specific areas to watch out for include tear-out, site preparation, protection of the property where you are working as well as any adjacent properties, and knowing utility locations.

Ask yourself the following questions as you scope out your next project. Keep in mind that realistic answers could affect how you tackle the project as well as how you bid it.

- How much must be torn out?
- What will I find once this area has been removed?
- Is it necessary to tear any of the structure apart?
- Can products be used that will allow construction right over the existing structure?
- What necessary steps will I have to take to prepare the site for construction?
- What is the soil like in this area?
- Will something special need to be done for footings and/or embedding columns or posts?
- Will heavy machinery be required for this project?
- Will this heavy machinery have to work in the back yard?
- Do I have full access to the back yard?
- Will I have to remove a fence?
- Will I have any access to the property from the neighbors?
- Is the ground soft and wet?
- Will the machinery leave impressions in the lawn?
- Will I need to cover the lawn with plywood in order to move heavy machinery across it?
- Will any trees need to be removed altogether or moved to another location?
- Will the project interfere with the main roots of any trees that need to remain?
- Where are utility lines located?
- Will I need to have utility lines moved?

Safety

When working around a customer's home, safety must be your top priority, especially if children are present. At all times the job site should be kept clean. Do not leave cut material scattered about as it is easy to trip over, so clean up as you work. Of course, if debris in-cludes lumber with nails or screws, remove those nails or screws or bend them over. Find an area in which to store debris until its proper disposal, and try to pick a site that will expedite its pick-up.

If your particular job site features installed glass near the floor level in the area where you are working, put a piece of plywood in front of the glass. This will protect the glass—and anyone who might be standing behind it—in case you slip with a pneumatic gun or a nail ricochets.

Tools themselves can be very dangerous, especially to children who might have been watching you work. Children are very curious about the tool you keep touching and turning on and off. To prevent accidents, unplug your tools, lower blades, and remove extension cords. If there is a lock-off button, remove it as well if you plan to be away from the tool for any length of time.

Remind yourself, "safety first!" Practice safety all the time and soon it will become automatic. Your customers will appreciate your emphasis on safety as well.

First aid kit

Your own safety is also important. You have probably been on a job site by yourself on many occasions. Maybe you got something in your eye or a sliver in your finger and there was no one around to help. Set yourself up with a first aid kit that can accommodate the unex-pected. Purchase the best one you can or assemble one yourself. You never know when you, or someone else on the site, will need help.

Eyewear

One area of particular concern should be your eyes. When you as-semble your first aid kit, be sure to include eyewash. There are so many airborne particles on a job site that it is very easy for some to land in your eyes. Some of these particles are abrasive. If something gets in your eye, do not rub it—you could scratch the surface of the eyeball. Use the eyewash anytime your eye(s) feel irritated. I can't stress this enough—your eyes are important!

A good way to protect your eyes is to wear safety glasses. Choose glasses that are comfortable to wear (adjustable) and provide protec-tion on the top and on the sides as well. Also look for coated lenses to help prevent fogging, static, and scratches and to help protect your eyes from UV radiation. If you wear prescription glasses, choose eye-wear that fits comfortably over your existing glasses.

Other safety concerns

While we are on the subject of safety, when was the last time you wore hearing protection, gloves, good work boots (not athletic shoes), and appropriate clothing? Maybe you haven't given these items much concern, or maybe you have. This is a safety reminder—you need to act on it. I am a firm believer that hearing protection should be worn when working with—or even near someone working with—power tools. However, hearing protection (plugs or muffs) can be hazardous if worn all the time because you will not be able to hear what is happening around the job site, nor will you be as alert as you should. Once you are through using a power tool or have moved away from someone who is, remove your hearing protection; but don't forget to use it when the power tools fire up again.

Interior protection

One item that often gets neglected is respect for the customer's property, both interior and exterior, as well as any neighboring property. There are now products on the market that can help protect the environment while construction is underway. The following products should help with your next project.

Foot traffic during construction can quickly tarnish carpet and scratch wooden floors. These areas need protection until the project is completed. Plastic can be slippery, doesn't stay put, and is not puncture-resistant. Protective Products offers a cost-effective surface protection with adhesive-backed polyethylene films. This product is extremely resistant to tearing, and the specially formulated pressure-sensitive adhesive on one side keeps the film in place (Fig. 7-13). It comes in widths of 24" and 36" (61 and 91 cm) and in lengths of 200' (61 m), 500' (152 m), and 1000' (305 m). Other areas of concern are door thresholds, clad trim, and other nonporous surfaces, areas that need protection from mortar, stucco, dirt from the job site, and foot traffic (Fig. 7-14). The downsized product for these areas is blue and available in four sizes: 1" (25 mm), 3" (76 mm), 4" (102 mm), and 6" (152 mm), all 108' (33 cm) long.

In bathrooms, plumbing fixtures such as tubs and sinks need temporary protection during construction. Repairing porcelain chips on a tub can be expensive, but replacing it is even more costly! Protect the customer's investment by using a temporary protective coating by AC Products, Inc. (Fig. 7-15). They have products that will protect such items as fiberglass and acrylic tubs, ceramic tubs and sinks, and window glass and metal frames from damage. The product can be applied by an airless sprayer or brushed/rolled.

7-13
Protect the carpet from tracked-in dirt. Protective Products

7-14
Thresholds also need protection during construction and remodeling. Protective Products

7-15
When the job has been completed, peel and pull to remove the protective film.
AC Products, Inc.

Another area of concern is dust. Whether from tear-out or from wallboard installation, dust will filter throughout a home, creating quite a mess. Don't forget the environmental impact it can have on the customer who has to breathe the air during the project. It would be best to confine the dust to the one area where you are working, and this can be done with the DustDoor and Wall System (Brophy Design, Inc.). This product contains dust in one area and provides you with an exit through a zippered door (Fig. 7-16). With the help of ArchGuard, a modular clamp-on system (plastic and hook and loop), the whole unit can be installed without tape, nails, or tacks, leaving the walls free of damage. Your customers will appreciate that.

Attaching a dryer hose (nylon/elastic sleeve) and a 200-CFM blower will allow you to blow the dust outdoors (see Fig. 7-17). It's one sure way to control dust in a difficult situation. However, before exhausting any dust outdoors, be sure to contact your local government agency that regulates "air control." You might be required to conform to air-quality regulations in your area.

7-16
A tough commercial vinyl with an industrial grade nylon zipper. Brophy Designs, Inc.

A

B

7-17 *(A) Depending on your blower system, the manufacturer can make accommodation for the proper size hose. (B) You may have to get creative when it comes to installing the blower.* Brophy Designs, Inc.

Asbestos

When working on any home, you might discover existing products containing asbestos. Asbestos (a mineral fiber) is most commonly found in older homes, in pipe and furnace insulation materials, asbestos shingles, millboard textured paints and other coating materials, and floor tiles including backing, lining felt, or asphaltic "cutback" adhesives. Elevated concentrations of airborne asbestos can occur after asbestos-containing materials are disturbed by cutting, sanding, or other remodeling activities. Improper attempts to remove these materials can release asbestos fibers into the air in homes, increasing asbestos levels and endangering people living in those homes. If you plan to install a new floor covering, for instance, and you want to tear up the old, consider sending a sample of the existing flooring to a testing laboratory for analysis. Until you know for sure, it is important not to cut into the floor covering with any power tools that could create dust.

The most dangerous asbestos fibers are too small to be visible. After they are inhaled, they can remain and accumulate in the lungs. Asbestos can cause lung cancer, mesothelioma (a cancer of the chest and abdominal linings), and asbestosis (irreversible lung scarring that can be fatal). Symptoms of these diseases do not show up until many years after exposure began. Most individuals with asbestos-related disease were exposed to elevated concentrations on the job; some developed disease from exposure to clothing and equipment brought home from the job sites.

Various government agencies have regulations governing the removal of in-place asbestos and its safe disposal—including both commercial and residential. Check with them to make sure you are in compliance. You might need to hire a certified contractor for asbestos removal.

Hardware

Anyone in this business knows there are times when solid backing is not necessary—and other times when you really wish it was there! Each product you install has its own set of rules to follow, and the type of material to which you are fastening that product determines the method you choose for a secure application. In some cases, you have to open walls to install backing. When doing a renovation, for instance, on a bathroom wall that might require grab bars in the future, consider sheeting the area or the entire wall with ¾" (19 cm) plywood. Another alternative would be to install blocking in specific areas. If you choose to do this, be sure to clearly document the location of any blocking before installing the finish wall.

Some products can be installed using special anchors, while other products provide their own hardware. Whatever the case, be sure to use proper, safe, and approved hardware for the application at hand.

Although I am not endorsing the following products, I have used them in the field in some of the listed applications. You might be aware of other (similar) products, but be sure the product you choose is approved for your particular application. The following information has been offered by the manufacturer, TOGGLER Anchor System, Div. of Mechanical Plastics Corp. For free samples and technical support, you may call them at 800-544-2552.

TOGGLER BRAND Toggle Bolts offer the following features:

- Four channel sizes: ³⁄₁₆"-24; ¼"-20; ⅜"-16; ½"-13 (some metric tappings are available).
- Available in Zinc-Plated Steel and 304 Series Stainless Steel.
- Can be reused in the same hole after fixture is removed for maintenance or repair.

- Type V anchor in Federal Specification FF-B-588D.
- Approved for all U.S. government project use.
- This anchor is specified by the state of California for installing handrails in hospitals.

Applications for this bolt include:
- Sinks
- Partitions
- Cabinetry
- Mirrors
- Lighting fixtures
- Shelving
- TV mounts/brackets
- Handrails
- Medical equipment
- Chair lifts
- Appliances
- Grab bars
- Toilets
- Sliding door tracks
- Furniture

This toggle bolt works in the following building materials:
- Concrete block
- Cinder block
- Wallboard
- Stucco
- Paneling
- Hollow brick
- Hollow block
- Plaster
- Fiberglass
- Cement board
- Composite panels

This product requires four easy steps to install (Fig. 7-18).

SUPER TOGGLER Hollow-Wall Anchors
- Six wall grip ranges from ⅛" (3 mm) to 1½" (38 mm), each needing only a ⁵⁄₁₆" (8 mm) diameter drill bit.
- Available with built-in hardware for specialty applications.
- Absorb vibration and shock and will not damage building material.
- Type IV anchor in Federal Specification FF-B-588D.
- Approved for all U.S. government project use.

Applications for these anchors include:
- Towel bars/rings
- First aid kits

Four easy steps to total anchoring security!

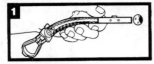

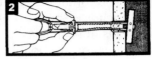

Drill appropriate sized hole. Hold metal channel flat alongside plastic straps and slide channel through hole.

With one hand, pull ring so metal channel rests flush behind wall as you slide plastic cap along straps with other hand until flange of cap is flush with wall.

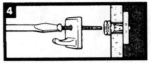

Place thumb between plastic straps. Push side to side snapping off straps flush with wall.

Insert bolt through item to be attached and tighten until flush with fixture. Minimum clearance behind wall: 1⁷/₈" (3¹/₂" for BBLC Toggle Bolt anchor).

7-18 *Four easy steps to total anchoring security!*
TOGGLER BRAND Anchor System, Division of Mechanical Plastics Corporation

- Fire extinguishers
- Soap dishes
- Soap dispensers
- Security systems
- Door stops
- Shelving
- Wall lamps
- Window treatments
- Mirrors
- Speakers
- Wall hooks
- Cabinets
- Shower doors

The hollow-wall anchor works in the following materials:

- Wallboard
- Thin paneling and fiberglass
- Acoustic ceilings
- Plasterboard
- Hardboard
- Sheet metal

- Hollow core doors
- Plaster

With this product you are three easy steps away from total anchoring security (Fig. 7-19).

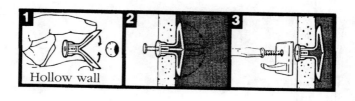

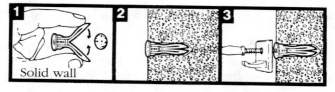

Instructions:

1. Drill $5/16$" (8mm Ø) hole. Fold anchor, insert anchor in hole and tap flush with wall.
2. Insert key to pop anchor open behind hollow wall (not necessary for thick or solid walls). Do not force or hammer key.
3. Place item over anchor. Insert screw and tighten until screw is flush with fixture.

7-19 *Three easy steps to total anchoring security!*
TOGGLER BRAND Anchor System, Division of Mechanical Plastics Corporation

TOGGLER BRAND ALLIGATOR Solid-Wall Anchors offer these features:

- Three drill diameters: $3/16$" (5 mm), $1/4$" (6 mm), and $5/16$" (8 mm).
- Two styles: with flange, or flush-mount for through-the-fixture installation.
- Patented "molding action" bonds anchor to wall for highest strength.
- Anti-rotation fins prevent anchor from sinking or spinning when installing the screw with a screw gun.
- Holds metal anchors of more than twice the diameter (in solid walls).
- Though specifically designed for solid substrates, they perform in a wallboard application as well.

Applications for these anchors include:

- Plumbing fixtures
- Electrical fixtures
- Handrails
- Corner guards
- Alarms
- Shower doors
- Door jambs
- TV brackets
- Framing
- Signs
- Shelving
- Cabinets
- Lighting
- Utility shelves
- Window frames
- Telephone equipment
- Ready-to-assemble furniture
- Partitions

The solid wall anchors work in the following materials:

- Concrete
- Brick
- Masonry
- Cinder block
- Stucco
- Ceramic tile
- Stone
- Plaster
- Patio block
- Wood
- Wallboard
- Particleboard

Solid wall anchors require only three easy steps to install (Fig. 7-20).

The same amount of energy to design the interior of a home should be spent on the exterior as well. Everyone needs to get out and enjoy life once in a while. Measures need to be taken so the same ease of comfort that is employed indoors is also available outdoors. The design should give users full access to the outdoor environment with all its benefits, enabling them to enjoy nature in total comfort. Consult with a licensed landscape architect who has experience in this field to help achieve the customer's goals. Don't forget to include the customer in this important phase of the project, because it is all being done for them.

Staying up-to-date on products that can make the project easier and safer to install is important and can have a tremendous impact on your work. Don't neglect your own safety or the safety of others on the job site, and keep in mind the wide variety of new products that can make your job easier and more satisfying to both you and your customer!

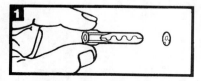

Drill hole same diameter as anchor.

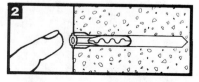

Push in anchor and tap flush.

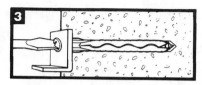

Insert screw and tighten. Anti-rotation fins eliminate spinning while ALLIGATOR anchor extrudes along screw.

7-20 *Three easy steps to total anchoring security!*
TOGGLER BRAND Anchor System, Division of Mechanical Plastics Corporation

8

Environmentally safe homes

Why go through all the trouble of building or remodeling a home for universal design if the products used or the property the home sits on is not environmentally safe? Interesting question, isn't it? Customers today are concerned about the quality of the air they breathe and the products used and whether or not they are harmful. As a professional, you might find yourself with no choice—you'll be pressured to use environmentally friendly building products brought on by state and federal environmental regulations. Americans today are concerned about their health!

"When you can't breathe, nothing else matters." No one understands the truth of this statement better than the American Lung Association (ALA); and the American Lung Association, Minneapolis Affiliate (see chapters 2 and 3), has worked to encourage healthy choices since the turn of the century. The Minneapolis Affiliate is America's oldest voluntary health agency, and it has an outstanding service record when it comes to issues concerning respiratory health. From tuberculosis to tobacco to airborne toxins, the ALA has led the way to lung health and disease prevention.

Since the early 1970s, the American Lung Association, Minneapolis Affiliate, has been a leader in the movement to improve our environment. Poor air quality can cause or trigger a number of diseases, most of them conditions of the lung. That is why air quality is critical to the association's work to fight, cure, and control lung disease.

A leader in the outdoor air quality debate, the ALA has been hard at work trying to solve indoor air quality problems as well. Their indoor air program took off in 1988 with a storm of telephone calls (thousands!) about radon gas. Since then, they have grown to provide a broad public information and consultation service in that field.

The ALA has become a resource for both consumers and professionals, providing information to individuals and groups through educational materials and presentations. Topics range from asbestos to dust mites to secondhand tobacco smoke and the diseases they cause: lung cancer, asthma, and allergies—all diseases that can strike people where they live. If you've ever seen anyone gasping for breath, you know why lung health and good air quality are so important to the American Lung Association and the people they serve.

Every year since 1993, the Minneapolis Affiliate has been involved in an ongoing project called HEALTH HOUSE:

> Health House is about choices: choices we make when we build or remodel; choices that make a difference in the levels of indoor air pollution; choices about environmentally friendly kinds of building materials.
>
> The purpose of Heath House '95 is to educate homeowners, builders and remodelers about choices that can improve indoor quality of living in our homes.
>
> As we have moved through the planning and building of Health House '95, we've learned that there are no absolutes. Instead, the project team has combined healthy building materials, thoughtful techniques and individual tastes and choices in a holistic approach to healthy as well as economical and comfortable living.

Indoor pollution

The following information was furnished by the American Lung Association, Minneapolis Affiliate (Health House '94 & '95), the Environmental Protection Agency (EPA, *The Inside Story: A Guide to Indoor Air Quality*, 1995), and Honeywell, Inc. (*Know Your IAQ: A Guide to Understanding Indoor Air Quality*, 1993).

Causes of indoor air problems

Indoor pollution sources that release gases or particles into the air are the primary cause of indoor air quality problems in homes. Inadequate ventilation can increase indoor pollutant levels by not bringing in enough outdoor air to dilute emissions from indoor sources and by not carrying indoor air pollutants out of the home. High temperature and humidity levels can also increase concentrations of some pollutants.

Pollutant sources

In any home there are many sources of indoor air pollution. The relative importance of any single source depends on how much of a given pollutant it emits and how hazardous those emissions are. In some cases, factors such as the age of the source and proper maintenance are significant. Common sources of pollution include:

- Combustion: One byproduct of combustion is carbon monoxide, released from improperly operating or unvented fuel-burning appliances (e.g., kerosene-fueled space heaters), furnaces (coal/oil/gas), gas water heaters, fireplaces, wood stoves, and vehicle exhaust. The burning of tobacco products is also included.

- Building materials and furnishings: Our homes and public buildings contain many sources of pollution such as asbestos (found in ceiling/flooring materials, wall/pipe insulation, pre-1974 spackling/plaster compounds); formaldehyde (found in particleboard/fiberboard/plywood, adhesives, fabrics, furniture, and urea-formaldehyde foam ([UFFI]) insulation); lead (found in paint, dust, soil, lead solder, and ceramic glazes); and wet or damp carpet.

- Volatile organic compounds (VOCs) and toxic chemicals found in cleaning agents, hobby-related products, glues, paints, personal care products, pesticides, and sealants.

- Heating, ventilating, and air-conditioning (HVAC) and household appliances such as air conditioners, air filters, cooling systems, dehumidification devices, humidifiers, and unvented (or improperly vented) dryers.

- Outdoor sources such as radon (found primarily in soil, but also in well water, and building materials), pesticides, and industrial air pollution.

You might be surprised to learn that some very familiar things pollute the air we breathe. The following common indoor air pollutants comprise only a partial list:

- Pollen and spores from household plants
- Infiltrating dust
- Viruses, bacteria, and fungi
- Dust mites and their carcasses and droppings
- Human skin flakes
- Pet dander
- Cooking smoke and airborne grease released by cooking
- Mildew and mold spores from damp basements and bathrooms

The air we breathe all day every day carries a mixture of millions of these tiny annoyances. In small concentrations, these particles and gases can make life miserable for all of us. In significant concentrations, they can make an individual sick.

It is interesting to consider that in the last several years, scientific evidence has indicated that the air within homes and other buildings can be more seriously polluted than the outdoor air in even the largest and most industrialized cities. This is no small matter because other research indicates that people spend approximately 90 percent of their time indoors. What this means is that for many people, the risks to health might be greater due to exposure to air pollution indoors than outdoors. It probably comes as no surprise that the young, the elderly, and the chronically ill, especially those suffering from respiratory or cardiovascular disease, are most susceptible to the effects of indoor air pollution.

A good number of particles settle out of the air onto furniture, drapes, and carpets before an air cleaner (if one is even present) can capture them. These settled-out particles are easily stirred up again by ordinary family activities such as normal traffic, playing children, and—especially—running a vacuum cleaner. One thing is certain: all the particulates are ultra-small. It takes an optical microscope, sometimes even an electron microscope, to see them at all. Among the millions of particles, you can see only 1 percent of the total, that is, over 99 percent of the particles contaminating indoor air can't be seen without a microscope. The bottom line, though, is that whether you can see them or not, they are annoying and harmful!

Lack of ventilation

Today professionals are building more energy-efficient homes than they did in the past and consumers are weatherizing their homes. The combination of energy awareness and new construction methods and techniques creates a "tighter" home, and it is this "tightness" that reduces the naturally occurring exchange of indoor air and outdoor air—ventilation. Fresh outdoor air stays out, and indoor air pollutants, such as dust and tobacco smoke particles, remain trapped inside.

Weatherization generally does not cause indoor air problems by adding new pollutants to the air (with a few exceptions, such as caulking, that can sometimes emit pollutants). However, measures such as installing storm windows, weather stripping, caulking, and blown-in wall insulation can reduce the amount of outdoor air infiltrating into a home. Consequently, after weatherization, concentrations of indoor air pollutants from sources inside the home can increase.

Unfortunately, making homes more energy efficient exacts an un-expected price. Inadequate ventilation can sometimes be detected by the presence of stuffy air, moisture condensation on cold surfaces, and/or mold and mildew growth.

Controlling the situation

The problem of indoor air pollution can be approached several different ways. Employing a combination of methods probably yields the best results.

Reduce emissions

Usually the most effective way to improve indoor air quality is to eliminate individual sources of pollution or to reduce their emissions. Some sources, like those that contain asbestos, can be sealed or encapsulated (the preferred term); others, like gas stoves, can be adjusted to decrease the amount of emissions. In many cases, source control is also a more cost-efficient approach to protecting indoor air quality than increasing ventilation, which increases energy costs.

Ventilation improvements

Another approach to lowering the concentrations of indoor air pollutants in a home is to increase the amount of outdoor air coming indoors. Most home heating and cooling systems, including forced-air heating systems, do not mechanically bring fresh air into the home. Opening windows and doors, operating window or attic fans when the weather permits, or running a window air conditioner with the vent control open increases the outdoor ventilation rate. Local bathroom or kitchen fans that exhaust outdoors remove contaminants directly from the room where the fan is located and also increase the outdoor air ventilation rate.

Let your customer know that it is particularly important to take as many of these steps as possible while they are involved in "short-term" activities that can generate high levels of pollutants. For example:

- Painting and paint stripping
- Heating with kerosene heaters
- Cooking
- Home maintenance activities
- Hobby activities such as welding, soldering, and sanding

If possible, perhaps these activities can be moved outdoors. This information doesn't just apply to the customer. Some of these activities will directly affect you as you undertake a renovation project. It is just as important to protect yourself from these pollutants as it is to protect the customer and the entire environment. Contain the pollutants to one area by sealing vents and cold air returns (but be sure to turn the heating system off; if this not possible, find an alternative method). Also block doors, open windows, and/or use a blower to remove pollutants while work is in progress.

Advanced designs of new homes are starting to feature mechanical systems that bring outdoor air into the home. Some of these designs include energy-efficient heat recovery ventilators (HRV, but also known as air-to-air heat exchangers). For more information about air-to-air heat exchangers, contact:

Energy Efficiency and Renewable Energy Clearinghouse
P.O. Box 3048
Merrifield, VA 22116
800-363-3732

The Comfort Ventilator (Carrier Corporation) addresses indoor air quality problems. It continually renews the indoor air supply by bringing fresh air into tightly constructed homes. The American Society of Heating, Refrigerating, and Air-Conditioning Engineers (ASHRAE) recommends a ventilation rate of 0.35 ach (air changes per hour) for new homes. This unit provides at least eight air changes per 24-hour period, which meets the requirements of ASHRAE Standard 62-1989. This unit effectively exhausts chemical and biological indoor air pollutants. In addition, it draws in fresh outside air through its incoming air filter, cleans it, and removes large airborne particles. The outside air is then warmed using heat recovered from the stale, exhausted air. The filtered, fresh air entering the home improves air quality and potentially reduces allergic reactions. The unit's acoustic design positions the motor for quiet operation, muffling sound and keeping vibrations to a minimum. Seven models ranging from 150 to 270 cubic feet per minute are available for residential application, accommodating various space requirements as well as different installation and comfort needs (Fig. 8-1).

Air cleaners

There are many types and sizes of air cleaners on the market, ranging from relatively inexpensive tabletop models to sophisticated and expensive whole-house systems. Some air cleaners are highly effective at particle removal, while others, including most tabletop models, are much less so. Air cleaners are generally not designed to remove gaseous pollutants.

The effectiveness of an air cleaner depends on how well it collects pollutants from indoor air (expressed as a percentage efficiency

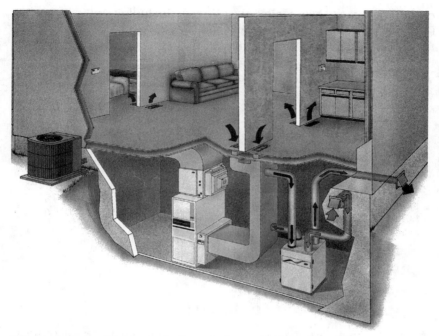

8-1 *Proper ventilation is the key to clean, fresh indoor air.* Used with permission of Carrier Corp.

rate) and how much air it draws through the cleaning or filtering element (expressed in cubic feet per minute). For example, a very efficient collector with a low air-circulation rate will not be effective, but neither will a less efficient collector with a high air-circulation rate. The right balance between efficiency rate and air-circulation rate must be achieved. Of course, the long-term performance of any air cleaner depends on maintaining it according to the manufacturer's directions.

Another important factor in determining the effectiveness of an air cleaner is the "strength" of the pollutant source. Tabletop air cleaners, in particular, might not remove satisfactory amounts of pollutants from strong nearby sources. Individuals who are sensitive to a particular source might find air cleaners helpful only in conjunction with concerted efforts to remove the source.

There might be times when central air cleaning simply isn't possible or practical. Honeywell Inc. has designed a portable unit, the Enviracaire, that removes more than 99.97 percent of indoor air particulates. The unit uses High Efficiency Particulate Air (HEPA) filters. When properly sized for the room area, these portable air cleaners are just as efficient at removing indoor air pollutants as a central air cleaning system. Many allergy sufferers, including my wife who (without fail) sneezes every morning at least 6 times in a row, have found that using such a unit in the bedroom gives them cleaner air to breathe as they sleep and helps their symptoms significantly. My wife's sneezing has been reduced to about once every two weeks, a vast improvement (Fig. 8-2).

8-2
In goes the bad air, out comes the good air . . . The unit draws dirty air from a 360° radius, then gently blows clean air at floor level distributing it throughout the room. Honeywell Inc.

Radon

The most common source of indoor radon is uranium in the soil or rock on which homes are built. As uranium naturally breaks down, it releases radon gas, which is colorless, odorless, and radioactive. Radon gas enters homes through dirt floors, cracks in concrete walls and floors, floor drains, and sumps. When radon becomes trapped in buildings and concentrations build up indoors, exposure to radon becomes a concern. In 1993, the EPA estimated that radon causes about 14,000 preventable lung cancer deaths each year; however, this number could range from 7,000 to 30,000 deaths per year.

Any home might have a radon problem, including homes that are new or older, well-sealed or drafty, with or without basements. Sometimes radon enters the home through well water. In a small number of homes, the building materials emit radon, but building materials rarely cause radon problems by themselves.

You can't see radon, but it's not hard to find out if there is a radon problem. It is important, especially in existing homes, that the premises be tested for radon levels before any remodeling takes place. In fact, if you are called in for an estimate, ask the potential customer if the home has been tested for radon and suggest that the homeowners have it done if they have not yet done so. If there is a problem, then corrective measures can be added into the bid.

The EPA has set a maximum threshold of 4.0 picocuries per liter (pCi/L) of air. If the home exceeds this level, it is recommended that the radon problem be mitigated. Based on the national residential radon survey completed in 1991, the average indoor level is 1.3 picocuries. Radon levels less than 4 pCi/L still pose a risk and in many cases can be reduced.

Inexpensive do-it-yourself radon test kits are available at hardware stores and retail outlets. Recommend to homeowners that they purchase a kit that has passed EPA's testing program or is state-certified. These kits usually display the phrase "Meets EPA Requirements." One such kit is EPA-certified Radon-Zone, developed in 1992 by Enzone Incorporated. To test homes, simply place the container in the home for 72 hours and then mail it along with a $10 lab analysis fee to the Enzone laboratory, where it will be professionally tested for radon contamination. You might want to carry a few of these kits with you as a convenience to your customers.

Another alternative is to hire a trained contractor to do the testing. These contractors should have met EPA's requirements and carry a special RMP identification card. The EPA Radon Measurement Proficiency (RMP) Program evaluates testing contractors.

The EPA provides a list of companies and individual contractors to state radon offices. You can call your state's radon office to obtain a list of qualified contractors in the area—call 800-SOS-RADON (767-72366) for a list of state radon offices. (Note: Although it looks odd, this is the correct number. Dial it like an ordinary phone number except dial five digits at the end instead of the usual four.)

There are simple solutions to radon problems, but lowering high radon levels requires technical skills and special skills. If radon is a problem, recommend that your customers use a contractor who has received special training in this area. If you are looking for a subcontractor to use for a particular job, contact the state radon office. The EPA Radon Contractor Proficiency (RCP) Program tests these contractors, and those listed by the EPA carry special RCP identification cards. A trained RCP contractor can study the problem and help select the correct treatment method.

Perhaps this is an area of interest for you and can be an added value to the division that handles your special needs projects. Be sure that you jump through all the hoops—contact the EPA office and see what it will take to get up to speed on this timely subject.

To learn more on the subject, read *Make Your House Radon Free* by Drs. Carl and Barbara Giles (ISBN 0-8306-3291-3, McGraw-Hill, 1990). The authors explain how to identify the factors that cause radon accumulation in the first place and help you weigh available remedies for their cost and effectiveness. They also make informed recommendations on reputable radon detection and deterrence products. You'll even find out how to build a radon-proof home. It should be noted that the EPA manuals and literature were of major assistance in providing information and line drawings used in *Make Your House Radon Free*.

The EPA has a variety of helpful materials relating to radon that you should add to your library. Contact your regional EPA office for further information. Addresses and phone numbers are at the end of this chapter.

Biological contaminants

Biological contaminants are everywhere and include such common materials as bacteria, molds, mildew, viruses, animal dander, cat saliva, house dust mites, cockroaches, and pollen. These pollutants have many sources. Pollens originate from plants, but viruses are transmitted by people and animals. Bacteria are carried by people and animals as well as soil and plant debris. Obviously household pets are the sources of saliva and animal dander. Did you realize that the protein in urine from rats and mice is a potent allergen? When it dries, it can become airborne. Standing water, water-damaged materials, or wet surfaces also serve as a breeding ground for molds, mildews, bacteria, and insects. House dust mites, the source of one of the most powerful biological allergens, grow in damp, warm environments. Contaminated central air handling systems can become breeding grounds for mold, mildew, and other sources of biological contaminants and can then distribute these contaminants throughout the home.

A good way to reduce exposure to many of these pollutants is to install and use exhaust fans that are vented to the outdoors in kitchens, bathrooms, and laundry rooms and vent clothes dryers outdoors. These actions can eliminate much of the moisture that builds up from everyday activities. There are exhaust fans on the market that produce little noise, an important consideration for some individuals. Another benefit to using kitchen and bathroom exhaust fans is that they can reduce levels of organic pollutants that vaporize from hot water used in showers and dishwashers.

Broan offers a direct discharge ventilator—a through-the-wall fan. The 512M is a 70 CFM exhaust fan that will handle ventilation performance for a bathroom up to 65 square feet. What makes this unit unique is that it requires no ducting. The 6" (15 cm) round flexible aluminum duct will accommodate walls from 4½" to 10" (11 to 25 cm) thick—great for almost any home (Fig. 8-3).

Another approach is to ventilate the attic and crawl spaces to prevent moisture build-up. Keeping humidity levels in these areas below

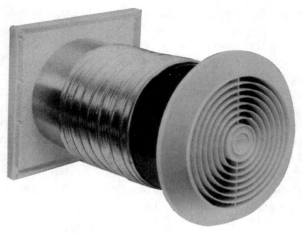

8-3 *The unit is UL listed for use over bathtubs and showers when connected to a GFCI circuit.*
Broan MFG. Co., Inc.

50 percent can prevent water condensation on building materials. In fact, the growth of some sources of biological contaminants can be minimized by controlling the relative humidity level in a home. A relative humidity of 30 to 50 percent is generally recommended for homes.

If you are using cool mist or ultrasonic humidifiers, clean appliances according to the manufacturer's instructions and refill with fresh water daily. Because these humidifiers can become breeding grounds for biological contaminants, they have the potential for causing diseases such as hypersensitivity pneumonitis and humidifier fever. Evaporation trays in air conditioners, dehumidifiers, and refrigerators should also be cleaned frequently.

Water-damaged carpets and building materials can harbor mold and bacteria. Thoroughly clean and dry water-damaged carpets and building materials (within 24 hours if possible) or consider their removal and replacement because it is very difficult to completely rid such materials of biological contaminants.

The contractor can only do so much. Once the home is constructed, it is up to the customer to keep it clean. House dust mites, pollens, animal dander, and other allergy-causing agents can be reduced, although not eliminated, through regular cleaning. Individuals who are allergic to these pollutants should strive for a clean house and use allergen-proof products such as a special encasement for the mattress. Allergic individuals should also leave the house while it is being vacuumed because vacuuming can actually increase airborne levels of mite allergens and other biological contaminants. A central vacuum system vented to the outdoors or a vacuum with high-efficiency filters might also be of help.

After 38 years of research and development, White-Westinghouse has introduced a line of central vacuums that features their exclusive Free-Flow Filtration System. This system utilizes a custom-designed two-ply disposable, primary micro-filter/dirt receptacle that is electrostatically charged and backed by a durable secondary nylon filter. It also utilizes high-velocity air movement and deep cleaning ability to effectively vacuum up allergens—ragweed pollen, plant spores, and most importantly, dust mites. White-Westinghouse central vacuums are designed for installation in any size home, new or existing, and are generally installed in the garage with inlets strategically placed throughout the home (Fig. 8-4).

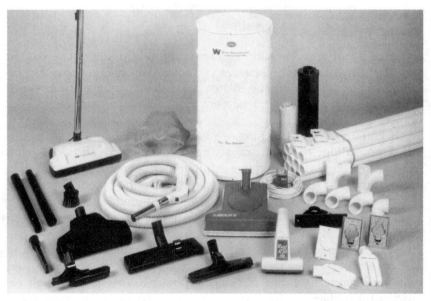

8-4 *With a central vacuum system, your customers will experience a cleaner, healthier indoor environment.* White-Westinghouse

Generally, installing a central vacuum system shouldn't be a problem, but if you run into a difficult case, advise the customer that there are portable vacuums on the market designed to help with indoor pollutants. One such product is the HEMS SB1410 by Singer (Ryobi Motor Products Corp.). This is an upright vacuum with the High-Efficiency Microfiltration System that is 99.3 percent efficient in removing bacteria, pollen, fungi, dust mites, and dust particles as small as 0.1 micron. The unique feature is the bag design. The HEMS filter uses specially designed and constructed inner and outer bags to trap these particles and prevent their release back into the indoor living environment. This unique design enhances performance, helping the homeowner rid the home of annoying allergens (Fig. 8-5).

Take steps to minimize biological pollutants in basements. Do not finish a basement below ground level unless all water leaks are patched and you are certain that your customer will adequately ventilate and heat the space. Encourage your customer to clean and disinfect the basement floor drains regularly. The relative humidity level in the basement is also important and should be kept between 30 and 50 percent. Your customer might need to operate a dehumidifier in the basement to keep relative humidity at an appropriate level.

8-5
The unit comes with a 10-amp motor and a 30' cord with on-board attachments. Ryobi North America

Stoves, heaters, fireplaces, and chimneys

In addition to environmental tobacco smoke, other sources of combustion products are unvented kerosene and gas space heaters, wood stoves, fireplaces, and gas stoves. The major pollutants released are carbon monoxide, nitrogen dioxide, and particles. Unvented kerosene heaters can also generate acid aerosols.

Combustion gases and particles also come from chimneys and flues that are improperly installed or maintained and cracked furnace heat exchangers. Pollutants from fireplaces and wood stoves with no dedicated outdoor air supply can be "backdrafted" from the chimney into the living space, particularly in weatherized homes.

Carbon monoxide

A colorless, odorless gas, carbon monoxide interferes with the delivery of oxygen throughout the body. At high concentrations, it can cause unconsciousness and death. Lower concentrations can cause a range of symptoms from headaches to episodes of increased chest pain in people with chronic heart disease. Fetuses, infants, elderly, and people with anemia or with a history of heart or respiratory disease can be especially sensitive to carbon monoxide exposures.

Nitrogen dioxide

Nitrogen dioxide is a colorless, odorless gas that irritates the mucous membranes in the eye, nose, and throat and causes shortness of breath after exposure to high concentrations. People at particular risk from exposure to nitrogen dioxide include children and individuals with asthma and other respiratory diseases.

Particles

When fuels are incompletely burned, particles can lodge in the lungs and irritate or damage lung tissue. A number of pollutants that can cause cancer attach to small particles that are inhaled and then carried deep into the lungs.

Reducing exposure to combustion

Now that you are aware of some of the dangers of indoor air pollution, take precautions in your own life and make appropriate recommendations to your customers when the topic turns to combustion-related fixtures. Your customers will appreciate both your knowledge and your concern.

Unvented fuel-burning space heaters

Consider the potential effects of indoor air pollution if an unvented kerosene or gas space heater is used. Follow the manufacturer's directions, especially the instructions regarding the proper fuel to use and the heater's proper adjustment. A persistent yellow-tipped flame is generally an indication of maladjustment and increased pollutant emissions. While a space heater is in use, open a door from the room where the heater is located to the rest of the home and open a window slightly.

Exhaust fans, gas stoves and fireplaces
Using a stove hood with a fan vented to the outdoors greatly reduces exposure to pollutants during cooking. Improper adjustment of the burners, often indicated by a persistent yellow-tipped flame, also causes increased pollutant emissions. Ask the gas company to adjust the burner so that the flame tip is blue. If a gas stove or range is part of the bid, then consider one that has a pilotless ignition, so there will be no pilot light burning continuously. Remind the customer that the gas stove should never be used to heat their home. In addition, they should ensure that the flue to their gas fireplace is open when the fireplace is in use. Consider fitting the fireplace opening with glass doors. Depending on how tight the unit is, the customer could leave the flue damper open all the time.

Wood stoves
If your customers are interested in installing a wood stove, guide them toward a properly sized new stove, one that is certified to meet EPA emission standards. Remind your customer that doors to their old wood stoves should be fitted tightly and that they should burn aged or cured (dried) wood only. It is also important that they follow the manufacturer's directions for starting, stoking, and putting out the fire in wood stoves. Pressure-treated lumber should never be burned indoors because of the chemicals used in the treating process.

HVAC maintenance
Blocked, leaking, or damaged chimneys or flues release harmful combustion gases and particles and even fatal concentrations of carbon monoxide. Regular inspection and timely repair are important. Strictly follow all service and maintenance procedures recommended by the manufacturer, including those that tell you how frequently to change the filter (possible once every month or twice during periods of use).

Household products
Organic chemicals are widely used as ingredients in household products. Paints, varnishes, and wax all contain organic solvents, as do

many cleaning, disinfecting, cosmetic, degreasing, and hobby products. Fuels are made up of organic compounds. All of these can release organic compounds when used and, to some degree, when they are stored.

Household chemicals are a way of life. We use them daily and yet really take no thought of the consequences of long-term exposure. With awareness, you and your customers can reduce exposure.

Follow label instructions
Potentially hazardous products often have warnings aimed at reducing user exposure. If a label says to use the product in a well-ventilated area, go outdoors or only use the product in areas equipped with an exhaust fan. Otherwise, open windows to provide the maximum amount of outdoor air possible.

Adopt safe disposal practices
Gases can leak even from closed containers, so this single step can help lower concentrations of organic chemicals in a home. When you are through with a job, do not continue to store unneeded household chemicals. Nor should you simply toss unwanted products in the garbage can. Find out if your local government or any organization in your community sponsors special days for the collection of toxic household wastes.

Buy limited quantities
If you use products only occasionally or seasonally, such as paints, paint strippers, and kerosene for space heaters or gasoline for generators, buy only as much as you will use right away.

Minimize exposure to methylene chloride
Products that contain methylene chloride include paint strippers, adhesive removers, and aerosol spray paints. Methylene chloride is known to cause cancer in animals. Also, methylene chloride is converted to carbon monoxide in the body and causes symptoms associated with exposure to carbon monoxide. When using products containing this chemical indoors, make sure the work area is well ventilated.

Minimize benzene exposure
Benzene is a known human cancer-causing agent. The main indoor sources of this chemical are environmental tobacco smoke, stored fuels and paint supplies, and automobile emissions in attached garages.

Actions that will reduce benzene exposure include eliminating smoking within the home, providing for maximum ventilation during painting, and discarding paint supplies and special fuels that will not be used immediately.

For me, this has been a touchy subject because I grew up in a smoker's environment. I do not smoke and never have, so when I visit my parents, I have a hard time sleeping because even though the bedding is clean, it is so tobacco-impregnated that it is uncomfortable. On the other hand, my grandmother smoked, but she was always considerate of nonsmokers. What bothers me is why it took open heart surgery to get her to quit. Frequently subcontractors who worked for me smoked—but what right did they have to smoke on a job site, throwing butts around? Out of respect for the customer, there should be no smoking on a job site unless the customer gives such permission, and if the contractor says "no smoking," then that's the final word on the subject. If there is smoking during breaks or lunchtime, then don't forget to pick up the butts.

Carpet

In recent years, a number of consumers have associated a variety of symptoms with the installation of new carpet. Scientists have not been able to determine whether the chemicals emitted by new carpets are responsible. If you are installing new carpet, you might wish to take the following steps:

- Request information on carpet emissions from the carpet dealer or supplier.
- Unroll and air out the carpet in a well-ventilated area before the carpet is installed.
- Ask for low-emitting adhesives, if adhesives are needed for installation.
- Ask the customer to leave the premises during and immediately after carpet installation.
- Be sure the installer (including yourself if you do the installation) follows the Carpet and Rug Institute's installation guidelines.
- During carpet installation, open doors and windows. Increasing the amount of fresh air in the home reduces exposure to most chemicals released from the carpet. During and after installation, use window fans, room air conditioners, or other mechanical ventilation equipment to exhaust fumes to the outdoors. Keep the equipment running for at least 48

to 72 hours after the new carpet has been installed.
- Contact the dealer if objectionable odors persist.
- Advise the customer to follow the manufacturer's instructions for proper carpet maintenance.

Formaldehyde

Formaldehyde is an important chemical used widely in the industry to manufacture building materials and numerous household products. It is also a by-product of combustion and certain other natural processes, so it might be present in substantial concentrations both indoors and out. Sources of formaldehyde in the home include building materials, burning tobacco products, household products, and the use of unvented fuel-burning appliances, like gas stoves or kerosene space heaters.

Formaldehyde, by itself or in combination with other chemicals, serves a number of purposes in manufactured products. For example, it adds permanent press qualities to clothing and draperies, is a component of glues and adhesives, and is a preservative in some paints and coating products.

In homes, the most significant sources of formaldehyde are likely to be pressed wood products made using adhesives that contain urea-formaldehyde (UF) resins. Pressed wood products made for indoor use include:
- Particleboard used as subflooring and shelving and in cabinetry and furniture
- Hardwood plywood paneling used for decorative wall covering and in cabinets and furniture
- Medium-density fiberboard (MDF) used for drawer fronts, cabinets, and furniture tops

Medium-density fiberboard contains a higher resin-to-wood ratio than any other UF pressed wood product and is generally recognized as being the highest formaldehyde-emitting pressed wood product.

Other pressed wood products, such as softwood plywood and flake or oriented strandboard, are products used for exterior construction and contain the dark or red/black-colored phenol-formaldehyde (PF) resin. Although formaldehyde is present in both types of resins, pressed woods that contain PF resin generally emit formaldehyde at considerably lower rates than those containing UF resin.

Since 1985, the Department of Housing and Urban Development (HUD) has permitted the use only of plywood and particleboard that conform to specified formaldehyde-emission limits in the construction of prefabricated and mobile homes. In the past, some of these homes had elevated levels of formaldehyde because of the large amount of high-formaldehyde-emitting pressed wood products used in their construction and because of their relatively small interior space.

The rate at which products such as pressed wood or textiles release formaldehyde changes over the life of the product, and formaldehyde emissions generally decrease as products age. When the products are new, high indoor temperatures or humidity can cause increased release of formaldehyde from these products.

During the 1970s, many homes had urea-formaldehyde foam insulation (UFFI) installed in the wall cavities as an energy conservation measure. However, many of these homes were found to have relatively high indoor concentrations of formaldehyde soon after the UFFI installation. Few homes are now insulated with this product. Studies show that formaldehyde emissions from UFFI decline with time so homes in which UFFI was installed many years ago are unlikely to have high levels of formaldehyde now.

Health effects

Formaldehyde, a colorless, pungent-smelling gas, can cause watery eyes, burning sensations in the eyes and throat, nausea, and difficulty in breathing in some humans exposed to elevated levels (above 0.1 part per million). High concentrations can trigger attacks in people with asthma. There is evidence that some people can develop a sensitivity to formaldehyde. It has also been shown to cause cancer in animals and might cause cancer in humans.

Reducing exposure

If you or your customer experience adverse reactions to formaldehyde, you might want to avoid the use of pressed wood and other formaldehyde-emitting products. Ask about the formaldehyde content of pressed wood products, including building materials, cabinetry, and furniture, before purchasing them. Even if you or the customer experience no reactions to formaldehyde, you should still minimize exposure by purchasing exterior-grade products, which emit less formaldehyde.

Some studies suggest that coating pressed wood products with polyurethane might reduce formaldehyde emissions for some period of time. To be effective, any such coating must cover all surfaces and edges and remain intact. Increase the ventilation and carefully follow the manufacturer's instruction while applying these coatings.

The rate at which formaldehyde is released is accelerated by heat and might also depend somewhat on the humidity level. Therefore, the use of dehumidifiers and air conditioning to control humidity and to maintain a moderate temperature can help reduce formaldehyde emissions. Increasing the rate of ventilation in the home will also help to reduce formaldehyde levels.

Lead

Lead has long been recognized as a harmful environmental pollutant. In late 1991, the Secretary of the Department of Health and Human Services called lead the "number one environmental threat to the health of children in the United States." There are many ways in which humans are exposed to lead:

- Air
- Drinking water
- Food
- Contaminated soil
- Deteriorating paint
- Dust

Airborne lead enters the body when an individual breathes or swallows lead particles or dust. Before it was known how harmful lead could be, it was widely used in paint, gasoline, water pipes, and many other products.

Old lead-based paint is the most significant source of lead exposure in the United States today. Harmful exposures to lead can be created when lead-based paint is improperly removed from surfaces by dry scraping, sanding, or open-flame burning. High concentrations of airborne lead particles in homes can also result when lead dust from outdoor sources enters the home, including contaminated soil tracked inside, and from the use of lead in certain indoor activities such as soldering and creating stained-glass.

Health effects of exposure

Lead affects practically all bodily systems. At high levels, it can cause convulsions, coma, and even death. Lower levels of lead can adversely affect the brain, central nervous system, blood cells, and kidneys.

The effects of lead exposure on fetuses and young children can be severe. They include delays in physical and mental development, lower IQ levels, shortened attention spans, and increased behavioral problems. Fetuses, infants, and children are more vulnerable to lead exposure than adults because lead is more easily absorbed into growing bodies and the tissues of small children are more sensitive to the damaging effects of lead. Children might also experience higher exposures because they are more likely to get lead dust on their hands and then put their fingers or other lead-contaminated objects into their mouths.

Ways to reduce exposure

To minimize lead dust exposure, keep areas where children play as dust-free and clean as possible. During and after a project, have your customer mop floors, and wipe window ledges and chewable surfaces (such as cribs) with a solution of powdered automatic dishwasher detergent (not a multipurpose household cleaner) in warm water. Dishwasher detergents are recommended because of their high phosphate content. Suggest that toys and stuffed animals be washed regularly and that children wash their hands before meals, naptime, and bedtime.

Most homes built before 1960 contain heavily leaded paint. Some homes built as recently as 1978 might also contain lead paint. This paint could be on window frames, walls, the outside of homes, or on other surfaces. Neither you nor your customer should burn painted wood since it might contain lead; take the responsibility for this and haul painted scrap material away. If you encounter lead-based paint on a job, leave it undisturbed if it is in good condition—do not sand or burn off paint that might contain lead. In good condition, lead paint is usually not a problem, except in places where painted surfaces rub against each other and create dust (for example, opening a window).

Do not remove lead paint. Individuals have been poisoned by scraping or sanding lead paint because these activities generated large amounts of lead dust. As with asbestos, paint should also be tested at a private laboratory to determine the presence of lead. Hire a subcontractor who specializes in lead paint removal. The homeowner, especially children and pregnant women, should leave the area until all work is completed and cleanup is done.

Do not bring lead dust into the home. If you work in construction, demolition, painting, or your hobby involves working with lead, you might unknowingly bring lead into the home on your hands or clothes. You might also be tracking in lead from soil around the home. Soil very close to homes might be contaminated from lead paint on the outside of the building. Soil by roads and highways might be contaminated from years of exhaust fumes from cars and trucks that used leaded gas. Wipe your feet before entering a home. If you work with lead, change your clothes before you enter a home (e.g., to estimate a job), and launder that clothing separately.

Find out about lead in drinking water. Well and city water does not usually contain lead. Water usually picks up lead inside the home from household plumbing that is made with lead materials. Since 1991, solder and plumbing parts that come into contact with potable (drinkable) water have been required to be lead-free or have very low percentages of lead in the valves. The only way to know if there is lead in drinking water is to have it tested. Contact the local heath department or the water supplier to find out how to get the water tested. For more information, contact the National Lead Information Center at 800-532-3394 and ask for *Lead Poisoning and Your Children*. If you want to talk to a specialist, call 800-424-5323.

Remodeling and new construction criteria

Today we are building homes more carefully to save heating and cooling dollars. We are putting in high-performance windows, better insulation, and wrapping our homes in protective coatings, all to create a "tighter" package for greater energy efficiency. However, with the construction of tighter homes, indoor air quality problems can develop from too little ventilation. It is important to stay on top of the home's mechanical system and how it will perform in order to provide better indoor air quality. The following 14 points comprise a comprehensive checklist regarding issues of healthy indoor environments, energy efficiency, and resource efficiency. Use this section as a guide to a better, healthier home:

1 Use sealed-combustion, energy-efficient appliances that meet energy/safety standards.

   During the installation of fuel-burning appliances, attach a duct system that connects to the outside of the house. This duct serves as an air intake source and provides the appliance with a supply of oxygen, which is required during the combustion process to eliminate backdrafting and combustion gases such as carbon monoxide from entering the house. There should also be a separate exhaust duct vented to the outside of the house.

2 Install whole house mechanical ventilation: air filtration, dehumidification, and air-to-air heat-recovery exchange systems.

   Install an air-to-air heat-recovery exchanger as a part of the home's overall mechanical system. It improves indoor air quality by providing air exchange for an entire house using fresh, filtered air, and dehumidification to control humidity and prevent molds, mildew and dust mites. While this could cost from $1,500 to $2,200 installed, there will be up to a 90 percent energy recovery from exhausted air.

3 Site house properly.

Study site and surrounding area for an understanding of orientation in regard to sun and wind patterns. A southeastern orientation would be optimal to take advantage of solar gain. In addition, locate the house away from pollution sources (e.g., soil and groundwater contamination). Minimize excavation for erosion control.

The homeowner will realize energy savings because maximizing daylight from a southeastern exposure reduces the demand for heat and light. Of course, these savings will vary by location of site. In addition, living away from pollution sources is better for your health. However, locating the house near conveniences decreases the demand for fossil fuels for gas.

4 Use building materials, finishes, and furnishings containing low volatile organic compounds.

Read material data sheets available from retailers and manufacturers for product make-up. Contact product manufacturers' consumer hotlines for more information on products. Be cognizant of indoor air pollutants and learn to recognize health symptoms/irritations that can occur after exposure to these irritants. ChemRex, Inc., has a construction adhesive, PL Premium, that stands up to strict environmental regulations (VOC compliance) but it is also nonflammable, waterproof, and works with all building materials.

Actively seeking out and using these products should minimize occupant irritation and health problems as a result of reaction to chemical compounds. There will also be less toxic waste to clean up.

5 Waterproof the foundation properly.

The waterproofing system involves three steps:

~First apply an asphalt-based polymer to the exterior side of the basement walls to create a waterproof seal.

~Over the polymer coating, apply an insulation board made from a dense fiberboard material that provides thermal protection and drainage qualities.

~Third, install drainage tile at the walls' footings to allow the water to drain to daylight or a drywell.

Another way to protect against water problems is to install a capillary break on top of the footing of the exterior wall. The capillary break material (made of polystyrene or other types of waterproof substances) acts as a barrier and prevents water from wicking up through the ground into the wall cavity. Overall, a foundation waterproofing system prevents biological contamination. Moisture control in the house also prevents deterioration of the structure. Insulative board does not rot and has an insulation value of 5 per inch.

6 Seal ductwork.

During ductwork installation, use a foil duct tape, a high-temperature flue tape, and a nonhardening sealant at the bypasses and joints to seal air and vapors. This procedure prevents contaminants from recirculating throughout the house. Indoor air quality should be better if the ducts are cleaned as well.

7 Use vapor barriers.

The air vapor barrier is made from a polystyrene material and is installed in each room over a framed house's insulation on the exterior walls. At the points where an exterior and interior wall meet, the polystyrene barrier is placed between the interior stud and the exterior wall to provide a continuous wrap. The barrier is taped and caulked at all seams and joints to provide a continuous vapor barrier. This procedure helps to prevent condensation and mold growth on exterior walls. It also decreases air infiltration, helping to conserve energy, which in turn reduces heating bills and reduces demand on fossil fuels.

8 Control radon emissions.

At the foundation level, cover sub-slab gravel (minimum 4" ([10 cm])) with a 6-mil polystyrene membrane to block radon gases from entering the basement through the slab. Over the sump basin, install a vented cover, connecting it to a vent pipe that vents (and is sealed) to the outside of the house. Should radon be detected, the plastic vent stack can be attached to the sump cover and power-vented to the outside of the house. The power venting action sucks out the gases from under that slab and vents them out of the house. Preventing cancer-causing radon from entering the house reduces and/or eliminates the health risks associated with radon gas.

9 Use high-efficiency (low-E, double-glazed) windows.

When possible, orient the house toward a southeastern exposure to maximize on the sun's light. Placement of windows on the south and east side of the house helps to capture the natural light. Special consideration should be given to windows placed on the north side of the home, particularly in northern climates, to ensure that the windows have insulative properties for decreased air infiltration and increased energy savings. Other considerations for windows include UV coating on windows to prevent damage to furnishings and low-emissivity (low-E) glass that reflects radiant heat. Careful attention to window selection and placement can produce a positive effect on both the mental and physical well-being of people who are exposed to and receive an adequate dose of natural light. It can also reduce heat loss, thus conserving energy and providing lower energy bills. Conserving energy reduces the demand on fossil fuels.

10 Use natural advantages in landscaping.

Visit local nurseries to learn about native species that are available and to determine if these species meet the requirements of your location's light, soil type, temperature, and maintenance time. When landscaping for energy conservation, consider the type of plant or tree (e.g., deciduous or coniferous), in terms of what you want to achieve. Strategic tree planting can reduce energy demands on your home by blocking the wind and sun during various times of the year and day. Careful selection of planting materials can reduce or eliminate the need for pesticides and herbicides, and also provides habitat for native wildlife. Using native plants is economically beneficial to indigenous horticulture businesses. Depending on the species selected, less water might be required, and strategic planting can save energy.

11 Use cellulose insulation with high R-value.

Insulation is blown into wall cavities to fill in gaps and tight spaces behind pipes, ducts, and wires. Cellulose insulation provides better full-coverage insulation and reduces air infiltration because of product density. For installation, a netting material is attached to the wall studs on the interior of the exterior walls to hold the insulation in place. With special blowing equipment, the insulation is blown into the netting to the wall cavity between the studs. The high R-value of cellulose insulation produces greater energy efficiency, thus saving on energy bills. Because the insulation material itself is recycled (e.g., newspaper cellulose), its use reduces overall consumption.

12 Use materials made from recycled materials or containing recycled contents.

Read product labeling and ask retailers/manufacturers of products about their products' contents. Additional information is available from sources such as the Center for Resourceful Building Technology and various building suppliers. Using recycled materials provides a market for them, thus encouraging the reduce/reuse/recycle idea. It also reduces our demand for precious natural resources and reduces pollution and landfill waste.

13 Install disposal and recycling systems.

Install recycling centers/systems in your home to accommodate the recyclable items that you consume. Contact your local neighborhood association or city officials to find out about local recycling facilities, drop-off sites, or curbside pick-up. This action also provides a market for recycled materials, reduces our demand for natural resources, and reduces pollution and landfill waste. It might also eliminate or reduce the health risks associated with the illegal dumping of toxic materials that can result in groundwater contamination and poor air quality.

14 Minimize construction waste.

As a contractor, consider setting up recycling/collection bins on construction sites. This requires educating the job supervisor and workers on what materials can and should be recycled, and it requires monitoring and responsibility on the part of those workers. Also involved are the time and costs of transporting materials to a recycling site. However, it also provides a market for recycled materials, thus encouraging reduce/reuse/recycle idea while it reduces demand for natural resources. Minimizing construction water also reduces ground/air/water contamination and landfill waste.

Interior design considerations

Selecting materials for the interior of a home can be a challenge if your customer is sensitive to the many chemicals often used in their production or preservation. Manufacturers should be able to provide you with material safety data sheets on their products before you purchase. Often these are available through the dealer where you purchase these items. When determining what materials to select for the interior of your customer's home, base your decision on the toxicity levels of the products and not solely on the "naturalness" of the product—and be sure to consult with the customer.

Wallcoverings

When selecting wallcoverings, search out products that have low toxicity levels. Make certain you follow through on this idea all the way, from wall preparation to finish coat for both paint and wallpaper on new and existing walls. If sanding is involved, use a sander that has been hooked up to a dust collector (vacuum cleaner). Carefully check the makeup of any additives, such as mildew-resistant chemicals added to paint.

Wallpaper

Many wallpapers and wallpaper adhesives are treated with fungicides. Ask for more information about the paper or adhesive from your supplier or from the wallpaper manufacturer. Vinyl wallpaper can produce vinyl and formaldehyde contamination plus various contaminants from the adhesive.

Paint

Make sure that the paint you choose has a low VOC level. All paints release trace amounts of gases that can be irritating to occupants for months after application. Paints with a high VOC level will off-gas and could cause respiratory irritations from the emissions. The lighter the pigment in the paint, the less toxic the paint is. The tint is the component likely to have a negative impact on the environment because of the potentially toxic compounds added to the paint to create the color, which is why pastel colors are preferred. Each paint color and product should be tested for compatibility with the customer. Purchase minimal quantities of paint in the colors chosen by the customer until the customer is satisfied, and don't forget to add these extra materials and labor into your bid.

Floor coverings

There are many types of floor coverings that can be used in a home. Of course, like anything else, you need to work with the customer to select the right flooring. For those who have allergies, carpet should be removed from those areas of the house where they spend most of their time.

Solid hardwood floors

This type of flooring is recommended because of its smooth, easy-to-clean surface. An important issue to consider is the type of finish that you use on the wood floor. There are many water-based finishes; however, some don't withstand heavy foot traffic and will require refinishing on a regular basis. If you select an oil-based finish, ensure that you have the proper ventilation in the area that you are finishing and that any fumes are exhausted from the home's interior. Another idea is to select your hardwood from a sustainable source. The source should be certified by the Scientific Certification Institute or the Rain Forest Alliance.

Bruce Hardwood Floors' Natural Reflections collection has 11 natural and decorator accent colors that make it easy to coordinate with any decor. The ⁵⁄₁₆" × 2¼" (8 mm × 57 mm) of solid oak strip flooring is prefinished with UV-cured urethane finish that has been formulated to maximize toughness and durability and minimize care. The Insta-Lock installation system results in much faster installation, so less time is spent on the job site (Fig. 8-6). The factory-finished floors eliminate the dust and fumes once associated with on-site sand-and-finish installations. Where possible, consider hardwood flooring for bedrooms as it creates a much less allergic environment. Your customers will certainly appreciate it!

8-6 *Hardwood flooring—just what the doctor ordered!* Natural Reflections by Bruce Hardwood Floors

Ceramic tile

Most ceramic tile is stable and considered a good material selection. Tile that has been glazed (make sure it is not a glaze containing lead) is recommended because it has been sealed and therefore has less chance of sheltering bacteria or other microorganisms.

Vinyl

One of the most readily available flooring materials, vinyl comes in sheet goods or individual squares. It is easy to clean and durable. To avoid potential respiratory irritations, ask for low-odor adhesive for installation.

Linoleum

Linoleum is made from linseed oil, pine resins, and wood flour on a jute backing. It contains no harmful toxins and can easily be cleaned. However, some people are sensitive to the pine resins used in linoleum and should avoid using it in their homes altogether.

Brick and stone

Both these materials are good selections for interior use because of their inert qualities.

Carpet

If you have to use it, keep carpeting to a minimum. Make sure you see a material safety data sheet on the product to get an idea of its chemical makeup. Formaldehyde is commonly used in carpets and is known to cause upper respiratory irritations and headaches. Often it takes two years or more for the formaldehyde to be out-gassed from the carpet. A quick way to tell if a particular carpet is irritating is to put a freshly cut sample in a glass jar and set it in direct sunlight. After a few hours, open the lid and have your customer smell the fumes; if the fumes seem offensive, consider selecting another carpet. Obviously, you do not want to purchase a carpet until you have had an opportunity to take a sample and perform this test. A word on wool carpet: although wool is a natural product, wool carpet is often treated with stain-resistant products and moth repellent—two substances that can be toxic to your health.

Carpet pads

Whether natural, rubber, or plastic, carpet pads can be irritating to people. Carpets and pads collect dust and some are potent sources of air contamination.

Cabinetry

To avoid problems from off-gassing formaldehyde, the best selection for cabinets is solid hardwood sealed with a low-VOC sealer. Many cabinets are made from particleboard that has a wood veneer finish glued to it. The particleboard and the bonding agent contain formaldehyde and can be an irritant to many people, until they completely off-gas in a few years. Another option to cabinetry is metal because of its inert qualities. When using MDF as a substrate for countertops, it is important that you take the necessary precautions and seal all areas that will not be covered in plastic laminate since MDF off-gasses at high VOC levels—this technique will reduce VOC levels.

Countertops

Use solid surfaces, such as glazed ceramic tile, marble, granite, or stainless steel for countertops for their inert qualities. Many countertops are particleboard covered with laminate (see above note on treatment of laminate). Particleboard off-gasses formaldehyde, but when covered and sealed with laminate, the emissions are lessened. A solid surfacing material is safe to use (e.g., Gibraltar by Wilsonart). If using a glazed ceramic tile, make sure you use a grout with no additives.

Interior fabrics

Encourage your customer to keep upholstery, drapes, and upholstered furniture to a minimum. Many of the fabrics used to make these items contain stain repellents, fungicides, and formaldehyde. Consider using natural, untreated fabrics such as cotton where applicable.

Recycled materials

Consider using nonbearing steel studs for interior walls. The steel stud can be used as a substitute for wood, is noncombustible, and is made from recycled steel. It is easy to use with standard tools, and traditional framing material can be attached to steel studs—especially around door openings. Plumbing and wiring can be routed through prepunched holes. Check with your local supply house to learn more about this product.

Consider using improved truss systems that use both steel and wood in their engineered design. Some wallboard papers are made entirely from recycled paper, and vinyl sidings are also improving their recycled content. Fiberglass can include recycled glass, rigid foam can contain up to 50 percent recycled materials, and cellulose insulation is almost totally recycled.

State and local organizations

Your questions or concerns about indoor air problems can frequently be answered by the government agencies in your area. Responsibilities for indoor air quality issues are usually divided among many different agencies. Call or write the agencies responsible for health or air quality control to begin your library on the subject. A good place to start is to contact the EPA office for your region.

EPA Region 1
JFK Federal Bldg.
1 Congress Street, Room 2203
Boston, MA 02202
617-565-3420
This regional office serves Connecticut, Maine, Massachusetts, New Hampshire, Rhode Island, and Vermont.

EPA Region 2
290 Broadway
New York, NY 10007
212-637-3000
This regional office serves New Jersey, New York, Puerto Rico, and the Virgin Islands.

EPA Region 3
841 Chestnut St.
Philadelphia, PA 19107
215-597-9800
This regional office serves Delaware, the District of Columbia, Maryland, Pennsylvania, Virginia, and West Virginia.

EPA Region 4
345 Courtland St., NE
Atlanta, GA 30365
404-347-4727
This regional office serves Alabama, Florida, Georgia, Kentucky, Mississippi, North Carolina, South Carolina, and Tennessee.

EPA Region 5
77 West Jackson Blvd.
Chicago, IL 60604
312-353-2000

This regional office serves Illinois, Indiana, Michigan, Minnesota, Ohio, and Wisconsin.

EPA Region 6
1445 Ross Ave.
12th Floor, Ste. 1200
Dallas, TX 74202
214-665-6444
This regional office serves Arkansas, Louisiana, New Mexico, Oklahoma, and Texas.

EPA Region 7
726 Minnesota Ave.
Kansas City, KS 66101
913-551-7000
This regional office serves Iowa, Kansas, Missouri, and Nebraska.

EPA Region 8
One Denver Place
999 18th St., Ste. 500
Denver, CO 80202
800-759-4372 (region)
303-293-1603
This regional office serves Colorado, Montana, North Dakota, South Dakota, Utah, and Wyoming.

EPA Region 9
75 Hawthorne St.
San Francisco, CA 94105
415-744-1500
This regional office serves Arizona, California, Hawaii, Nevada, American Samoa, and Guam.

EPA Region 10
1200 Sixth Ave.
Seattle, WA 98101
800-424-4372 (region)
206-553-1200
This regional office serves Alaska, Idaho, Oregon, and Washington.

EPA Headquarters
401 M St. SW
Washington, DC 20460
202-260-2090
Other organizations that might be a source of useful information include:

Indoor Air Quality Information Clearinghouse (IAQ INFO)
P.O. Box 37133
Washington, DC 20013-7133
800-438-4318
This line operates Monday to Friday from 9 a.m. to 5 p.m., Eastern Standard Time (EST). IAQ INFO distributes EPA publications, answers questions on the phone, and makes referrals to other nonprofit and governmental organizations.

Consider reading any or all of the following EPA publications:
- *The Inside Story: A Guide to Indoor Air Quality*
- *A Citizen's Guide to Radon: The Guide to Protecting Yourself and Your Family from Radon*
- *Home Buyer's and Seller's Guide to Radon*
- *Asbestos in Your Home*
- *What You Should Know About Combustion Appliances and Indoor Air Pollution*

Access and accommodations

An environmentally safe home should be designed with changing lifestyles in mind. The universal design and environmentally safe home concepts can be interwoven to accommodate the occupants for ease of living as they age or become physically disabled. Here is a partial list of some of the features that have been discussed in *Accessible Housing* and still need to be considered during the design phases of your project:
- Wider hallways and doorways for easy maneuverability
- Ramps to the outside of the house from the garage entrance and other doors
- Closet in the front entry that can be adapted for an elevator or lift to other floors
- Master bedroom on the first floor
- Crank-out windows instead of double-hung
- Lever-style handles instead of knobs
- Laundry room on the first level
- The main floor all on one level
- Direct-glue carpet (or no carpet) for wheelchair users

So, now that you've read *Accessible Housing*, how do you feel about universal design? Is this an area that needs your expertise and skills?

> Whoever acquires knowledge and does not practice it resembles him who ploughs his land and leaves it unsown.
>
> Saadi

A

Contributing agencies, associations, organizations, and vendors

Agencies and organizations

ANSI
11 West 42nd St.
New York, NY 10036

Building Officials and Code
 Administrators International
 (BOCA)
4051 West Flossmoor Rd.
Country Club Hills, IL 60478-5795

Burglary Prevention Council
221 North LaSalle St., Ste. 3500
Chicago, IL 60601-1520

Center for Accessible Housing
School of Design
North Carolina State University
Box 8613
Raleigh, NC 27695-8613

Chicago Botanic Garden
P.O. Box 400
Glencoe, IL 60022
708-835-8243

Easter Seal Society of Washington
State Office
521 2nd Ave. W.
Seattle, WA 98119

Eastern Paralyzed Veterans
  Association
75-20 Astoria Blvd.
Jackson Heights, NY 11370-1177

Health House Project
American Lung Association/MPLS
1829 Portland Ave.
Minneapolis, MN 55404

HUD USER
P.O. Box 6091
Rockville, MD 20850

International Conference of
  Building Officials (ICBO)
5360 South Workman Mill Rd.
Whittier, CA 90601

NAHB Research Center
400 Prince George's Blvd.
Upper Marlboro, MD 20772-8731

National Conference of States on
  Building Codes and Standards,
  Inc. (NCSBCS)
505 Huntmar Park Dr., Ste. 210
Herndon, VA 22070

National Easter Seals Society
230 West Monroe St., Ste. 1800
Chicago, IL 60606-4802

National Kitchen and Bath
  Association
687 Willow Grove St.
Hackettstown, NJ 07840

WELCOME, H.O.M.E., Inc.
P.O. Box 586
Newburg, WI 53060

Appliances

AMI, Inc.
P.O. Box 1782
Stanwood, WA 98292
360-629-9269

Dwyer Products Corp.
418 North Calumet Ave.
Michigan City, IN 46360
800-348-8508

GE Appliances
AP4-240
Louisville, KY 40225

King Refrigerator Corp.
76-02 Woodhaven Blvd.
Glendale, NY 11385
718-897-2200

Ryobi Motor Products Corp.
1424 Perman Dairy Rd.
Anderson, SC 29625
800-845-5020

The Jenn-Air/Magic Chef
3035 North Shadeland Ave.
Indianapolis, IN 46226-0901
800-673-5262

Whirlpool Corp.
2303 Pipestone Rd.
Benton Harbor, MI 49022

White-Westinghouse
Central Vacuum Systems
P.O. Box 786
Webster City, IA 50595
515-832-3398

Books/magazines/plans

American Standard Literature
Department
P.O. Box 639
Hanover, MD 21076

Architectural and Transportation
Barriers Compliance Board
1331 F St. NW, Ste. 1000
Washington, DC 20004

Building Officials and Code
Administrators International
(BOCA)
4051 West Flossmoor Rd.
Country Club Hills, IL 60478-5795

Center for Accessible Housing
School of Design
North Carolina State University
Box 8613
Raleigh, NC 27695-8613

Dri-View Manufacturing (GE
Company)
4700 Allmond Ave.
Louisville, KY 40209

Easter Seal Society of Washington
State Office
521 2nd Ave. W.
Seattle, WA 98119

Eastern Paralyzed Veterans
Association
75-20 Astoria Blvd.
Jackson Heights, NY 11370-1177

Health House Project
American Lung Association/MPLS
1829 Portland Ave.
Minneapolis, MN 55404

HomeStyles Publishing and
Marketing
275 Market St., Ste. 521
Minneapolis, MN 55405
800-547-5570

HUD USER
P.O. Box 6091
Rockville, MD 20850

International Conference of
Building Officials (ICBO)
5360 South Workman Mill Rd.
Whittier, CA 90601

NAHB Research Center
400 Prince George's Blvd.
Upper Marlboro, MD 20772-8731

National Conference of States on
Building Codes and Standards,
Inc. (NCSBCS)
505 Huntmar Park Dr., Ste. 210
Herndon, VA 22070

National Easter Seal Society
230 West Monroe St., Ste. 1800
Chicago, IL 60606-4802

National Kitchen and Bath
Association
687 Willow Grove St.
Hackettstown, NJ 07840

Southern Building Code Congress
International (SBCCI)
900 Montclair Rd.
Birmingham, AL 35213

Taylor Publishing Co.
1550 West Mockingbird Ln.
Dallas, TX 75235
800-759-8120

The Tauton Press, Inc.
63 South Main St.
Newtown, CT 06470
800-283-7252

WELCOME, H.O.M.E., Inc.
P.O. Box 586
Newburg, WI 53060

Whirlpool Corp.
2000 North State Rt. 63
Benton Harbor, MI 49022-2692

Workbench Magazine
700 West 47th St., Ste. 310
Kansas City, MO 64112
816-531-5730

Cabinets/products

Accessible Work Systems, Inc.
2295 CR 292
Bellevue, OH 44811
800-321-4053

Asko, Inc.
903 North Bowser, #200
Richardson, TX 75081
800-367-2444

KraftMaid Cabinetry, Inc.
16052 Industrial Pkwy.
Middlefield, OH 44062
800-654-3008

Lee/Rowan
Building Products Division
6333 Etzel Ave.
St. Louis, MO 63133
800-325-6150

Vance Industries, Inc.
7401 West Wilson Ave.
Chicago, IL 60656
708-867-6000

White Home Products, Inc.
P.O. Box 340
Smyrna, GA 30081
800-200-9272

Yorktowne, Inc.
100 Redco Ave.
Red Lion, PA 17356-0231
717-244-4011

Firms—architects/ designers/contractors

CK&B
1661 Glenroy Dr., #101
San Jose, CA 95124

Easter Seals Construction
4301 South Pine, Ste. 57
Tacoma, WA 98409

Extended Home Living Services, Inc.
3445 Carol Ln.
Northbrook, IL 60062
708-824-1999

Geise Architects
81 Vine St., Ste. 202
Seattle, WA 98121
206-441-1440

GUYNES DESIGN, Inc.
1555 East Jackson
Phoenix, AZ 85034
800-264-0390

Habitat, Inc.
6031 South Maple Ave.
Tempe, AZ 85283

Harvey's Kitchen & Baths
22560 Glenn Dr., Ste. 115
Sterling, VA 20164
703-444-0871

Horticulture Therapy Services
Chicago Botanic Garden
P.O. Box 400
Glencoe, IL 60022
708-835-8243

Kitchen Bath Design
1000 Bristol St. North
Newport Beach, CA 92660
714-955-1232

LifeStyle HomeDesign Services
275 Market St., Ste. 512
Minneapolis, MN 55405

Mary Jo Peterson, CKD, CBD
Design Consultant
3 Sunset Cove Rd.
Brookfield, CT 06804

Northwest Hospital
1550 North 115th St., MS H020A
Seattle, WA 98133

Hardware

Fiberstars, Inc.
2883 Bayview Dr.
Fremont, CA 94538
800-327-7877

Mechanical Plastics Corp.
444 Saw Mill River Rd.
Elmsford, NY 10523
800-544-2552

Power Access Corp.
42 Bridge St.
Collinsville, CT 06022
800-344-0088

Stanley Hardware
480 Myrtle St.
New Britain, CT 06053
800-337-4393

Weiser Lock—A Masco Co.
6700 Weiser Lock Dr.
Tucson, AZ 85746
800-677-5625

Health care products

ARJO Inc.
8130 Lehigh Ave.
Morton Grove, IL 60053
800-323-1245

DMI—DURO-MED Industries, Inc.
155 Polifly Rd.
Hackensack, NJ 07602
800-526-4753

Electric Mobility Corp.
#1 Mobility Plaza
Sewell, NJ 08080
800-662-4548

Enzone, Inc.
P.O. Box 290480
Davie, FL 33329-0480
800-448-0535

Frohock-Stewart
455 Whitney Ave.
Northboro, MA 01532
800-343-6059

Guardian Products, Inc.
4175 Guardian St.
Simi Valley, CA 93063
800-423-8034

Hewi, Inc.
2851 Old Tree Dr.
Lancaster, PA 17603
717-293-1313

Lindustries, Inc.
P.O. Box 295
Auburndale, MA 02166
617-237-8177

Lubidet USA, Inc.
1980 South Quebec Street, Ste. 4
Denver, CO 80231-3234
800-582-4338

Makita U.S.A., Inc.
14930 Northam St.
La Mirada, CA 90638-5753
800-462-5482

Rampit, Inc.
P.O. Box 286
Coldwater, MI 49036
800-876-9498

Rubbermaid, Inc.
1147 Akron Rd.
Wooster, OH 44691-6000
216-264-6464

T.F. Herceg, Inc.
982 Route 1
Pine Island, NY 10969
800-724-5305

Heating/fireplace

Carrier Corp.
Dept. ACLS
108 Metropolitan Park Dr.
Liverpool, NY 13088
800-227-7437 (Dealers)
315-457-9333 (Information)

Heat-N-Glow Fireplace Products,
  Inc.
6665 West Hwy. 13
Savage, MN 55378
612-882-3737

Honeywell, Inc.
Home and Building Control
1985 Douglas Dr. North
Golden Valley, MN 55422
800-345-6770

SSHC, Inc.
146 Elm St.
Old Saybrook, CT 06475
203-388-3848

Lifts/elevators

Access Industries, Inc.
4001 East 138th St.
Grandview, MO 64030
800-925-3100

Aquatic Access, Inc.
417 Dorsey Way
Louisville, KY 40223
800-325-5438

Bruno Independent Living Aids,
  Inc.
1780 Executive Dr.
Oconomowoc, WI 53066
800-882-8183

Garaventa (Canada) Ltd.
P.O. Box 1769
Blaine, WA 98231-1769
800-663-6556

Spectrum Pool Products
9600 Inspiration Dr.
Missoula, MT 59802
800-776-5309

Waupaca Elevator Company, Inc.
P.O. Box 246
Waupaca, WI 54981
800-238-8739

Materials

Bruce Hardwood Floors
16803 Dallas Pkwy.
Dallas, TX 75248
800-722-4647

ChemRex, Inc.
889 Valley Park Dr.
Shakopee, MN 55379
612-496-6000

Pittsburgh Corning
800 Presque Isle Dr.
Pittsburgh, PA 15239-2799
412-327-6100

The R.C.A. Rubber Co.
P.O. Box 9240
Akron, OH 44305
800-321-2340

Wilsonart International, Inc.
P.O. Box 6110
Temple, TX 76503-6110
800-433-3222

Phone/notification/ security systems

Aiphone Corp.
1700 13th Ave. N.E.
Bellevue, WA 98009
206-455-0510

AMERIPHONE, Inc.
7231 Garden Grove Blvd., Ste. E
Garden Grove, CA 92641-4219
714-897-0808

Essex Electronics, Inc.
1130 Mark Ave.
Carpinteria, CA 93013
800-539-5377

Plumbing/products for bathrooms/kitchens

Alsons Corp.
42 Union St.
Hillsdale, MI 49242
800-769-2744

American Standard
P.O. Box 6820
Piscataway, NJ 08855-6820
800-752-6292

Aqua Glass Corp.
P.O. Box 412
Adamsville, TN 38310
800-542-5806

Broan MFG. Co., Inc.
P.O. Box 140
Hartford, WI 53027-0140
800-558-1711

E.L. Mustee & Sons, Inc.
5431 West 164th St.
Cleveland, OH 44142
216-267-3100

Florestone Products Co.
2851 Falcon Dr.
Madera, CA 93637
800-446-8827

Franke, Inc.
Kitchen Systems Division
212 Church Rd.
North Wales, PA 19454
215-699-8761

Gemini Bath & Kitchen Products
3790 East 44th St., Ste. 228
Tucson, AZ 85713
800-262-6252

Grohe America, Inc.
241 Covington Dr.
Bloomingdale, IL 60108
708-582-7711

Hansgrohe, Inc.
1465 Ventura Dr.
Cummings, GA 30103
800-719-1000

Hinge-It Corp.
3999 Millersville Rd.
Indianapolis, IN 46205
800-599-6328

Kohler Co.
444 Highland Dr.
Kohler, WI 53044
414-457-4441

Interbath, Inc.
665 North Baldwin Park Blvd.
City of Industry, CA 91746
818-369-1841

International Cushioned Products
#202-8360 Bridgeport Rd.
Richmond, BC Canada V6X 3C7
800-882-7638

Jacuzzi Whirlpool Bath
2121 North California Blvd.,
 Ste. 475
Walnut Creek, CA 94596
800-678-6889 (Literature)
510-938-7070 (Corporate)

Maax, Inc.
600 Cameron
Sainte-Marie, Beauce

Quebec, Canada G6E 1B2
418-387-3646

Pedal Valves, Inc.
13625 River Rd.
Luling, LA 70070
800-431-3668

PPP Manufacturing Co.
3868 Providence Rd.
Newtown Square, PA 19073
800-473-1803

Resources Conservation, Inc.
P.O. Box 71
Greenwich, CT 06836-0071
800-243-2862

Robern, Inc.
1648 Winchester Rd.
Bensalem, PA 19020
800-877-2376

Ultraflo Corp.
P.O. Box 2294
Sandusky, OH 44870
419-626-8182

Universal-Rundle Corp.
217 North Mill St.
New Castle, PA 16103-0029
800-955-0316

Silcraft Corp.
528 Hughes Dr.
Traverse City, MI 49686
800-678-7100

Sterling Plumbing Group
Market/Communications
 Department
2900 Golf Rd.
Rolling Meadows, IL 60008
800-895-4774

Tub-Master Corp.
413 Virginia Dr.
Orlando, FL 32803-1892
407-898-2881

Protective products

AC Products, Inc.
172 East La Jolla St.
Placentia, CA 92670
800-238-4204

Brophy Design, Inc.
524 Green St.
Boylston, MA 01505
508-393-7166

Protective Products
401 Indian Ridge Trail
Wauconda, IL 60084
800-831-1380

Tools

Calculated Industries, Inc.
4840 Hytech Dr.
Carson City, NV 89706
800-854-8075

Swanson Tool Company, Inc.
1010 Lambrecht Rd.
Frankfort, IL 60423
815-469-9453

Windows/lights/skylights

Andersen Windows, Inc.
100 Fourth Ave. North
Bayport, MN 55003-1096
612-439-5150
800-426-4261 (for the nearest retailer)

Pella Corp.
102 Main St.
Pella, IA 50219
800-847-3552

SOLATUBE North America Ltd.
5825 Avenida Encinas, Ste. 101
Carlsbad, CA 92008
800-773-7652

Tempo Industries, Inc.
2002-A South Grand Ave.
Santa Ana, CA 92705
714-641-0313

Velux-America Inc.
P.O. Box 5001
Greenwood, SC 29648-5001
800-283-2831

B

Special offer

To order the 3- and 4-page itemized bid sheets discussed in chapter 4 and other helpful business forms, complete and mail the order form on the next page. Also available are Extra Work and/or Change Order Sheets and Contractor/Agreement Sheets. The Complete Contractors Helping Hands™ Packet contains one of each type of form.

TO ORDER FORMS:

	Product	Price (Ea.)	Quantity	Amount
Extra Work and/or Change Order Sheets	1EWCO	1.75	_____	_____
Contract/Agreement Sheets	2CA	1.75	_____	_____
Itemized Bid Sheets (3-Page Set)	3IBS	3.50	_____	_____
Itemized Bid Sheets (4-Page Set)	4IBS	4.75	_____	_____
Complete Contractors Helping Hands™ Packet	5CHHP	10.00	_____	_____
Shipping & Handling (Orders Up to 6)				3.50
			SUBTOTAL	_____

TO ORDER BOOK:

	Product	Price (Ea.)	Quantity	Amount
The Helping Hands™ Guide To Hiring A Remodeling Contractor	HHG	14.00	_____	_____
Shipping & Handling (Orders Up to 2)				2.25
			SUBTOTAL	_____
			WA (Only) 8% Tax	_____
			TOTAL	_____

Make Check or Money Order Payable To:

C.R.S., Inc.
P.O. Box 4567
Spokane, WA 99202-0567
Phone: (509) 926-1724

Name _____

Address _____

City _____ State _____ Zip _____

Phone _____

C.R.S., Inc.

C

Measurements

Multipliers That are Useful to the Trade

To change	To	Multiply by
Inches	Feet	0.0833
Inches	Millimeters	25.4
Feet	Inches	12
Feet	Yards	0.3333
Yards	Feet	3
Square inches	Square feet	0.00694
Square feet	Square inches	144
Square feet	Square yards	0.11111
Square yards	Square feet	9
Cubic inches	Cubic feet	0.00058
Cubic feet	Cubic inches	1728
Cubic feet	Cubic yards	0.03703
Cubic yards	Cubic feet	27
Cubic inches	Gallons	0.00433
Cubic feet	Gallons	7.48
Gallons	Cubic inches	231
Gallons	Cubic feet	0.1337
Gallons	Pounds of water	8.33
Pounds of water	Gallons	0.12004
Ounces	Pounds	0.0625
Pounds	Ounces	16

C-1 *Trade multipliers.*

To change	To	Multiply by
Inches of water	Pounds per square inch	0.0361
Inches of water	Inches of mercury	0.0735
Inches of water	Ounces per square inch	0.578
Inches of water	Pounds per square foot	5.2
Inches of mercury	Inches of water	13.6
Inches of mercury	Feet of water	1.1333
Inches of mercury	Feet of water	0.4914
Ounces per square inch	Pounds per square inch	0.127
Ounces per square inch	Inches of mercury	1.733
Pounds per square inch	Inches of water	27.72
Pounds per square inch	Feet of water	2.310
Pounds per square inch	Inches of mercury	2.04
Pounds per square inch	Atmospheres	0.0681
Feet of water	Pounds per square inch	0.434
Feet of water	Pounds per square foot	62.5
Feet of water	Inches of mercury	0.8824
Atmospheres	Pounds per square inch	14.696
Atmospheres	Inches of mercury	29.92
Atmospheres	Feet of water	34
Long tons	Pounds	2240
Short tons	Pounds	2000
Short tons	Long tons	0.89285

C-1 *Continued.*

Metric Symbols

Quantity	Unit	Symbol
Length	Millimeter	mm
	Centimeter	cm
	Meter	m
	Kilometer	km
Area	Square millimeter	mm^2
	Square centimeter	cm^2
	Square decimeter	dm^2
	Square meter	m^2
	Square kilometer	km^2
Volume	Cubic centimeter	cm^3
	Cubic decimeter	dm^3
	Cubic meter	m^3
Mass	Milligram	mg
	Gram	g
	Kilogram	kg
	Tonne	t
Temperature	Degree Celsius	°C
	Kelvin	K
Time	Second	s
Plane angle	Radius	rad
Force	Newton	N

C-2 *Metric symbols.*

Quantity	*Unit*	*Symbol*
Energy, work, quantity of heat	Joule	J
	Kilojoule	kJ
	Megajoule	MJ
Power, heat flow rate	Watt	W
	Kilowatt	kW
Pressure	Pascal	Pa
	Kilopascal	kPa
	Megapascal	MPa
Velocity, speed	Meter per second	m/s
	Kilometer per hour	km/h
Revolutional frequency	Revolution per minute	r/min

C-2 *Continued.*

Decimal Equivalents of Fractions of an Inch

Inches	Decimal of an inch	Inches	Decimal of an inch
1/64	0.015625	11/64	0.171875
1/32	0.03125	3/16	0.1875
3/64	0.046875	13/64	0.203125
1/16	0.0625	7/32	0.21875
5/64	0.078125	15/64	0.234375
3/32	0.09375	1/4	0.25
7/64	0.109375	17/64	0.265625
1/8	0.125	9/32	0.28125
9/64	0.140625	19/64	0.296875
5/32	0.15625	5/16	0.3125

NOTE: To find the decimal equivalent of a fraction, divide the numerator by the denominator.

C-3 *Decimal equivalents of fractions of an inch.*

Inches Converted to Decimals of Feet

Inches	*Decimal of a foot*	*Inches*	*Decimal of a foot*
1/8	0.01042	1 5/8	0.13542
1/4	0.02083	1 3/4	0.14583
3/8	0.03125	1 7/8	0.15625
1/2	0.04167	2	0.16666
5/8	0.05208	2 1/8	0.17708
3/4	0.06250	2 1/4	0.18750
7/8	0.07291	2 3/8	0.19792
1	0.08333	2 1/2	0.20833
1 1/8	0.09375	2 5/8	0.21875
1 1/4	0.10417	2 3/4	0.22917
1 3/8	0.11458	2 7/8	0.23959
1 1/2	0.12500	3	0.25000

NOTE: To change inches to decimals of a foot, divide by 12. To change decimals of a foot to inches, multiply by 12.

C-4 *Inches converted to decimals of feet.*

Board Lumber Measure

Nominal size	Actual size	Board feet per linear foot	Linear feet per 1000 board feet
1 × 2	¾ × 1½	⅙ (0.167)	6000
1 × 3	¾ × 2½	¼ (0.250)	4000
1 × 4	¾ × 3½	⅓ (0.333)	3000
1 × 6	¾ × 5½	½ (0.500)	2000
1 × 8	¾ × 7¼	⅔ (0.666)	1500
1 × 10	¾ × 9¼	⅚ (0.833)	1200
1 × 12	¾ × 11¼	1 (1.0)	1000

C-5 *Board lumber conversions.*

Dimensional Lumber Board Measure

Nominal size	Actual size	Board feet per linear foot	Linear feet per 1000 board feet
2 × 2	1½ × 1½	⅓ (0.333)	3000
2 × 3	1½ × 2½	½ (0.500)	2000
2 × 4	1½ × 3½	⅔ (0.666)	1500
2 × 6	1½ × 5½	1 (1.0)	1000
2 × 8	1½ × 7¼	1⅓ (1.333)	750
2 × 10	1½ × 9¼	1⅔ (1.666)	600
2 × 12	1½ × 11¼	2 (2.0)	500

C-6 *Board measures.*

Approximate Weights of Building Materials

Material	Lbs./sq. ft.
Roof with wood or asphalt shingles	10
Roof with ³⁄₁₆ slate	15
Roof with tar and gravel	15
Concrete wall—8"	100
Concrete wall—10"	125
Concrete wall—12"	150
Concrete block wall—8"	55
Brick wall—4"	35
Brick wall—8"	75
Exterior wood frame wall (4" studs)	10
Interior partitions (per sq. ft. of floor area)	20

C-7 *Weights of building materials.*

Residential Live Loads

Area/activity	Live load, psf
First floor	40
Second floor and habitable attics	30
Balconies, fire escapes, and stairs	100
Garages	50

C-8 *Residential live loads.*

Design Loads

Usage	Live load (lbs./sq. ft.)
Bedrooms	30
Other rooms (residential)	40
Ceiling joists (no attic use)	5
Ceiling joists (light storage)	20
Ceiling joists (attic rooms)	30
Retail stores	75–100
Warehouses	125–250
School classrooms	40
Offices	80
Libraries	
Reading rooms	60
Book stacks	150
Auditoriums, gyms	100
Theater stage	150
Most corridors, lobbies, stairs, exits, fire escapes, etc. in public buildings	100

C-9 *Design loads.*

Screw Lengths and Available Gauge Numbers

Length	Gauge numbers	Length	Gauge numbers
¼"	0 to 3	1¾"	8 to 20
⅜"	2 to 7	2"	8 to 20
½"	2 to 8	2¼"	9 to 20
⅝"	3 to 10	2½"	12 to 20
¾"	4 to 11	2¾"	14 to 20
⅞"	6 to 12	3"	16 to 20
1"	6 to 14	3½"	18 to 20
1¼"	7 to 16	4"	18 to 20
1½"	6 to 18		

C-10 *Screw lengths.*

		Nail Sizes and Number Per Pound		
Penny size "d"	Length	Approximate number per pound, Common	Approximate number per pound, Box	Approximate number per pound, Finish
2	1"	875	1000	1300
3	1¼"	575	650	850
4	1½"	315	450	600
5	1¾"	265	400	500
6	2"	190	225	300
7	2¼"	160		
8	2½"	105	140	200
9	2¾"	90		
10	3"	70	90	120
12	3¼"	60	85	110
16	3½"	50	70	90
20	4"	30	50	60
30	4½"	25		
40	5"	20		
50	5½"	15		
60	6"	10		

NOTE: Aluminum and c.c. nails are slightly smaller than other nails of the same penny size.

C-11 *Nail sizes.*

Converting Inches to Decimals of a Foot

Inches	Decimals of a foot	Inches	Decimals of a foot
1"	0.083	7"	0.583
2"	0.167	8"	0.667
3"	0.250	9"	0.750
4"	0.333	10"	0.833
5"	0.417	11"	0.917
6"	0.500	12"	1.0

C-12 *Conversion for inches to decimals of a foot.*

Decimals to Millimeters

Decimal equivalent	Millimeters	Decimal equivalent	Millimeters
0.0625	1.59	0.5625	14.29
0.1250	3.18	0.6250	15.87
0.1875	4.76	0.6875	17.46
0.2500	6.35	0.7500	19.05
0.3125	7.94	0.8125	20.64
0.3750	9.52	0.8750	22.22
0.4375	11.11	0.9375	23.81
0.5000	12.70	1.000	25.40

C-13 *Decimals to millimeters.*

Conversion Table

0.001 in.	0.025 mm	1 mi.^{2}	2.590 km^2
1 in.	25.400 mm	1 in.^{3}	16.387 cm^3
1 ft.	30.48 cm	1 ft.^{3}	0.0283 m^3
1 ft.	0.3048 m	1 yd.^{3}	0.7647 m^3
1 yd.	0.9144 m	1 U.S. oz.	29.57 ml
1 mi.	1.609 km	1 U.S. pint	0.4732 l
1 in.^{2}	6.4516 cm^2	1 U.S. gal.	3.785 l
1 ft.^{2}	0.0929 m^2	1 oz	28.35 g
1 yd.^{2}	0.8361 m^2	1 lb.	0.4536 kg
1 acre	0.4047 ha		

C-14 *Conversion table.*

Measurement Conversions

Imperial to Metric

Length	1 inch	25.4 mm
	1 foot	0.3048 m
	1 yard	0.9144 m
	1 mile	1.609 km
Mass	1 pound	0.454 kg
	1 U.S. short ton	0.9072 tonne
Area	1 ft²	0.092 m²
	1 yd²	0.836 m²
	1 acre	0.404 hectare (ha)
Capacity	1 ft³	0.028 m³
Or	1 yd³	0.764 m³
Volume	1 liquid quart	0.946 litre (l)
	1 gallon	3.785 litre (l)
Heat	1 Btu	1055 joule (J)
	1 Btu/hr	0.293 watt (W)

C-15 *Measurement conversions.*

Inches to Millimetres

Inches	Millimetres	Inches	Millimetres
1	25.4	11	279.4
2	50.8	12	304.8
3	76.2	13	330.2
4	101.6	14	355.6
5	127.0	15	381.0
6	152.4	16	406.4
7	177.8	17	431.8
8	203.2	18	457.2
9	228.6	19	482.6
10	254.0	20	508.0

C-16 *Converting inches to millimeters.*

Fractions to Decimals

Fractions	Decimal equivalent	Fractions	Decimal equivalent
1/16	0.0625	9/16	0.5625
1/8	0.1250	5/8	0.6250
3/16	0.1875	11/16	0.6875
1/4	0.2500	3/4	0.7500
5/16	0.3125	13/16	0.8125
3/8	0.3750	7/8	0.8750
7/16	0.4375	15/16	0.9375
1/2	0.5000	1	1.000

C-17 *Converting fractions to decimals.*

Square Inches to
Approximate Square Centimeters

Square inches	Square centimeters	Square inches	Square centimeters
1	6.5	8	52.0
2	13.0	9	58.5
3	19.5	10	65.0
4	26.0	25	162.5
5	32.5	50	325.0
6	39.0	100	650.0
7	45.5		

C-18A *Converting square inches to square centimeters.*

Square Feet to Approximate Square Meters

Square feet	Square meters	Square feet	Square meters
1	0.925	8	0.7400
2	0.1850	9	0.8325
3	0.2775	10	0.9250
4	0.3700	25	2.315
5	0.4650	50	4.65
6	0.5550	100	9.25
7	0.6475		

C-18B *Converting square feet to square meters.*

Decimal Equivalents of Fractions

Fraction	Decimal	Fraction	Decimal
1/64	0.015625	13/64	0.203125
1/32	0.03125	7/32	0.21875
3/64	0.046875	15/64	0.234375
1/20	0.05	1/4	0.25
1/16	0.0625	17/64	0.265625
1/13	0.0769	9/32	0.28125
5/64	0.078125	19/64	0.296875
1/12	0.0833	5/16	0.3125
1/11	0.0909	21/64	0.328125
3/32	0.09375	1/3	0.333
1/10	0.10	11/32	0.34375
7/64	0.109375	23/64	0.359375
1/9	0.111	3/8	0.375
1/8	0.125	25/64	0.390625
9/64	0.140625	13/32	0.40625
1/7	0.1429	27/64	0.421875
5/32	0.15625	7/16	0.4375
1/6	0.1667	29/64	0.453125
11/64	0.171875	15/32	0.46875
3/16	0.1875	31/64	0.484375
1/5	0.2	1/2	0.5

C-19 *Decimal equivalents of fractions.*

Fraction	Decimal	Fraction	Decimal
$\frac{33}{64}$	0.515625	$\frac{5}{8}$	0.625
$\frac{17}{32}$	0.53125	$\frac{41}{64}$	0.640625
$\frac{35}{64}$	0.546875	$\frac{21}{32}$	0.65625
$\frac{9}{16}$	0.5625	$\frac{43}{64}$	0.671875
$\frac{37}{64}$	0.578125	$\frac{11}{16}$	0.6875
$\frac{19}{32}$	0.59375	$\frac{45}{64}$	0.703125
$\frac{39}{64}$	0.609375		

C-19 *Continued.*

Circumference of Circle

Diameter (inches)	Circumference	Diameter (inches)	Circumference
⅛	0.3927	3¾	11.78
¼	0.7854	4	12.56
⅜	1.178	4½	14.13
½	1.570	5	15.70
⅝	1.963	5½	17.27
¾	2.356	6	18.84
⅞	2.748	6½	20.42
1	3.141	7	21.99
1⅛	3.534	7½	23.56
1¼	3.927	8	25.13
1⅜	4.319	8½	26.70
1½	4.712	9	28.27
1⅝	5.105	9½	29.84
1¾	5.497	10	31.41
1⅞	5.890	10½	32.98
2	6.283	11	34.55
2¼	7.068	11½	36.12
2½	7.854	12	37.69
2¾	8.639	12½	39.27
3	9.424	13	40.84
3¼	10.21	13½	42.41
3½	10.99	14	43.98

C-20 *Circumference of a circle.*

Diameter (inches)	Circumference	Diameter (inches)	Circumference
14½	45.55	24	75.39
15	47.12	24½	76.96
15½	48.69	25	78.54
16	50.26	26	81.68
16½	51.83	27	84.82
17	53.40	28	87.96
17½	54.97	29	91.10
18	56.54	30	94.24
18½	58.11	31	97.38
19	59.69	32	100.5
19½	61.26	33	103.6
20	62.83	34	106.8
20½	64.40	35	109.9
21	65.97	36	113.0
21½	67.54	37	116.2
22	69.11	38	119.3
22½	70.68	39	122.5
23	72.25	40	125.6
23½	73.82		

C-20 *Continued.*

Surface Measure			
144 sq. in.	1 sq. ft.	160 sq. rd.	1 acre
9 sq. ft.	1 sq. yd.	640 acres	1 sq. mile
30½ sq. yd.	1 sq. rd.	43,560 sq. ft.	1 acre

C-21 *Surface measure.*

Area of Circle

Diameter	Area	Diameter	Area
⅛	0.0123	3¾	11.044
¼	0.0491	4	12.566
⅜	0.1104	4½	15.904
½	0.1963	5	19.635
⅝	0.3068	5½	23.758
¾	0.4418	6	28.274
⅞	0.6013	6½	33.183
1	0.7854	7	38.484
1⅛	0.9940	7½	44.178
1¼	1.227	8	50.265
1⅜	1.484	8½	56.745
1½	1.767	9	63.617
1⅝	2.073	9½	70.882
1¾	2.405	10	78.54
1⅞	2.761	10½	86.59
2	3.141	11	95.03
2¼	3.976	11½	103.86
2½	4.908	12	113.09
2¾	5.939	12½	122.71
3	7.068	13	132.73
3¼	8.295	13½	143.13
3½	9.621	14	153.93

C-22 *Area of a circle.*

Diameter	Area	Diameter	Area
14½	165.13	24	452.39
15	176.71	24½	471.43
15½	188.69	25	490.87
16	201.06	26	530.93
16½	213.82	27	572.55
17	226.98	28	615.75
17½	240.52	29	660.52
18	254.46	30	706.86
18½	268.80	31	754.76
19	283.52	32	804.24
19½	298.6	33	855.30
20	314.16	34	907.92
20½	330.06	35	962.11
21	346.36	36	1017.8
21½	363.05	37	1075.2
22	380.13	38	1134.1
22½	397.60	39	1194.5
23	415.47	40	1256.6
23½	433.73		

C-22 *Continued.*

Conversion Factors in Converting from Customary (U.S.) Units to Metric Units

To find	Multiply	By
Microns	Mils	25.4
Centimeters	Inches	2.54
Meters	Feet	0.3048
Meters	Yards	0.19144
Kilometers	Miles	1.609344
Grams	Ounces	28.349523
Kilograms	Pounds	0.4539237
Liters	Gallons (U.S.)	3.7854118
Liters	Gallons (imperial)	4.546090
Milliliters (cc)	Fluid ounces	29.573530
Milliliters (cc)	Cubic inches	16.387064
Square centimeters	Square inches	6.4516
Square meters	Square feet	0.09290304
Square meters	Square yards	0.83612736
Cubic meters	Cubic feet	2.8316847×10^{-2}
Cubic meters	Cubic yards	0.76455486
Joules	BTU	1054.3504
Joules	Foot-pounds	1.35582
Kilowatts	BTU per minute	0.01757251
Kilowatts	Foot-pounds per minute	2.2597×10^{-5}
Kilowatts	Horsepower	0.7457
Radians	Degrees	0.017453293
Watts	BTU per minute	17.5725

C-23 *Converting customary units to metric units.*

Inch and Metric Scales

Scales used for detail drawings		
Inch scale		Metric scale
1"	is full size	1:1
3"	is closest to	1:5
1½"	is closest to	1:10*
¾"	is used for	1:10*
½"	is closest to	1:20
Scales used for building plans		
Inch scale		Metric scale
¼"	is closest to	1:50
⅛"	is closest to	1:100
Scale used for site plans		
Inch scale		Metric scale
¹⁄₁₆"	is closest to	1:200

*The 1:10 is used for both ¾" and the 1½" scales.

C-24 *Inch and metric scales.*

Cubic Measure

1728 cu. in.	1 cu. ft.
27 cu. in.	1 cu. yd.
128 cu. ft.	1 cord

C-25 *Cubic measures.*

Metric-Customary Equivalents

1 meter	39.3 inches 3.28083 feet 1.0936 yards
1 centimeter	0.3937 inch
1 millimeter	0.03937 inch, or nearly ⅟₂₅ inch
1 kilometer	0.62137 mile
1 foot	0.3048 meter
1 inch	2.54 centimeters 25.40 millimeters
Measures of surface	
1 square meter	10.764 square feet 1.196 square yards
1 square centimeter	0.155 square inch
1 square millimeter	0.00155 square inch
1 square yard	0.836 square meter
1 square foot	0.0929 square meter
1 square inch	6.452 square centimeter 645.2 square millimeter
Measures of volume and capacity	
1 cubic meter	35.314 cubic feet 1.308 cubic yards 264.2 U.S. gallons (231 cubic inches)
1 cubic decimeter	61.0230 cubic inches 0.0353 cubic feet
1 cubic centimeter	0.061 cubic inch
1 liter	1 cubic decimeter 61.0230 cubic inches

C-26 *Measurement conversions.*

	0.0353 cubic foot 1.0567 quarts (U.S.) 0.2642 gallon (U.S.) 2.2020 lb. of water at 62°F
1 cubic yard	0.7645 cubic meter
1 cubic foot	0.02832 cubic meter 28.317 cubic decimeters 28.317 liters
1 cubic inch	16.383 cubic centimeters
1 gallon (British)	4.543 liters
1 gallon (U.S.)	3.785 liters
Measures of weight	
1 gram	15.432 grains
1 kilogram	2.2046 pounds
1 metric ton	0.9842 ton or 2240 pounds 19.68 cwts. 2204.6 pounds
1 grain	0.0648 gram
1 ounce avoirdupois	28.35 grams
1 pound	0.4536 kilograms
1 ton or 2240 lb.	1.1016 metric tons 1016 kilograms

C-26 *Continued.*

Formulas

Circle
Circumference = diameter × 3.1416
Circumference = radius × 6.2832
Diameter = radius × 2
Diameter = square root of; (area ÷ 0.7854)
Diameter = square root of area × 1.1283
Diameter = circumference × 0.31831
Radius = diameter ÷ 2
Radius = circumference × 0.15915
Radius = square root of area × 0.56419
Area = diameter × diameter × 0.7854
Area = half of the circumference × half of the diameter
Area = square of the circumference × 0.0796
Arc length = degrees × radius × 0.01745
Degrees of arc = length ÷ (radius × 0.01745)
Radius of arc = length ÷ (degrees × 0.01745)
Side of equal square = diameter × 0.8862
Side of inscribed square = diameter × 0.7071
Area of sector = area of circle × degrees of arc ÷ 360
Cone
Area of surface = one half of circumference of base × slant height + area of base.
Volume = diameter × diameter × 0.7854 × one-third of the altitude.

C-27 *Formula functions.*

Cube
Volume = width × height × length

Cylinder
Area of surface = diameter × 3.1416 × length + area of the two bases
Area of base = diameter × diameter × 0.7854
Area of base = volume ÷ length
Length = volume ÷ area of base
Volume = length × area of base
Capacity in gallons = volume in inches ÷ 231
Capacity of gallons = diameter × diameter × length × 0.0034
Capacity in gallons = volume in feet × 7.48

Ellipse
Area = short diameter × long diameter × 0.7854

Hexagon
Area = width of side × 2.598 × width of side

Parallelogram
Area = base × distance between the two parallel sides

Pyramid
Area = ½ perimeter of base × slant height + area of base
Volume = area of base × ⅓ of the altitude

Rectangle
Area = length × width

Rectangular prism
Volume = width × height × length

C-27 *Continued.*

Sphere
Area of surface = diameter × diameter × 3.1416
Side of inscribed cube = radius × 1.547
Volume = diameter × diameter × diameter × 0.5236
Square
Area = length × width
Triangle
Area = one-half of height times base
Trapezoid
Area = one-half of the sum of the parallel sides × the height

C-27 *Continued.*

Weights & Measures

Linear measure

12 inches = 1 foot

3 feet = 1 yard

5½ yards = 1 rod

320 rods = 1 mile

1 mile = 1760 yards

1 mile = 5280 feet

Square measure

144 sq. inches = 1 sq. foot

9 sq. feet = 1 sq. yard

1 sq. yard = 1296 sq. inches

4840 sq. yards = 1 acre

640 acres = 1 sq. mile

Cubic measure

1728 cubic inches = 1 cubic foot

27 cubic feet = 1 cubic yard

Avoirdupois weight

16 ounces = 1 pound

100 pounds = 1 hundredweight

20 hundredweight = 1 ton

1 ton = 2000 pounds

1 long ton = 2240 pounds

C-28 *Weights and measures.*

Liquid measure
4 gills = 1 pint
2 pints = 1 quart
4 quarts = 1 gallon
31½ gallons = 1 barrel
1 gallon = 231 cubic inches
7.48 gallons = 1 cubic foot
1 gallon water = 8.33 pounds
1 gallon gasoline = 5.84 pounds

C-28 *Continued.*

Weights of Building Materials

Framing and Floor

Component	Material	Load, psf
Framing (16" oc)	2 × 4 and 2 × 6	2
	2 × 8 and 2 × 10	3
Floor-ceiling	Softwood, per inch	3
	Hardwood, per inch	4
	Plywood, per inch	3
	Concrete, per inch	12
	Stone, per inch	13
	Carpet	0.5
	Drywall, per inch	5

C-29 *Weights of various building materials.*

Estimating Cubic Yards of Concrete for Slabs, Walks and Drives

Slab thickness Inches	Slab area Square feet				
	10	50	100	300	500
2	0.1	0.3	0.6	1.9	3.1
3	0.1	0.5	0.9	2.8	4.7
4	0.1	0.6	1.2	3.7	6.2
5	0.2	0.7	1.5	4.7	7.2
6	0.2	0.9	1.9	5.6	9.3

C-30 *Estimating concrete needs.*

Grades for Traffic Surface

Surface	Minimum	Maximum
Driveways in the north	1%	10%
Driveways in the south	1%	15%
Walks	1%	4%
Ramps		15%
Wheelchair ramps		8%
Patios	1%	2%

C-31 *Recommended elevation grades.*

Wheelchair Ramps

Maximum slope	1 in 12
Minimum clear width	3'0"
Minimum curb height	2"
Railing	2'8"
Maximum length	30'0"
Minimum width of passage	2'8"
Approximate length of chair	3'8"
Seat height	17" to 18"
Maximum comfortable reach	5'4"
Eye level	3'9" to 4'3"

C-32 *Suggestions for wheelchair ramps.*

- *Polyurethane:*
  ~Expensive
  ~Resists water
  ~Durable
  ~Scratches are difficult to hide
- *Varnishes:*
  ~Less expensive than polyurethane
  ~Less durable than polyurethane
  ~Resists water
  ~Scratches are difficult to hide
- *Penetrating sealers:*
  ~Provide a low-gloss sheen
  ~Durable
  ~Scratches touch up easily

C-33 *Qualities of various wood finishes.*

Reconstituted Wood Panels with Typical Uses

Particleboard	Wood particles and resin. a. Industrial grade—Cabinets and counter tops under plastic laminates. b. Underlayment—Installed over subfloor under tile or carpet.
Wafer board	Wood wafers and resin. Inexpensive sheathing, craft projects, etc.
Oriented Strand Board (OSB)	Thin wood strands oriented at right angles with phenolic resin. Same uses as above.
Hardboard	Wood fiber mat compressed into stiff, hard sheets. a. Service—Light weight—Cabinet backs, etc. b. Standard—Stronger with better finish quality. c. Tempered—Stiffer and harder for exterior use.
Fiberboard (Grayboard)	Molded wood fibers—Underlayment, sound deadening panels.
Composite plywood	A core of particleboard with face and back veneers glued directly to it.

C-34 *Typical uses of wood panels.*

Types of Plywood with Typical Uses

Softwood veneer	Cross laminated plies or veneers— Sheathing, general construction and industrial use, etc.
Hardwood veneer	Cross laminated plies with hardwood face and back veneer— Furniture and cabinet work, etc.
Lumbercore plywood	Two face veneers and 2 crossband plies with an inner core of lumber strips—Desk and table tops, etc.
Medium-density overlay (MDO)	Exterior plywood with resin and fiber veneer—Signs, soffits, etc.
High-density overlay (HDO)	Tougher than MDO—Concrete forms, workbench tops, etc.
Plywood siding	T-111 and other textures used as one step sheathing and siding where codes allow.

C-35 *Typical uses of plywood.*

Potential Life Spans for Gutters

Material	Expected life span	Material	Expected life span
Aluminum	15 to 20 years	Copper	50 years
Vinyl	Indefinite	Wood	10 to 15 years
Steel	Less than 10 years		

All estimated life spans depend on installation procedure, maintenance, and climatic conditions.

C-36 *Potential life spans of gutters.*

Price Ranges for Gutters

Material	Price range	Material	Price range
Aluminum	Moderate	Copper	Very expensive
Vinyl	Expensive	Wood	Moderate to expensive
Steel	Inexpensive		

All estimated life spans depend on installation procedure, maintenance, and climatic conditions.

C-37 *Price ranges of gutters.*

Index

Illustrations are in **boldface**.

About the author

Photograph of the author taken by James McClintock.

Leon A. Frechette has over 20 years' experience in construction, re-modeling, and related fields. He has appeared on many TV and radio talk shows, providing practical know-how to both consumers and construction professionals. Over the course of his career he has filmed demonstration and training videotapes, provided expert testimony in court cases, and designed a toy collection. He has a broad range of expertise and is a noted expert within the construction industry.

Leon's interests lie in the tool business: designing and testing new products, refining structure and technique. He has tested many hand and power tools as well as other construction-related products and submitted written evaluations for in-house company use and articles for both newsstand and industry publications. His column, "Frechette on Tools," runs monthly in *Tech Directions*, a publication for vocational educators, and he has published many other magazine articles. Leon won the 1995 National Association of Home and Workshop Writers (NAHWW)/Stanley Tools "do-it-yourself" Writing Contest (the "Golden Hammer" award) for Best Short Subject.

Leon authored and published *The Helping Hands™ Guide to Hiring a Remodeling Contractor*, which featured his simplified business forms. He's the author of *The Pre-Development Handbook* for the City of Spokane and the Spokane Housing Authority, a user-friendly guide for builders and developers to the many agencies overseeing construction and rehabilitation within the city. His book, *Bathroom Remodeling*, was published by TAB Books/McGraw-Hill in 1994, and the *Builder's Guide to Decks* will be out in late 1995, also with McGraw-Hill. Other book projects are currently in development.